PRAISE FOR *SHOW THE STORY*

Human beings are wired to absorb information through stories. Words alone are not enough. Visuals are the way we learn best. *Show the Story* provides an in-depth look at the strategy and psychology of presenting a case visually. Hundreds of images show you real cases and how to best communicate the story. It is a breakthrough book for today's attorneys.

—Lisa Blue, PhD, JD, forensic psychologist, named in the
top 50 women lawyers by *National Law Journal*

If you ever questioned how to visually prepare your case, this book is the answer! In my years as a trial attorney and consultant, I have never seen a presentation that so brilliantly illustrates how to message the story of your case. The Bailey brothers lucidly demonstrate how visually communicating the story engenders the understanding necessary to be successful. A great read and reference.

—Gregory S. Cusimano, past president of the Alabama Association for Justice,
Lifetime Achievement Award from the American Association for Justice

The lawyers who have used this visual format win and win big . . . an extremely authentic and original approach with a profound humanity and generosity of spirit.

—Joshua Karton, Communication Arts, Gerry Spence
Trial Lawyers College, and California Western School of Law

The Bailey brothers are legal visionaries with a passion to help trial lawyers become better. This meticulous, fascinating work on the use of visuals to tell the story stands alone as the single best resource of its kind.

—Karen Koehler, *Best Lawyers in America* 2006–present,
member of the American Board of Trial Advocates

This book has great insights into the art of visual storytelling. It teaches you how to transform your case from dry facts and a few exhibits to an engaging visual story that really comes to life. The Bailey brothers show you how to visually engage a jury and keep them engaged. A must read for every trial lawyer.

—Nancy La Vista, past president of the
Palm Beach County Chapter of ABOTA

You've pioneered a radical way to look at our cases. This book shows not only how to make a winning visual story, but how to persuade through sequencing information properly. Your methods have helped us obtain millions in verdicts for our clients.

—Robert F. Linton, Jr., past president of the Cleveland Academy of
Trial Attorneys, named an Ohio Super Lawyer 2007–2011

The Bailey brothers have written an encyclopedia of information about showing your clients story to the jury through visual presentations with clear instructions about how to do it correctly. It should be in every trial lawyer's library. It's a winner.

—Paul Luvera, past president of the Inner Circle of Advocates,
member of the International Academy of Trial Lawyers

The Bailey brothers have made an invaluable contribution to the trial bar and those we serve. *Show the Story* is for those who aspire to be the very best.

—Tommy Malone, member of the International Society of
Barristers, named in *Best Lawyers in America* 1989–present

A valuable roadmap that teaches us how to visually frame and sequence our trial and settlement presentations. The lessons of *Show the Story* will definitely enhance our likelihood of success.

—Mark Mandell, past president of the
American Association for Justice

In this age when visual persuasion and storytelling are the hallmarks of successful litigation, William and Robert Bailey have captured the essence of the genre. This is a comprehensive and highly valuable book, rich with ideas, illustrations and superb content. It will benefit all trial lawyers, whether novice or experienced.

—Howard L. Nations, president of the National Trial Lawyers Association,
Adjunct Law Professor at South Texas College of Law

If lawyers employ the sophisticated visual strategies presented in this book they will have a distinct advantage over those who do not. All will benefit greatly from this text. Bravo!

—Kathleen Flynn Peterson, fellow of the American College of Trial
Lawyers, past president of the American Association for Justice

I highly recommend that practicing attorneys in the field of personal injury and wrongful death litigation read and use *Show the Story*. It explains how to use visual tools and techniques to tell the story of the case.

—Ron Rouda, Lifetime Achievement Award, American Board of Trial Advocates, 2011, and fellow of the International Academy of Trial Lawyers

This is one book that will be on my bookshelf and will be required reading for all lawyers in my firm. Accomplished trial lawyer William Bailey gives us all the tools we need to tell the visual story of the trial. Trial consultant Robert Bailey is the best visual trial storyteller in the country. Thank you for showing us the visual story.

—Paul Scoptur, co-chair of the National College of Advocacy Board of Trustees, Adjunct Professor of Law at Marquette University Law School

I love it! It is a classic. It will be bought by every real trial lawyer in the country. This is the Bible for using visuals in trial. Wow!

—Mike Wampold, Adjunct Professor at the University of Washington School of Law, National Institute of Trial Advocacy Instructor, 2003–present

Robert is a trial consultant with a film-director-like brilliance in presenting the story. William is one of those rare trial lawyers who understands how to use visual imagery to persuade. Together the Bailey brothers teach us how to transform our case into a winning visual story. Every trial lawyer needs this book!

—David A. Wenner, co-creator of the Jury Bias Model™

SHOW
THE STORY
The Power of Visual Advocacy

SHOW
THE STORY

The Power of Visual Advocacy

by

William S. Bailey & Robert W. Bailey

TRIAL GUIDES™

TRIAL GUIDES, LLC

Trial Guides, LLC, Portland, Oregon, 97205

© 2011 Trial Guides, LLC

ISBN: 978-1-934833-38-4

Library of Congress Control Number: 201192959

Please see illustration credits on page 393 for information on the creators of the illustrations in this book. All works used with permission.

Trial Guides, LLC
Attn: Permissions
2400 SW Park Place
Portland, OR 97205
(800) 309-6845
www.trialguides.com

Cover design by Robert W. Bailey

Jacket layout by Theodore Marshall

Interior design by Laura Lind Design

This book is printed on acid-free paper.

I dedicate this book to my wife, Sylvia, who always has supported me to follow my dreams, even when the going gets tough.

—William S. Bailey

For my lovely partner, Michaela.
Your love is a gift and I am forever grateful.

—Robert W. Bailey

Contents

ACKNOWLEDGMENTS

WILLIAM S. BAILEY

This book would not have happened without the support and encouragement of many people. Aaron DeShaw of Trial Guides was willing to take a risk on a new idea, and the editorial skill and unfailing good nature of Tina Ricks helped us to turn it into reality.

United States District Court Chief Judge Marsha J. Pechman and King County (Washington) Superior Court Judge William L. Downing have presided over hundreds of jury trials and have a firm grasp on what juries and judges want. They provided me with keen insight into this.

Professor Robert Aronson of the University of Washington School of Law and Professors David Boerner and John Mitchell of Seattle University School of Law have given me wise counsel throughout my career and were most generous in expanding on evidentiary and ethical issues. Professor Margaret Chon of Seattle University School of Law was very helpful in acquainting me with other legal issues.

The clients I represent are the center of my professional life. I am grateful to Nathan Malkow; Ray and Kerrie Moore; Roger Murray; George, Kathy, and Zoe Philippides; and Claude States for permitting me to use events from their lives. The kind and generous heart of the late Yianni Philippides continues to inspire me. He was taken from us far too soon. I also thank Kevin Biglow and John Mabrey, who allowed me to use information from their cases.

Fellow lawyers in the trial bar have been a consistent source of ideas and inspiration. I am grateful to the lawyers whose work is featured in this book: Mimy A. Bailey, Michael J. Bond, Marilyn B. Brenneman, Kathy A. Cochran, Randolph I. Gordon, Bradley S. Keller, Jonathan Lee, Michael D. Myers, and Michael Reiss.

Computer graphics and animation consultants have been an essential part of my practice. Special thanks are due Duane Hoffmann, who not only has provided me creative, dynamic images in multiple cases, but also devoted hundreds of hours to the custom illustrations in this book. Patrick O'Neill, Jay Syverson, and Aaron Weholt are enormously talented providers of illustrations and animations to the legal community, whose work appears either in this book or the DVD that accompanies it.

Special thanks go to my mentor and longtime friend Paul N. Luvera, one of the best trial lawyers in America; Justice Tom Chambers, a great trial lawyer and jurist who I greatly admire; my former law partner and longtime friend Steve Fury; Doria Reagan, PhD, a bodhisattva; Stefanie Lindgren, for her word processing speed and unfailing good nature in the face of doing yet another draft; my legal assistant Tonya Arico, for constantly retrieving information from the archives of past cases; my friends and talented trial lawyers Karen Koehler, Reed Schifferman, and Mike Wampold, who read a draft of the book and gave me valuable feedback. Vonda Sargent, my friend and teaching partner at Seattle University, Rick Friedman, Judy Proller, Jesse Robison, and Tom Vesper all were generous in sharing their thoughts and providing encouragement.

I also want to acknowledge the sources that helped me to track down information for the book: Walter Dauber, Yakima, Washington, lawyer; David Dilgard of the Everett Public Library; Freemantle Media, Ltd.; Creators Syndicate; University of Washington Library System; and the Ronald W. Reagan Presidential Library.

The editors of *Trial* magazine have been my strong supporters and friends throughout the years. An article that appeared in *Trial* in August 1991, "Lessons From L.A. Law: Winning Through Cinematic Techniques" was the initial inspiration for doing this book; Professor Richard E. Mayer of the University of California at Santa Barbara, an authority on multimedia learning, was most generous with his time.

Thanks to Greg Smith and Darla Upchurch of the National Institute for Trial Advocacy, who gave us considerable time, advice, and encouragement. The friendship and advice of Professor Frederick Moss of Southern Methodist University has been invaluable to me.

My friend Steve Bremner was invaluable as a source of both sage advice and moral support throughout the writing of this book.

ROBERT W. BAILEY

The idea for writing a book with my brother began a decade ago, but it wasn't until recent years that we actually began the work. I want to thank my brother, Bill Bailey, for all his hard work and dedication to making this book a reality. It required more to accomplish this dream than either one of us ever imagined and he gave it 100 percent.

I also want to thank attorneys Robert Tourtelot and Tom Warner for graciously allowing me to write about the cases that I included in this book. May the lessons learned from these cases help in the representation of others who have been seriously injured.

My gratitude also goes to attorneys David Wenner, Jim Lees, Robert Linton, and John Feder. Your thoughtful feedback helped make this a better book and I am grateful for your valuable insights.

A special thanks goes to Aaron DeShaw, editor Tina Ricks, and all the staff at Trial Guides. Thank you for your assistance in bringing this book to press.

Thanks also to Darla Upchurch of the National Institute for Trial Advocacy. I appreciate your creative suggestions and time.

Along the way there have also been a number of people who have directly or indirectly supported my work. I want to thank Scott Moyer for his support through the years. Thanks also to Jay Marshall and Carol Wood for being there when it all began. I thank Evan Naylor and Harrison Fong for their talented support.

I also want to acknowledge and thank the attorneys, clients, and fellow consultants that I have had the opportunity to work with over the years. Each of you touched my life in unique ways and I have grown as a man and as a human being through knowing you.

Finally, I want to acknowledge and thank Michaela McGivern. More than anyone, she knows what it took for me to write this book. I deeply appreciate all her editorial support, suggestions, and wise counsel.

Authors' Note

This book includes illustrative examples drawn from actual cases. However, except where otherwise expressly stated, the names and certain other identifying details of all cases, litigants, witnesses, counsel, and other participants have been changed. For these reasons, any similarity between the fictionalized names, and other particulars in this book, and real individuals, companies, and cases is strictly coincidental.

PUBLISHER'S NOTE

This book is intended for practicing attorneys. This book does not offer legal or other professional advice and does not take the place of consultation with an attorney or other professional with appropriate expertise and experience.

Attorneys are strongly cautioned to evaluate the information, techniques, ideas, and opinions set forth in this book in light of their own research, experience, and judgment, to consult applicable rules, regulations, procedures, cases, and statutes (including those issued after the publication date of this book), and to make independent decisions about whether and how to apply such information, techniques, ideas, and opinions to a particular case.

Quotations from published works, cases, pleadings, discovery, and other sources are for illustrative purposes only and may not be suitable for use in litigation in any particular case.

All references to copyrighted works and trademarks of third parties are strictly informational and for purposes of instruction and commentary. No sponsorship or endorsement by, or affiliation with, the copyright or trademark owners is claimed or implied by the authors or publisher of this book.

The authors and publisher disclaim any liability or responsibility for loss or damage resulting from the use of this book or the information, ideas, or opinions contained in this book.

INTRODUCTION

This book provides a behind-the-scenes look at what it takes to become a visual storyteller. It explores the visual strategies used by successful writers, animators, and film directors and shows you how to apply similar techniques to create persuasive visual presentations for trial or settlement.

Hundreds of pictures reveal the step-by-step creative process. We analyze actual cases, displaying and explaining their visual constructions. You'll learn new ideas that will transform your cases into compelling visual stories that engage jurors, judges, insurance adjusters, and corporate decision makers. In short, this book provides a comprehensive picture of what it takes to become a visual advocate.

The contents are presented in four parts. Each part is self-contained and can be read independently.

The contents are presented in four parts. Each part is self-contained and can be read independently.

PART ONE: VISUAL LEARNING

The first part of the book surveys our visual world and explains how it has changed the communication techniques that you must use to be effective, both in and out of the courtroom. It explores the importance of using words and images to build multimedia messages that engage jurors, using the latest brain research from neurological science.

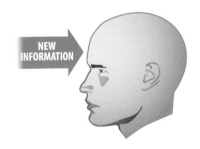

PART TWO: SHOW THE STORY

The second part contains practical information on how to show the story in opening statements and settlement presentations. It includes case profiles and easy-to-follow steps that reveal how to think like a film director, establish the story's settings, introduce the defendants, set up the conflict, show the standards,

show the defendant's actions, build suspense, re-create climactic moments, and integrate the theme visually through the case. The strategies outlined in this section will enhance the visual presentation of any case.

Part Three: Visual Tools and Techniques

The third part discusses the use of specific visual tools including computer illustrations, animations, and video re-creations. We describe the process of creating better work-product through more successful partnerships with legal media consultants. We focus on actual cases, so you can apply the information to the cases you are handling.

Part Four: Visual Foundation

The fourth part looks at the foundation, evidentiary, and ethical issues created by the use of modern-day visuals in the courtroom. We offer suggestions on how to get visual exhibits into evidence, as well as how to keep out those offered by your opponent.

Individually and collectively, these parts cover a variety of techniques that modern trial attorneys need to master in order to become more effective visual communicators. Using the ideas and strategies presented will change how you prepare cases for trial or settlement.

Appendices

The defense communicates visually also. It is to your advantage to study your opponents' methods. The appendices briefly describe how the defense uses some of the techniques presented in this book. Using these appendices, you can begin to think visually about the defense's point of view and to anticipate what they may use against you.

PART
ONE

Visual Learning

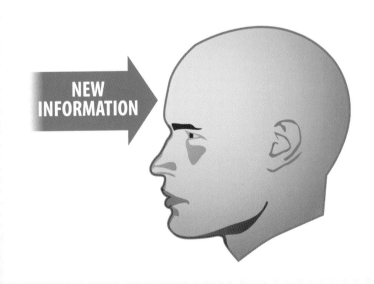

1

OUR VISUAL WORLD

The digital revolution is far more significant than the invention of writing or even printing.

—Douglas Engelbart

In the twenty-first century, information must be visually interesting in order to effectively persuade an audience. Yet most lawyers lack the necessary training and experience to communicate visually.

PREDOMINANCE OF VISUAL IMAGERY

Communication in the modern world is shifting steadily toward a visual, nonverbal basis. People are much more visually sophisticated today than at any other time in history. We want and expect communication to include images; that's what fills the screens of our personal computers, televisions, and cell phones and dominates our popular culture.

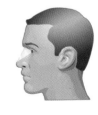

Modern Life is Visual

Advertising and marketing bombard us every day, from the junk mail that comes to our houses, to computer solicitations that pop up on our screens, to commercials with glamour-filled

sequences of people and products on network television. The advertising industry spends billions of dollars each year in search of powerful symbolic images to stimulate and motivate us to buy things.

TELEVISION HAS FOREVER CHANGED COMMUNICATION

More than any other medium in modern life, television dominates our expectations on how information should be presented. Television requires that information be communicated in an informal, interesting, and compact form, with high entertainment and production values. Modern audiences have been conditioned by the fast pace and visual shorthand of television, resulting in shrinking attention spans and a demand that presenters get to the point quickly.

The average television news story lasts only about a minute and a half, with pictures flashing on the screen as the broadcast journalist narrates. Sound bites are in; long speeches are out.

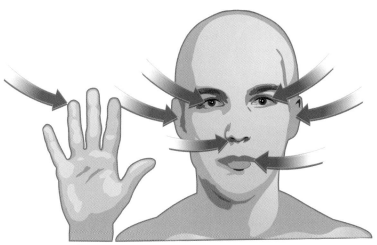

Experience from senses

THE IMPORTANCE OF VISUALIZING LEGAL CASES

So how does all of this affect you when representing a client in the modern world?

Law is about not only critical thinking and problem solving but also effective communication. With so many competing points of view, if you can capture the attention and respect of a decision maker, you'll be the one who gets the best result for your client. Visual-communication strategies aren't just for the mass media; they offer many advantages to lawyers, too, including:

1. Showing things that language alone often cannot.

2. Increasing attention, comprehension, and retention.

3. Adding power, dramatic effect, and interest.

4. Shortening the time required to communicate.

THE PREDOMINANCE OF THE VISUAL

Our eyes are the windows into our brains, the pathways by which most new information arrives, allowing us to recognize patterns and make informed decisions. This is how we learn,

from the routine tasks of daily life to the most complicated new information. The information we get from our eyes is what we rely on most to make sense of the world.

Jurors have to quickly take in large quantities of new, unfamiliar information that lawyers in the case have spent years collecting. For this volume of new information to be understood and absorbed by the jury, a lawyer has to be an effective communicator. Saturation bombing of details will not work. How do good teachers educate their students? They write new information on the board or show it on a screen, so that it can be *seen*. They also draw analogies to what students already know. An effective lawyer has to be a good teacher, using the same techniques that work in the classroom. Alan Morrill recognized decades ago that jurors without visuals are likely to be clueless:

> With anything more than a simple set of facts involving an intersection collision, it is probably safe to say that... [with] words alone, not one juror has a clear picture in his mind as to how the accident occurred.[1]

BEYOND INFORMATION COLLECTING

Lawyers are proficient information collectors, using the rules of discovery to accumulate a large volume of documents and depositions filled with details. As the information piles up, it becomes harder and harder to know what to do with it. Where is the story buried within this mound of paper? Where are the themes that will be critical to the jury in sorting things out? Most lawyers find it difficult to create a compelling story out of the information they have collected. Yet that is exactly what the jury most wants and needs to hear and see—the story, not the details. As media advisor Roger Ailes once admonished President Ronald Reagan before a critical televised debate:

1. Alan E. Morrill, *Trial Diplomacy*, 2nd ed. (Chicago: Court Practice Institute, 1974).

You didn't get elected on details. You got elected on themes. Every time a question is asked, relate it to one of your themes.[2]

SALES RESISTANCE

Beyond the capacity of visuals to educate and inform, they bridge the persuasion gap between words and images. Jurors today are sophisticated, heavily filtering what they hear, knowing instinctively that you are advocating for a client's point of view. Words are the suspect agents of a sales pitch.

However, seeing is believing, and in that images are directed to our nonverbal subconscious minds, they are more resistant to juror skepticism than words. This is why modern advertising is much more focused on the images, with only minimal words.

JUDICIAL PERSPECTIVE: MAKE IT MORE VISUAL

While even experienced judges typically don't tell you how to try your cases, many of them are well informed on what jurors want. The judicial perspective on courtroom communication includes the need to make cases more visual, in the same way that teachers show things to make information come across better to a class. Without images to guide the message, many judges know that the traditional oral-advocacy approach is likely to lead to confusion, a view articulated by Judge Warren Wolfson of Chicago, Illinois:

> [Often] the jury hasn't the slightest idea what the lawyer is talking about. Lawyers can't rely on words only. . . . Juries will retain best, and believe best, what they see and hear at the same time. Most lawyers just don't know how to do that.[3]

2. Roger Ailes, *You Are the Message* (Homewood, IL: Dow Jones-Irwin, 1988), 22.
3. "Interview with Judge Warren Wolfson, 'How to improve your courtroom performance,'" *Trial Diplomacy Journal*, Vol. 8, No. 3 (1985): 7.

VISUAL ADVOCACY—TWENTY-FIRST CENTURY PERSUASION

The multimedia approach of using words and images in communication is the modern way of persuasion. Visual advocacy puts the information of a legal case in the same visual-verbal format that judges and jurors are used to in the outside world.

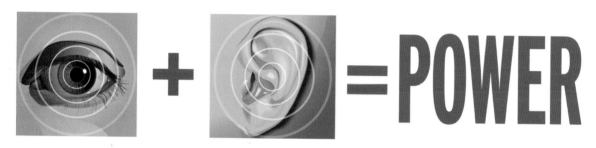

Combining the traditional forms of oral advocacy with images results in a powerful, persuasive form of communication. Done correctly, visual advocacy can become the tipping point of any case, dramatically increasing audience attention and involvement. The ability to use visuals with skill and sophistication has become one of the emerging hallmarks of professionalism for attorneys. This book is dedicated to putting the tools of multimedia communication into your hands.

2

COMMUNICATING VISUALLY

The medium is the message.

—Marshall McLuhan

At its essential core, a trial or settlement conference is a battle between two mutually exclusive interpretations of reality. How well each side communicates these realities has a lot to do with the outcome. The use of visuals is essential in this process.

A small number of innovative trial lawyers figured out the importance of visuals in the 1950s, successfully incorporating photos, models, and drawings into their courtroom presentations. One of these, Melvin Belli, wrote a pioneering book in 1955, *"Ready for the Plaintiff!"*[1] featuring not only his own work but also that of his peers. His explanation then of why visuals matter so much in persuading jurors remains true today:

What a jury could see, a jury could understand.

Since the time of Mr. Belli's book, television, film, and computers have cranked the level of visual exhibits in court way up. Trials now incorporate poster-size exhibits and digital images on screens or panels. But what are things that need to

---

1. Melvin Belli, *"Ready for the Plaintiff!"* (New York: Holt, 1956).

J. P. "Pete" Tonkoff, innovator featured in
"Ready for the Plaintiff!"

happen behind the scenes to work up a case visually? How do you determine what visuals to use? When is the best time to use them? These are a few of the many questions you need to answer as you develop a case visually. And the answers vary.

An animation may be the key to success in one case and a waste of money in another. An illustration may be all you need in one case, while another case may need a video. Resolving these issues requires that you understand how different visual media express information. It also means that you need to learn how to construct the story that your visuals will tell the jury.

There is growing evidence that the instant gratification of electronic devices and the Internet is rewiring our brains. This expresses itself in a number of ways, including a dramatic shortening of attention span. We now think in terms of seconds-long sound bites. Modern jurors have a stopwatch ticking in their brains—get to the point and keep it interesting, or they'll tune you out.

Before we go any further, it is important to have a basic knowledge of why visuals are so critical to the jury's learning process. Various researchers have shown that as much as 80 percent of all learning takes places through the eyes, with visual memory the most crucial ingredient.[2] Visuals allow an audience to decode and store information better.[3]

In the early 1960s, experimental psychologists Michael Gazzaniga and Roger W. Sperry first established that the human brain has two different ways of thinking.[4] On average, the right brain does better with visuals, remembering faces, spatial relationships, and things that depend on words. The right brain

LEFT BRAIN

Verbal
Logical/Analytical
Time
Sequential
Systematic
Linear
Facts & words
Abstract/Symbolic
Rational
Objective
Masculine

Recognizes:
Words
Letters
Numbers

RIGHT BRAIN

Nonverbal
Creative/Intuitive
Spatial
Random
Free
Holistic
Visual & colors
Sensory /Concrete
Emotional
Subjective
Feminine

Recognizes:
Faces
Places
Objects

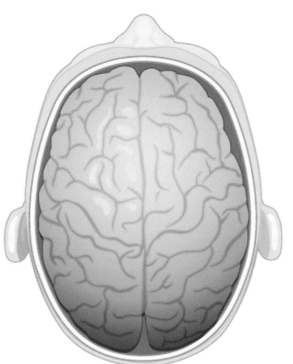

2. Robert R. Farrald and Richard G. Schamer, *Journal of Learning Disabilities* 6 (1973).

3. Peter Putnis and Roslyn Petelin, *Media Relations: Issues and Strategies* (1996); Patricia Baggett, "Understanding Visual and Verbal Messages," in *Knowledge Acquisition from Text and Pictures,* ed. Heinz Mandl and Joel R. Levin (North-Holland, 1989), 119.

4. Richard M. Restak, *The Brain* (New York: Bantam, 1984), 246-48. Though many books have been written about left and right brain research, none is more compelling than Dr. Leonard Shlain's *The Alphabet Versus the Goddess* (Penguin/Arkana 1998).

Traditional lawyering focuses on facts

processes information in a more intuitive and simultaneous way, looking first at the whole picture and then the details. In general, the left brain is more verbal, logical, and analytical, important for language and certain motor skills.[5]

You are no doubt most comfortable presenting information in the linear, logical, and analytical style of the left brain. Even when you use state-of-the-art media technology, you probably gravitate to the fact-driven, linear, and verbal.

5. Although subsequent research has shown that the divisions are not as polarized or as simple as once thought, it remains accepted that the right and left sides of the brain respond to different kinds of information.

A dry recitation of facts offers very little to the more nonverbal, creative, and intuitive right part of the brain, which is not reached by words alone.

In less visual times, the lawyer tradition of linear communication worked well enough. After the media revolution, this no longer is so. Jurors demand that presenters show and tell, engaging the whole brain. If you don't, they will check out on you quickly.

If you learn how to better use the creative part of your brain in working up a case (in addition to the logical part), you will be able to present the visual story of your case in much more sophisticated ways. The audience (whether jury, judge, or corporate insurance adjuster) will be more engaged and have an easier time learning and remembering your story's message.

This is at the heart of what visual advocacy is all about: presenting the story more holistically.

Visual advocacy engages both the creative power of the emotions and a sense of logic to produce an integrated message that both educates and persuades.

The lesson in all this is inescapable—you must move beyond word-driven appeals with too many details.

Engaging both the logical and creative sides of your audience will make your story more persuasive and memorable. Jurors want and need to see visuals along with words. Logical detail combines powerfully with photographs, illustrations, and videos. The result is an appealing presentation directed to the whole brain.

RECEIVER

INFORMATION FIELD

Send information to both sides of the brain.

SENDER

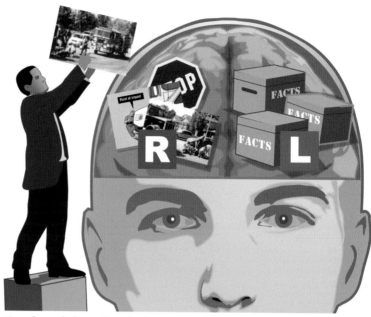

Combine left and right brain appeals.

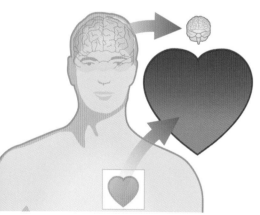

Head versus heart: the heart always wins.

Better audience engagement is the goal of visual advocacy, creatively integrating an emotional message with a logical one. The emotional component is particularly important, as no matter what people tell themselves, emotion and heart often trump logic.

Remember this simple equation: seeing plus hearing equals power—the power to persuade and the power to communicate more effectively.

So how do you work up a case visually? The answer to this question is critical because just using modern technology to show documents on a screen with a few added illustrations is not going to persuade your audience. What we are talking about, instead, is presenting a client's story in a whole new way. To work up and present a case visually, you need to start thinking more like a film director. We'll look at this in the next chapter.

TAKEAWAYS—COMMUNICATING VISUALLY

- *At its core, a case involves competing views of reality.*

- *A jury will make a decision based on which version is the most persuasive.*

- *What a jury can see, a jury can understand.*

- *The media revolution has upped the level of the game, requiring greater thought about the visuals in a case.*

- *You must appeal to both the emotion and the logic of the human brain.*

PART
TWO

Show the Story

3

THINKING LIKE A
FILM DIRECTOR

If you don't know where you are going, you'll wind up somewhere else.

—Yogi Berra

The availability of cameras, computers, projectors, and presentation software has all combined to make visual storytelling more accessible than ever before. But these tools alone are not what make a story compelling; rather, it is the way a story is crafted and visually presented. Even the most advanced technology cannot make a poorly designed story good.

With this in mind, we begin part 2 with suggestions on how to improve the visual design of a case by thinking more like a film director.

Film directors are responsible for the creative process of translating words into pictures. To accomplish this metamorphosis, they read the script multiple times and imagine what each scene might look like. Once they have a vision for the film, they work closely with other members of the production team

Even the most advanced technology cannot make a poorly designed story good.

21

to make that vision a reality. They work with storyboard artists to develop the look of each scene. They consider how they will establish settings and introduce the story's characters. They plan how to capture the audience's interest during the story's beginning. They give thought to the story's theme and how they will visualize it. They discuss camera angles with the director of photography, and once the footage is shot, they work with the editor to help create the final look of the film. These are just a few of the many ways that a film director guides the creative process of turning a script into a movie.

In order to guide the visualization of a trial story, you must utilize some of these same skills and think more like a film director. To find out how to do this, let's begin by looking at eight creative steps you can take to visually develop your case like a film director.

CREATIVE STEP 1—WRITE THE STORY

Early in discovery, once you have a basic idea of the facts of a case, write a rough draft of the story in the present tense. Use short sentences, and develop the story's theme. Include such elements as the rules that were broken, the settings where the action took place, the standards, the choices characters made that created the conflict, the outcome of the conflict, and so forth. When this rough draft is finished, go back and number each sentence sequentially as shown in the example below.

1. Mr. Logan walks out of his house to get in his truck and begin another day of work for the city.

2. He climbs into his cab and starts the engine.

3. He looks at his dash and sees the air-pressure gauge for his brakes is zero.

CREATIVE STEP 2—VISUALIZE THE FACTS

Read each numbered sentence and imagine what images could be used to visualize each important fact. Sometimes an element of the story is best shown by using a photograph. At other times, a graph, illustration, video, or document may be the better way to communicate a fact. Write your ideas beside each sentence and work through your entire rough draft. If you have more than one visual idea and are not sure which one to use, make a note and decide later which is the best one. In the example below, the need for specific photos was noted beside each sentence.

1. Mr. Logan walks out of his house to get in his truck and begin another day of work for the city.
   [Get photo of entire truck.]

2. He climbs in his cab and starts the engine.
   [Get photo of truck's cab on driver's side.]

3. He looks at his dash and sees the air-pressure gauge for his brakes is zero.
   [Get photo of the dash. Get a close-up photo of the air gauge on the dash.]

CREATIVE STEP 3—COLLECT THE IMAGES

Once you have identified the story's visuals, begin collecting those images. Talk with experts about what exhibits will best illustrate their opinions. Determine whether the expert or someone else is the best person to create the exhibits that are needed. (Don't assume that just because experts are knowledgeable in their professional fields that they are also experts in visual communication.) Do site inspections and take photographs. Create illustrations and graphics. Acquire X-rays, scans, and so forth. Add visuals as new facts are learned and your story develops.

The example below shows the photographs that were identified and collected for the facts in the first portion of the story.

> PHOTO 1: Mr. Logan walks out of his house to get in his truck and begin another day of work for the city.

> PHOTO 2: He climbs into his cab and starts the engine.

Add visuals as new facts are learned and your story develops.

PHOTO 3: He looks at his dash and sees the air-pressure gauge for his brakes is zero.

CREATIVE STEP 4—DOCUMENT THE SETTINGS

Visit the settings where important events happened in the story. These include places where defendants made choices, crashes occurred, and clients are trying to recover. Take photographs or video clips from different points of view. Review these visuals and decide which medium best shows the story.

The photograph below shows the setting where a defendant driver failed to stop at the stop limit line.

Visit the settings where important events happened in the story.

CREATIVE STEP 5—SEQUENCE THE IMAGES

Sequence the story's most important visuals on big pieces of foam core. You can also mount them on a wall in your office. (If your case is document intensive, you can sequence the visuals and documents in a notebook.) At different times of the day, take a moment to look at the sequencing of these images. If something is missing, add it. If something needs to be changed, change it. Show the visuals to partners and/or staff. Elicit questions and comments. Make additional changes as needed.

At different times of the day, take a moment to look at the sequencing of your images.

CREATIVE STEP 6—FOCUS THE VISUALS

Test the visual story as well as the oral story with a focus group. Be willing to see and hear the feedback the focus group provides. Sometimes this feedback is different from one's own ideas about "the way it should be." Be willing to adapt the story visually or orally to accommodate insightful feedback. Use the valuable ideas of others to improve the quality of the story and the information it is communicating.

Test the visual story as well as the oral story with a focus group.

CREATIVE STEP 7—EDIT THE STORY

Once you have gotten feedback on your presentation, edit the words and images to reflect this feedback. If appropriate, focus the presentation again. For example, an important moment in a story involving a personal injury was when one of the defendants made a risky choice not to look out his driver's side window. During a focus-group presentation, one person observed that the photograph that was being used during this part of the story showed the passenger window but not the driver's side window.

Original Story Photo

After the focus group was over, the photographs from a site inspection were reviewed and an image was found that showed the driver's side window. This image was then used to replace the original photo because it communicated the visual story in a much more accurate way.

Edited Story Photo

CREATIVE STEP 8—PREPARE FOR THE OPENING

Motion the court pretrial to get the visuals you've created approved for use in the trial. If the judge orders you to make changes in any of the visuals or develop additional foundation, you have time to do so. After you've taken any corrective measures, renew your motion, explaining all you've done to meet the judge's concerns.

Check out the logistics of your courtroom or settlement conference location ahead of time. What equipment, if any, will you need to bring? Are there any compatibility problems? Where is the optimal place to position yourself so everyone can see you and the visuals at the same time?

In summary, you must be a master of the visual story as well as the oral story. Those who use sophisticated visual strategies to present the case story will have a distinct advantage over

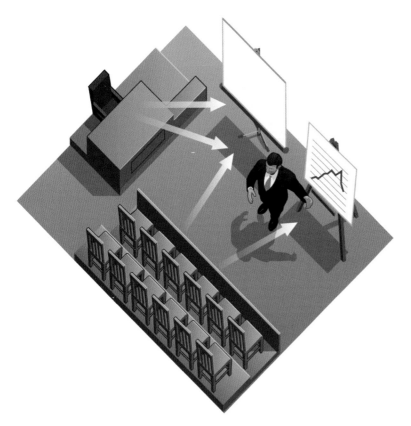

Position yourself so everyone can see you and the visuals at the same time.

those who do not. By following these eight creative steps you will begin thinking more like a film director. The chapters that follow are all designed to help you become better at creating the visual story. They include: establishing the story's settings, introducing characters visually, presenting the story's rule or theme, setting up the conflict, showing the standards, identifying character choices, re-creating climactic moments, and seeing the big picture. We begin by taking a detailed look at how to visually establish the important settings of a case.

You must be a master of the visual story as well as the oral story.

TAKEAWAYS—THINKING LIKE A FILM DIRECTOR

 ◆ *Write a rough draft of the case story.*

 ◆ *Number each sentence in the story and imagine what image could be used to visually complement each important fact.*

 ◆ *Obtain the visuals that best illustrate the story.*

 ◆ *Document important settings.*

 ◆ *Sequence the key visuals.*

 ◆ *Show others your visual story and get feedback.*

 ◆ *Present to a focus group.*

 ◆ *Edit the oral and visual story.*

 ◆ *Motion the court pretrial to get the visuals you've created approved for use in the trial.*

 ◆ *Determine the optimal place to position yourself so everyone can see you and the visuals.*

4

ESTABLISHING THE
STORY'S SETTINGS

*Telling a good story is like giving a mini-documentary of
what you have seen so others can see it, too.*

—Annette Simmons

When a screenwriter writes a script, he or she describes the
settings where the action takes place at the beginning of
each scene. Once the script goes into production, a location
scout looks for physical settings that reflect these descriptions.
When the film director and director of photography begin
shooting, they give each setting its final look in terms of lighting, camera angles, and so forth. In *Raiders of the Lost Ark* the
setting of the opening scene is described like this:

EXTERIOR: SOUTH AMERICA-HIGH JUNGLE-DAY

Mountains peak against sky in dense, lush rain forests
filled with the varied sounds of the jungle. Ragged, jutting
canyon walls are half-hidden by the thick mists. A group of
men make their way along a narrow trail across the green
face of the canyon.

At the head of the party is an American, INDIANA JONES. He wears a short leather jacket, a flapped holster, and a brimmed felt hat; there is a whip swinging at his hip.[1]

Once this setting is established, the script describes Indiana Jones walking toward a temple that is thousands of years old. After he reaches it and goes inside, the scene changes from an exterior jungle to the interior of a temple. This change in the story's settings allows the audience to visually follow where the action is occurring. This same technique of visualizing a story's settings can also be used to help jurors follow the events in an opening statement. In an opening, the jury wants to see where the action of the story is taking place. As the action changes to a different setting, they want to see what the new setting looks like.

This allows the jurors to see the places where important events occur. It also allows them to see where the story's "characters" make decisions and act in ways that create conflict and impact the lives of others. Although the settings of a case are the same whether one is a plaintiff's attorney or a defense attorney, how the settings are used will differ depending on one's point of view. Plaintiff's attorneys use settings to focus the jury's attention on the actions of the defendant. Defense attorneys use the same settings to focus on the plaintiff. The following case studies provide examples of how to identify and use the important settings in an opening. They are presented from the plaintiff's point of view so they are focused on the defendant.

CASE STORY: *MASON*

In the case of *Mason,* there are two defendants: the city and a truck driver. When multiple defendants are involved in a case, sometimes the settings for the story are the same and sometimes they can be different. Since there are two defendants in this case, let's look first at the settings for the defendant city.

The story's action begins in the office of a City Street Services Department. This is the setting where a city employee

> Plaintiff's attorneys use settings to focus the jury's attention on the actions of the defendant.

---

1. Lawrence Kasdan, *Raiders of the Lost Ark: The Illustrated Screenplay* (New York: Ballantine Books, 1981).

breaks rules and makes a risky decision to renew a driver's yearly contract without reviewing his driving record. Since this decision is related to a serious injury that occurs later in the story, a photograph of the office building is used to show the jury the setting where the defendant city made its decision.

Office Setting

In the middle of the story, the action shifts to an intersection. It is here that the driver hired by the city runs a stop sign. A photograph of the intersection shows the jury the setting where this action occurs.

Intersection Setting

During the story's ending, the injured plaintiff is taken to a hospital. The hospital setting is important because it is the place where the jury sees the extent of the plaintiff's injuries as doctors, specialists, and therapists diagnose them.

Hospital Setting

We now have identified three different settings where the action of this story takes place, with regard to the defendant city. Document each of these settings visually during discovery so you can use them later in the opening.

Setting 1

Setting 2

Setting 3

By showing these settings during opening, the jurors get to see for themselves the places where the defendant's decisions and actions endangered and harmed the plaintiff. (If the jurors are *not* shown these settings, they will likely create different pictures in their minds about what these settings look like and how the events occurred.)

As mentioned earlier, when a case has multiple defendants, sometimes the settings can vary for each party. In *Mason,* the other defendant was the driver who made risky choices while driving his truck for the city. Since the place where the defendant driver made these risky decisions was inside his truck's cab, a photograph of the truck's cab is a critical setting to include during this part of the story.

Truck Cab Setting

If we add this truck-cab setting to the settings for the defendant city, the story's combined settings now look like this:

Setting 1

Setting 2

Setting 3

Setting 4

Now that we have seen how the settings of a story can be used to show the places where the decisions and actions of the defendants occurred, let's see how the settings are determined in an entirely different case.

CASE STORY: *TUCKER*

In *Tucker,* the action of the story begins inside the defendant hospital where the ER staff is examining a patient who has just arrived complaining of throat pain. Since it may not be possible to visually document the interior of a hospital's emergency room, a photograph of the exterior of the hospital was used instead to establish the setting where the action is occurring.

Hospital Setting

As the story continues, the patient is admitted and transferred to a room on the fifth floor. This reflects a change in the location of the story's action. Since this new setting and what occurred there is critical to the story, a photograph was taken of the patient's room.

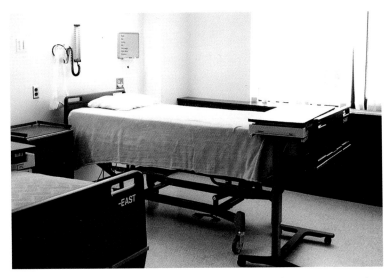

Room Setting

During the middle of the story, some of the action takes place inside the patient's throat. If an expert is going to testify about what the patient's throat looked like at this time based on the medical records, an illustration can be used to show the interior setting of the plaintiff's throat.

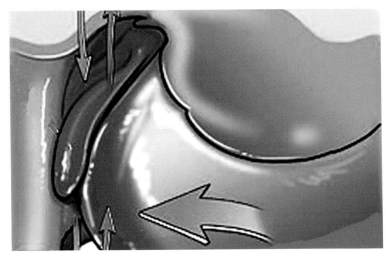

Interior Mouth Setting

During the ending of the story, we needed to show a series of rapidly changing settings to document the action. These included the hospital elevator, the basement hallway, and the operating room.

*Elevator
Setting*

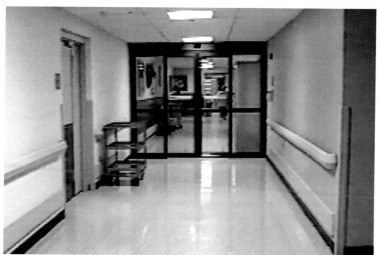

*Hallway
Setting*

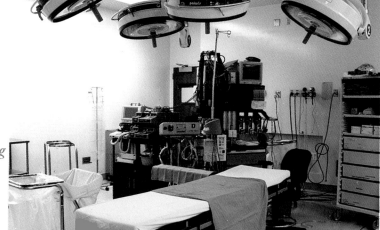

*Operating
Room
Setting*

Each of these photographs played a significant role in showing the jury how the defendant put the patient at risk and caused a serious injury.

If we combine the settings for this story, they look like this:

Setting 1

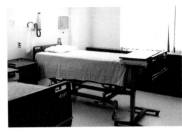

Setting 2

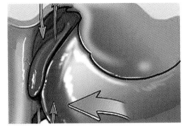

Setting 3

Setting 4

Setting 5

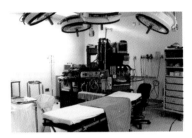

Setting 6

In summary, no matter what type of trial story you are presenting, the story has settings that you need to present visually to the jurors so they can see where the action is taking place. Identify these images and document them during discovery so you can use them later for settlement and/or trial presentations. Now that we have seen the importance of establishing a story's settings, let's explore how to show the story's characters.

Takeaways—Establishing the Story's Settings

- *Identify and document the key settings in a case.*

- *If there are multiple opposing parties, document the important settings for each party.*

- *When the action of the story changes to a new location, show the jury the new setting.*

5

INTRODUCING CHARACTERS VISUALLY

All drama is conflict. Without conflict, you have no action. Without action, you have no character. Without character, you have no story.

—Syd Field

Somewhere during the beginning of a movie, the main character of the story is visually introduced to the audience. In *Star Wars IV: A New Hope,* the hero, Luke Skywalker, is introduced as a young man living on a remote planet, where he is helping his aunt and uncle farm their land. What the audience soon learns, however, is that Luke dreams of leaving this farm and joining the Academy to help fight the evil Galactic Empire that is oppressing the land.

Once Luke has been introduced, the action of the story continues to focus on his character so the audience realizes he is the main character in the story. As a result, the decisions he makes and the actions he takes are of particular importance to the audience. The reason for this is that his decisions and actions reflect his internal values and communicate the message (theme) of the story. As the story progresses and the audience's experience of Luke's character deepens, their relationship and feelings toward him change as well. By the end of the film, as a result of seeing the choices and actions that Luke has made, the audience understands his rite of passage from adolescent to Jedi knight. The audience is able to see this change in his character because they see his decisions, actions, and values. So a good film director communicates the message (theme) of a film by accentuating how an audience experiences the story's characters.

Attorneys, like film directors, have the ability to visually introduce a "character" in a story. By using visual techniques similar to those used in filmmaking, you can focus attention on the decisions and actions of a particular character so that the jury understands who is the main character in the story. For plaintiff's attorneys, the main character of the story is the defendant, so the focus of the story is on the defendant's choices and actions. For defense attorneys, the focus is on the plaintiff. Presenting the story from the plaintiff's point of view will be discussed in this chapter and the remaining chapters in part 2.

When developing the visual story of a case, if you want to think more like a film director, you need to decide how you are going to visually portray the defendant. If the defendant is an individual, you can, of course, grab a frame from his video deposition and use it to represent him. If the defendant is a corporation, other types of images can be used. For example, if one of the defendants is a city, you might use a city logo or photo of the building where a city's administration department is based. Once an image has been selected to personify or represent a defendant, it can be used periodically throughout the opening whenever you want to refer to that defendant. In the case of *Mason*, a photo of the city's administration headquarters was used to represent the defendant city.

As the story develops and the city makes decisions that break rules and violate standards, this same image can be used to show the jury "who" is making these poor decisions. This simple visual technique allows the jurors to recognize,

Defendant City

experience, and react to the defendant's character, because they can see an image that visually represents the city. Sometimes the visual icon that is used to represent a defendant is the same image that is used to establish a setting. In *Mason,* the image that was selected to represent the defendant city was the same image used to show the setting where the city performed contractual services. The fact that this same image was used in a dual capacity is perfectly acceptable.

If there is more than one defendant in a case, a different visual image needs to be selected for each defendant. For example, in *Mason,* the second defendant was the driver of a truck. The image used to represent this defendant was a close-up photograph of the truck's cab where the defendant was driving at the time a crash occurred.

Defendant Driver

We now have selected two icons that represent each defendant in this trial story. These images will be used throughout the opening whenever we want to anchor important information and facts about liability or damages to these defendants.

Using a visual icon to personify the defendant and link him to the risky decisions and actions he made is a powerful communication tool. If, at different points of the story, the jury sees the image of the defendant and hears that the pictured defendant's poor decisions put others at risk, the jury is more likely to disapprove of the defendant's character and will assign negative feelings to the person or entity whose image is shown. When you use this type of visual anchoring throughout the opening, at some point when the jury sees the image of the defendant, it will likely trigger those strong feelings.

In *Tucker,* the defendant doctor and medical team were introduced and visualized by a photograph of the exterior of the hospital where they worked. This was the only image used to personify the defendants since other images were not available.

Using a visual icon to personify the defendant and link him or her to the risky decisions and actions made is a powerful communication tool.

Defendant Doctor and Medical Team

In summary, one of the ways you can think more like a film director is by introducing the defendant (or plaintiff) visually so the jury can see what the "character" looks like. By using this simple visual technique, you can anchor the key facts about a defendant to this image. It can also help the jurors link their thoughts and feelings about this character to this image. Great film directors and screenwriters use this same visual technique when working with the characters in their films. As a result, the audience comes to like some characters (Luke Skywalker as the hero) and dislike other characters (Darth Vader as the villain).

TAKEAWAYS—INTRODUCING CHARACTERS VISUALLY

◆ *No matter what type of trial story is being presented, a visual image needs to be selected to represent the defendant and/or plaintiff.*

◆ *If there is more than one defendant and/or plaintiff in the story, use a separate image to represent each "character."*

◆ *The defendant(s) in a story can be visually represented through the use of photographs, logos, graphics, video, still frames, and so forth.*

◆ *Once an image has been selected to represent the defendant and/or plaintiff, repeatedly use this same image whenever you want to anchor important facts about this defendant in the minds and emotions of the jury.*

6

PRESENTING THE STORY'S RULE OR THEME

You have to learn the rules of the game. And then you have to play better than anyone else.

—Albert Einstein

When film directors make a movie, they constantly consider the theme of the story and how to communicate that theme to the audience. The theme is the key to the audience's understanding of the story, and it reflects the point of view of the screenwriter as well as the interpretations of the director.

In the 1942 film *Casablanca,* directed by Michael Curtiz, the story communicates the timeless themes of self-centeredness and loving unconditionally. The main character, Rick Blaine (Humphrey Bogart), struggles to come to terms with the bitterness he feels toward life. The audience does not initially know why Rick is so bitter, but they eventually learn Rick had once lived in Paris, where he had fallen in love with a woman named Ilsa Lund (Ingrid Bergman). One day, without explanation, Ilsa had left Rick without saying good-bye. As a result, Rick had closed his heart and made the decision to never love

The theme is the key to the audience's understanding of the story.

again. This decision has impacted not only his own life, but also his relationships with others ever since.

As the story goes, Rick eventually relocates to Casablanca, where he owns a nightclub. Even though his business brings him in contact with many people, Rick's heart remains shut down, and he continuously demonstrates his unwillingness to stick his neck out for anybody. As fate would have it, Ilsa unexpectedly reenters his life with her husband, Victor Laszlo. Laszlo is part of the underground war effort, and the Nazis are seeking to capture him. As a result, the couple has traveled to Casablanca to get out of Europe and go to America.

One evening at the nightclub, Ilsa seeks Rick's help and confronts him. During this scene, Ilsa tells Rick the real reason for her abrupt departure in Paris. When she had become involved with Rick in Paris, she had thought her husband was dead. Then she received news that he was alive and in hiding. Upon learning this information, she had immediately left to find him.

Once Rick hears Ilsa's explanation and experiences that she is still in love with him, he begins to open his heart again and eventually decides to help Ilsa and her husband escape from the Nazis. In doing so, he takes important steps that allow him to reclaim his heart and his humanity once again. So it is through Rick's decisions and actions that the film communicates its theme: one must move beyond self-centeredness in order to love unconditionally. For attorneys, organizing the facts of a case so the story has a strong theme is just as important as it is for the screenwriter and director of a major motion picture.

> For attorneys, organizing the facts of a case so the story has a strong theme is just as important as it is for the screenwriter and director of a major motion picture.

Presenting the Theme

Publications such as *Moe Levine on Advocacy,*[1] *Rules of the Road,*[2] and *David Ball on Damages*[3] have all suggested strategies

---

1. Moe Levine, *Moe Levine on Advocacy* (Portland, OR: Trial Guides, 2009).
2. Rick Friedman and Patrick Malone, *Rules of the Road* (Portland, OR: Trial Guides, 2010).
3. David Ball, *David Ball on Damages* (South Bend, IN: National Institute for Trial Advocacy, 2001, 2005).

for how to begin an opening statement. One of their recommended strategies is to state a rule the defendants have violated. This rule must be broad in scope, easy to understand, and only a couple of sentences long. It must also be presented without any mention of the defendant's name. By identifying this rule at the opening's beginning, it is intended to act like a lens through which the jury will view the facts of the case. When used in this way, the rule is like a theme, because it suggests the story's subject. Let's examine how this rule or theme can be visualized to reinforce its importance to the jury.

Visualize the theme to reinforce its importance.

CASE STORY: *MASON*

In the story of *Mason,* the defendant city makes decisions that break at least two important rules. One of those rules says that the city must review a driver's driving history before renewing his or her annual contract. The other rule says that the city must periodically inspect a truck's paperwork to make sure its brakes have been inspected and are safe. During this story, the city makes choices that break both of these rules.

The defendant driver also makes decisions that break important rules like not stopping at a stop sign. As a result the public is put at risk.

The theme of this case has to do with the needless endangerment of the public. The word "needless" is used because the story might have been different if the city and driver had followed the rules instead of making risky choices. This theme guides the entire content of the story.

All the facts, questions, stories, and exhibits from *voir dire* to closing argument repeatedly focus the jury on the subject of risky choices, broken rules, and the actions that contributed to the harm.

Now that we know the theme of this story, we want to introduce it to the jury in a few simple sentences that are stated in the form of a rule at the opening's beginning. Here is the rule or theme for *Mason,* presented in two panels that are displayed sequentially on the screen.

> A city and its employees are not allowed to needlessly endanger the public.

Panel 1

> If a city and its employees needlessly endanger the public and someone is hurt, they are responsible for the harm.

Panel 2

Using a rule or theme to begin the opening sets the tone of the story, allowing jurors to reach their own conclusions rather than telling them what they should think.

These panels focus the jury's attention on the rule or theme. The jury does not yet know all the details of "what happened," but the jurors do understand that the subject of the story they are about to see (from the plaintiff's point of view) is going to be about someone needlessly being harmed. By displaying a rule like this at the beginning of the opening, your initial relationship with the jury is to act like a guide who introduces the case's theme in the form of a rule. Using a rule or theme to begin the opening sets the tone of the story, allowing jurors to reach their own conclusions rather than telling them what they should think.

Now that we have seen how a rule can be used like a theme to begin an opening, let's look at how this technique is used in an entirely different case.

CASE STORY: *TUCKER*

Hospital doctors know that if a patient can't breathe as a result of a blockage in his throat, they need to immediately perform an emergency airway procedure. Hospital doctors know that this relatively simple procedure can be done anywhere in a hospital, including the patient's room. In *Tucker,* a defendant doctor puts a patient at risk because he breaks this rule and makes decisions that endanger his patient. This is the theme of this trial story, and, like the previous example, it guides the opening (as well as the entire trial) both orally and visually. What we now want to do is articulate this theme in the form of a rule that the jury can see on a screen.

Once the jury sees this rule, they know that they are being asked to decide whether the defendant in this case "needlessly endangered" the plaintiff as a result of poor choices. From the very beginning of the opening, this rule focuses attention on the theme of this case.

To summarize, using a rule or theme at the opening's begin-

A physician is not allowed to needlessly endanger a patient.

If a physician needlessly endangers a patient and the patient is hurt, the physician is responsible for the harm.

Panel 1

Panel 2

ning informs the jury about the subject of the trial. Once this rule or theme is introduced, the next step is to focus the jury's attention on an incident where the defendant makes a risky decision that puts the plaintiff at risk. By sequencing the story in this way, a strong relationship is created between the rule or theme and an incident that expresses this theme.

TAKEAWAYS—PRESENTING THE STORY'S RULE OR THEME

- *Start the opening by presenting a rule that the defendants have violated. This rule should be broad enough that it also communicates the theme of the case.*

- *Display the rule or theme on the screen using one sentence at a time.*

- *Visualize the rule, using a font like Arial. Make the font size large (for example 40 point) so it is easy to read.*

- *Keep the rule simple.*

- *Remember that the word "needlessly" is an essential part of the rule or theme's language.*

- *When presenting the rule, do not mention the defendants' names.*

7

SETTING UP THE CONFLICT

*People screen out a lot of commercials because they open with
something dull. . . . When you advertise fire-extinguishers,
open with fire.*

—David Ogilvy

In filmmaking, the director sets up the story's conflict visually at the beginning of the movie. This is typically done with
what is called an "inciting incident." In the film *Raiders of the
Lost Ark,* during the first few minutes Indiana Jones enters an
ancient Peruvian temple and retrieves a golden artifact. He then
narrowly escapes a series of traps as he runs out of the temple
only to confront a rival archeologist who takes the artifact.
Empty-handed, Indy runs to a nearby airplane and narrowly
escapes death from the natives who are chasing him.

Within the first few minutes of this film, the inciting incident sets up the conflict of this story: an adventurous battle
between the forces of good and evil. It also focuses the audience's attention on the main character, Indiana Jones. In the
presentation of a trial story, an inciting incident sets up the
conflict between the defendant and the plaintiff. It also can be

> The inciting
> incident sets up the
> conflict between
> the defendant and
> the plaintiff.

used to focus attention on the defendant. Let's see how this is done in *Mason*.

CASE STORY: *MASON*

In *Mason,* the opening begins with the establishment of the case rule or theme: "A city and its employees are not allowed to needlessly endanger the public." Once this rule or theme has been established, the next objective is to create an inciting incident that introduces the defendant and shows a choice or action the defendant makes that puts the plaintiff at risk. Let's look at how this was done.

> Let me take you back for a moment. The year is 20XX. It is early summer in the city of Trent, and we are in the downtown office of Ms. Brenda Archer. She is the contract truck coordinator for the City of Trent's Street Services Department.

Presentation Strategy: Defendant City

The jury is immediately introduced to one of the defendants, a city employee named Brenda Archer. Since her deposition was not taped and we do not have a picture of her, a visual icon is needed to represent her as a city official. So a photograph of the building's exterior where she works was used. This photograph serves as a visual anchor to represent the defendant city. Once identified, this same image is used throughout the opening whenever we want the jury to refer to the defendant city.

Let's continue with the story.

The city has a program that enables its Street Services Department to hire dump-truck drivers and rent privately owned dump trucks for the hauling of asphalt and other materials for street repairs.

The story and visuals immediately introduce one of the defendants.

As the contract truck coordinator for the city's Street Services Department, one of Brenda Archer's responsibilities is reviewing a driver's performance history prior to renewing his or her yearly contract.

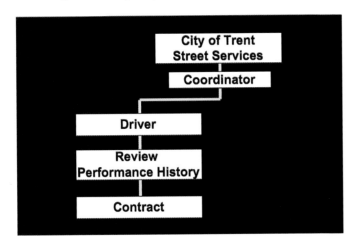

Presentation Strategy: Responsibility Chart

A simple graphic is used to visualize this information and to anchor the supervisor's responsibility of reviewing a driver's performance history prior to the renewal of driving privileges.

One of Brenda Archer's other responsibilities is reviewing the safety inspections of a truck's brakes. It is a city policy that this review must take place before a truck's yearly contract is renewed.

A simple graphic visually anchors one of the defendant's responsibilities.

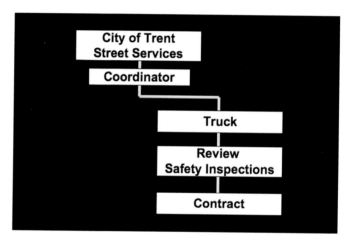

Presentation Strategy: Responsibility Chart

This graphic visually emphasizes the need for the city to do a safety inspection of the truck prior to renewing its contract.

On June 16, 20XX, a truck driver named John Logan Jr. is sitting in Brenda Archer's office. He has come to renew his yearly contract to drive for the city and use his truck to do work for the city.

As he sits in Brenda Archer's office, Mr. Logan knows that just one week prior to this meeting, he was involved in a collision. He also knows that fourteen months earlier, he was involved in another collision that caused substantial injuries.

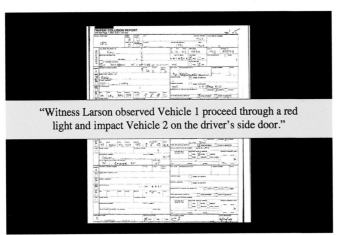

"Witness Larson observed Vehicle 1 proceed through a red light and impact Vehicle 2 on the driver's side door."

Presentation Strategy: Collision Report

The traffic-collision report is projected briefly to show the jury that it exists and that the driver of vehicle #1 (driven by Mr. Logan) drove through a red light. In order to keep the story moving, this exhibit is not discussed in detail at this time.

Mr. Logan also knows he has not had his truck's brakes inspected by the highway patrol for three years, and he does not have a current safety-inspection sticker on his truck.

The defendant has not had his brakes inspected for three years.

Now before we talk about what the contract coordinator says to this driver regarding these violations, and whether she renews his yearly contract or suspends his driving privileges, I want to take a moment to discuss the city's rules and written policies regarding the renewal of contracts for drivers and trucks.

Inciting Incident Summary

This inciting incident has now set up the story's conflict and focused attention on the defendants. The jury now wants to know what the city contract coordinator is going to do. If she revokes his driving privileges and suspends the use of his truck because its brakes have not been inspected, she has followed city rules and protected the public. If, on the other hand, she renews his driving privileges and the use of his truck, she breaks city rules and jeopardizes the public. At this point of the story, the jurors don't know what decisions she makes, but their curiosity and interest have been aroused.

The inciting incident in this story is displayed in seven different images.

Image 1

Image 2

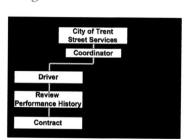

Image 3

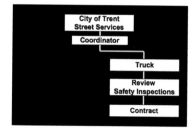

Image 4

Image 5

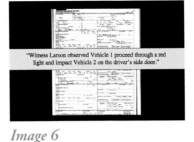

"Witness Larson observed Vehicle 1 proceed through a red light and impact Vehicle 2 on the driver's side door."

Image 6

Image 7

Viewing these panels as a whole, we see that photographs, documents, and simple graphics have been used to set up the conflict. The average time that any one of these panels is shown on the screen is five seconds. This means that this inciting incident is presented in less than one minute. With this fast pacing, the jury is continuously stimulated with new visual information that enhances the oral story.

Now that we have seen how an inciting incident can be used to set up the conflict in a story and focus attention on the defendant, let's look at the inciting incident in a medical-malpractice case.

The jury is continuously stimulated with new visual information that enhances the oral story.

CASE STORY: *TUCKER*

In *Tucker,* the opening begins with the establishment of the case rule or theme: "A physician is not allowed to needlessly endanger a patient." Once this rule or theme has been established, our next objective is to create an inciting incident that introduces the defendant and shows a choice or action the defendant makes that puts the plaintiff at risk.

Let me take you back for a moment. It is Saturday morning, August 24, 20XX. An ER doctor in the St. Koda Hospital is examining a twenty-two-year-old man who has a toothache. The patient's name is Ricky Tucker.

Presentation Strategy: Hospital Photo

This photograph of the hospital immediately establishes the setting where the action of the story is taking place.

> The ER doctor examines Mr. Tucker and notes that he has severe swelling in his throat and may need to see an ear, nose, and throat specialist the following morning if his condition does not improve. St. Koda Hospital then admits Mr. Tucker and assigns him to a room on the fifth floor.

The medical record shows the patient may need to se an ENT in the morning.

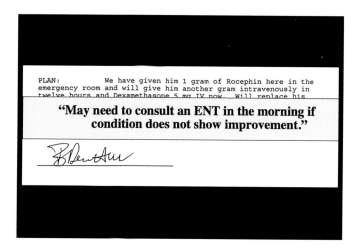

PLAN: We have given him 1 gram of Rocephin here in the emergency room and will give him another gram intravenously in twelve hours and Dexamethasone 5 mg IV now. Will replace his

"May need to consult an ENT in the morning if condition does not show improvement."

Presentation Strategy: Medical Record

Only one sentence from this medical record is selected to emphasize that the hospital was aware that this patient might need to see an ENT specialist on day two.

> On the morning of day two, Mr. Tucker's condition has not improved and a nurse notes this in his chart. At no time during the day does a nurse request that a physician see Mr. Tucker. At no time during this day does an ENT or any other physician come to Mr. Tucker's room to examine him.

EMERGENCY CARE SERVICES

E# *7 23 7266*

"Condition has not improved. Tonsils are enlarged and Patient is drooling. Left cheek is swollen."

PAST MEDICAL HX:

MEDICATIONS:

ALLERGIES: NKA

SMOKER / NON SMOKER   LMP   SANROX   PAIN   MIGRAINE   LAST TETANUS   TRIAGE NURSE SIGNATURE *A. Harrell*

The following morning, the patient's condition has not improved.

Presentation Strategy: Medical Record

This document establishes that the hospital knew that the patient's condition had not improved.

> On the morning of day three, Dr. Sienna, an ENT, arrives to examine Mr. Tucker for the first time. Dr. Sienna stands beside Mr. Tucker's bed and has him open his mouth so he can observe his throat. When Dr. Sienna looks inside Mr. Tucker's mouth, he sees that his throat is so swollen that it is almost completely blocked. Dr. Sienna knows this is a life-threatening situation. If the patient's throat becomes completely blocked he won't be able to breathe through his mouth or his nose. Dr. Sienna also knows that there is a simple procedure he can perform in the patient's room to immediately help him breathe.

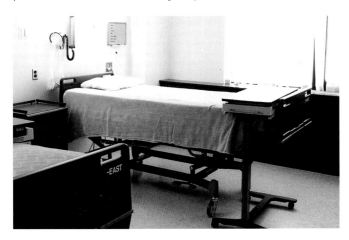

Now before we discuss what Dr. Sienna decides to do for this patient, I want to take a moment to talk about emergency airway procedures for patients who can't breathe.

Inciting Incident Summary

By the time this doctor sees this patient for the first time on day three, the patient's throat has already become so swollen that he is in danger of not being able to breathe. The jurors don't know what course of action this ENT will take, but their interest in the story is very high because the patient is in danger of not breathing. This inciting incident with its use of photographs and a few documents sets up the conflict in this story and informs the jury what the subject of this story is: a physician who breaks rules creates conflict and causes harm to a patient.

Viewing these panels as a whole, we see that they look very different from *Mason*, yet their purpose is the same: to set up the conflict and focus attention on a specific character in the story (in this case a physician).

The inciting incident in this story is displayed in four different visuals.

Image 1

Image 2

Image 3

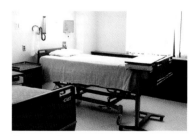

Image 4

Now that we have seen how an inciting incident can be used to set up the story's conflict and focus attention on a specific character in the story, the next chapter explores the importance of showing the standards.

TAKEAWAYS—SETTING UP THE CONFLICT

- Use an inciting incident at the beginning of the opening to establish a setting, introduce the defendant, and show a choice or action the defendant makes that violates the rule or theme.

- When presenting the inciting incident, use the visual icon that has been selected to represent the defendant. (Use this same visual icon throughout the story whenever you want to refer to the defendant).

- Keep the pacing of the story quick when presenting the inciting incident.

- Avoid too much detail during this portion of the opening. Simple is better.

8

SHOWING THE STANDARDS

Art is not what you see, but what you make others see.

—Edgar Degas

When an audience views a film, it sometimes needs to know information about a character's past in order to better understand the events that are unfolding in the present. In *Casablanca,* the audience discovers at the story's beginning that Rick doesn't seem to care about the needs of others. But it is not until an event from Rick's past is revealed (Ilsa's leaving him in Paris without saying good-bye) that viewers get some insight into why he acts the way he does. The introduction of this background information helps the audience to understand Rick's character and keeps the audience focused on the story's theme: the journey from self-centeredness to loving unconditionally.

In courtroom storytelling, this technique of providing background information so the jury understands the events of the story also applies. For example, if a case involves a defendant who breaks rules regarding the safe hiring of drivers, then the jury needs to know what these rules are *before* the defendant's

When structured properly, the standards portion of the opening reinforces the theme of the entire trial.

side presents its story. The jury will also need to know the potential risks involved if these rules are broken. Once this background information has been communicated and the story begins, the jury will be sensitized to these rules and the risks involved if the defendant breaks them. The delivery of this type of background information has the ability to influence the way the jury views the events throughout the story.

Let's look at how the standards can be visualized, giving particular attention to how they set up the story and influence the way the jury views the story's "characters." As we shall see, the standards are another opportunity to anchor the story's thematic message.

CASE STORY: *MASON*

As previously discussed, *Mason* involves two defendants: the City of Trent and a truck driver. In order for the jurors to understand this case, you need to educate them about the standards before they hear what happened. Specifically, the jury needs to know that the city has written policies and rules regarding the power to contract trucks and drivers. In particular, there are two rules that need to be defined. Rule BCT-5 specifies, among other things, how the city should do a performance evaluation of a truck driver prior to renewing his or her contract for city work. Rule BCT-7B specifies how the city should review the safety of a truck prior to contracting it for city work.

Since one of the challenges of this case was to make complex city rules easy for the jury to understand, let's look at the oral story, line by line, and see how the visual story was developed to complement it.

> The city has specific rules with regard to its contracts with owner-drivers like Mr. Logan. These rules spell out the city's duty to govern and control its relationship with drivers and their trucks.

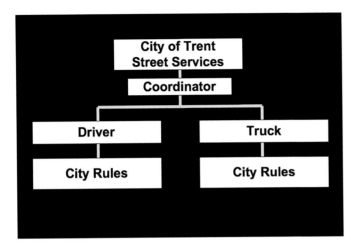

Presentation Strategy: General Rules

This simple demonstrative graphic shows that the City of Trent Street Services Department has two branches: drivers and trucks. Beneath each of these branches are the same words: "City Rules." This graphic emphasizes the fact that the city's drivers and trucks are both governed by rules. Continuing with the story:

> There are two rules I want to discuss: Rule BCT-5 and Rule BCT-7B. Let's look first at Rule BCT-5.

The city's drivers and trucks are both governed by rules.

Presentation Strategy: Detailed Rule

Simple enlarged type is all that is needed to focus the jury on the two rules that are now going to be discussed.

City Rule BCT-5 requires each contract truck owner to have a performance evaluation conducted by a city supervisor thirty days before being offered a new yearly contract.

The rules are presented in a simple way that is easy to understand.

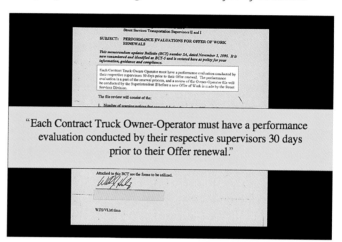

Presentation Strategy: Detailed Rule

A document showing the city's rule that is being discussed is presented here. The language of the contract is reentered in a text box that is filled with yellow to make the black type easy to read. In this example, the font Arial is used, large enough (for example, twenty-four point) so the words are easy to read.

Even though the city's rules are complex, the way they are visually introduced to the jury makes them seem easy to understand and follow. This makes it more likely that the jurors will say to themselves: "If I can follow this rule, then so can the city."

If, on the other hand, the presentation of these rules is hard to understand or uses language that is difficult for the jury to get, the jury is more likely to believe that the rule might have been hard for the city to understand as well. If this happens, the jurors will say to themselves: "If I can't understand these rules, maybe the city couldn't understand them either." For these reasons, the city's rule is presented in a very simple and straightforward manner.

> The city supervisor conducting the review of a truck owner must also do a performance evaluation to evaluate the driver's driving record during the previous twelve months. The form they use looks like this:

Showing the defendant's checklist allows the viewer to see it for themselves.

Presentation Strategy: Document

This document allows the jury to see that the city has an easy-to-use form with check boxes to evaluate a driver's performance. Showing this form so the jurors can see it for themselves is all that is necessary at this time in the story. (If you stop the story and go through this document in detail, it will bog the jurors down with too much detail that they don't need to know at this point.)

> City Rule BCT-5 also requires the city's contract truck supervisor to review the general fitness of the contracted dump truck and its equipment prior to renewing the yearly contract for the truck.

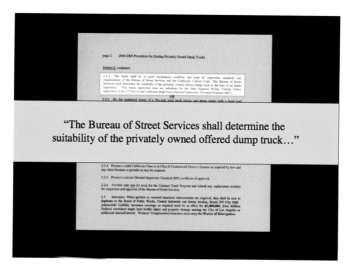

Presentation Strategy: Detailed Rule

In a style that is visually familiar, the jury is shown a new exhibit with a city rule that says the city is responsible for determining the suitability of a privately owned dump truck.

> The city contract truck supervisor must inspect the truck and make sure that a Commercial Vehicle Safety Association (CVSA) sticker is visibly placed on the truck showing that the highway patrol has inspected its braking system and found it to be in compliance.

The supervisor is required to make sure the truck has a current brake sticker.

Now let's look at another of the city's rules: Rule BCT-7B. This rule also requires city supervisors to routinely check contracted trucks to make sure that a current CVSA certificate is placed visibly on the truck.

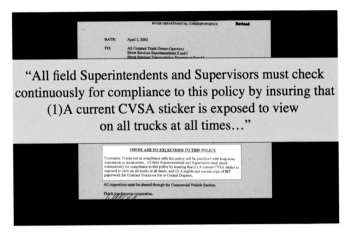

The city's rules state that any dump trucks not in compliance with this rule should be immediately suspended or terminated.

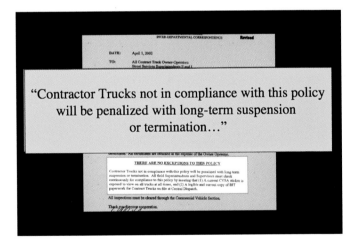

The city believes that this rule is so important that it states: "there are no exceptions to this policy." *[pause]*

There are no
exceptions to
this policy.

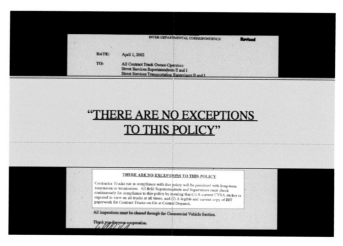

This "no exceptions" visual panel reinforces the importance the city places on supervisor compliance with its rules.

Standards Summary

The standards for this case have now been visualized in a series of panels showing documents, photographs, simple type, and graphics. When combined, they keep the jury focused on the defendant and set up the part of the story that later discloses the city's decisions to disregard these standards.

If we place these exhibits together, they look like this.

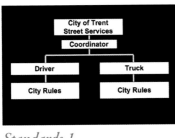

Standards 1

Standards 2

Standards 3

Standards 4

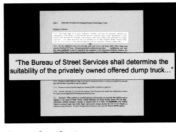

Standards 5

Standards 6

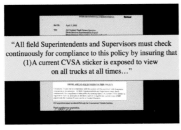

Standards 7

Standards 8

Standards 9

These case rules visually establish the standards for the jury, allowing the jurors to see them with their own eyes. Now let's analyze the standards in *Tucker*.

CASE STORY: *TUCKER*

In *Tucker,* the jurors learn at the beginning of the opening (during the rule or theme presentation) that, "A physician is not allowed to needlessly endanger a patient." They then learn through the inciting incident that an ENT did not see the patient with severe swelling in his throat for three days after being admitted. At that time, the patient's throat was almost completely blocked. We then suspended the presentation of the story for several reasons. One of them is to deliberately make the jury wait to find out what is going to happen. The other reason is to introduce the standards so that once the story is resumed, the jury will better appreciate the meaning of the events in the story.

Let's look at how this was done in *Tucker*.

I want to take a moment to talk about emergency airway puncture procedures for patients who can't breathe. *[pause]* The epiglottis is the small piece of tissue that dangles down from the roof of the soft palate.

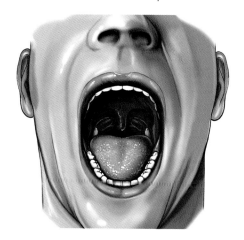

The illustration shows what a normal mouth looks like.

Presentation Strategy: Normal Throat

In order for the jury to fully appreciate the liability of this case, a medical illustration is used to show what the setting inside a normal mouth looks like.

The epiglottis closes automatically when we eat or drink to prevent food from going down the airway.

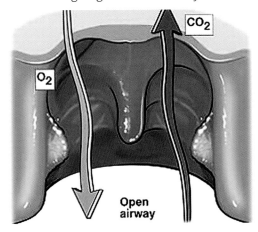

Experts will testify at the trial that sometimes, due to an infection, the walls at the back of the throat can swell, pushing the epiglottis to one side.

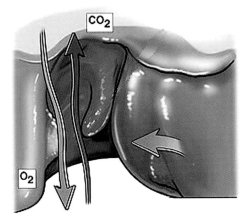

Presentation Strategy: Inflamed Throat

The previous illustration shows the jury how the walls at the back of the throat can swell due to an infection. It contrasts with the image of a normal throat, and the long narrow arrows show there is less space for the exchange of oxygen and carbon dioxide due to the severe swelling.

If the infection is not controlled and the walls at the back of the throat continue to swell, the swelling can completely obstruct the airway.

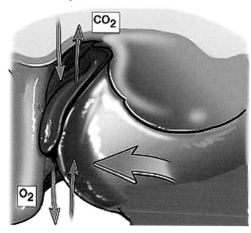

If the infection and swelling are not controlled, the airway can be completely obstructed.

Experts will testify that this is a life-threatening condition because it prevents a patient from breathing through his mouth or nose.

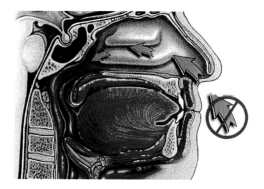

If a doctor sees that a wall at the back of a patient's throat has obstructed the patient's airway and he can no longer breathe, a doctor must immediately use a scalpel or sharp instrument to make a small incision on the patient's throat below the blockage. Once the incision is made, a small tube should be inserted through the incision and into the trachea so the patient can get oxygen.

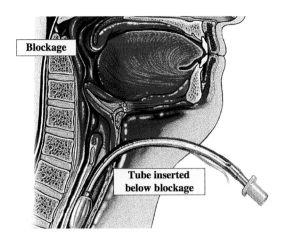

Experts will testify that inserting a tube into the mouth of a patient whose throat is blocked will not help the patient get air. That is why the incision and tubing must be inserted below the blockage.

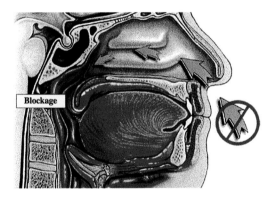

When a patient's airway is blocked and this type of procedure needs to be performed, doctors know that time is of the essence. If the patient's airway is not opened and the patient cannot breathe, carbon dioxide will begin building up in the body's tissues. If the necessary emergency procedure is not performed and carbon dioxide continues to build up, this can lead to brain damage or death in a matter of minutes. This is why doctors know that this emergency airway procedure must be performed immediately.

A doctor must immediately use a scalpel or sharp instrument to make a small incision.

Time is of the essence.

The scalpels or sharp instruments needed to perform such an operation can be found on crash carts located in a room near the nurse's station on each floor of the hospital.

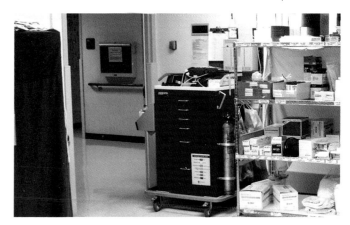

This room is designed for these types of emergency situations and has sharp instruments in labeled drawers for quick access.

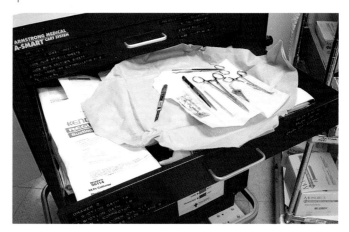

If a scalpel or crash cart is not available, any type of knife or sharp instrument can be used. Patients do not have to be taken to an operating room to perform this procedure. It can be safely done right in the patient's room. The most important thing is to get the patient breathing as quickly as possible.

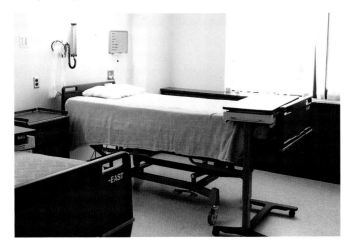

The operation can be done right in the patient's room.

Presentation Strategy: Procedure Standards

This photograph of the patient's bed is used here to emphasize the fact that an emergency airway procedure can be done anywhere, including the patient's room. The introduction of these standards keeps the jury focused on the defendant and sets up the expert's opinion about how a physician should act to refrain from needlessly endangering a patient. Showing the standards helps the jury to understand how a reasonable doctor should care for his or her patient in an emergency situation.

Standards Summary

The standards part of this opening has now established the expert's opinion about the danger of not performing an emergency airway procedure in a timely manner. As a result, the jury is now aware of the severe consequences that can result if this procedure is not performed in a timely manner.

Showing the standards helps the jury to understand how a reasonable doctor should care for his or her patient in an emergency situation.

If we combine the visuals used to show the standards for *Tucker,* they look like this:

Standards 1

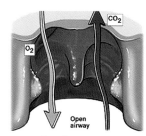

Standards 2

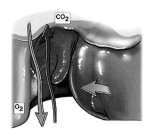

Standards 3

Standards 4

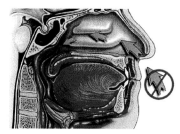

Standards 5

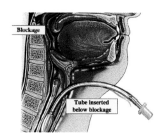

Standards 6

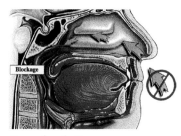

Standards 7

Standards 8

Standards 9

Standards 10

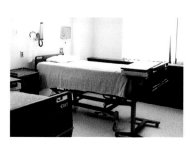

Standards 11

The visualization of these standards, when combined with the oral story, provides the jury with a basis for understanding the consequences of the defendant's decision (which occurs later in the story) to delay performing the emergency airway procedure on a patient with a blocked airway.

In summary, no matter what type of case you are presenting, providing the standards visually sensitizes the jury to the rules in a case. Once the jurors see these rules and understand them, they will further appreciate the risky choices made when the defendant chose not to follow these standards.

Now that you have seen the importance of showing the standards and providing background information for the story, in the next chapter we will look at the use of images to show the defendant's choices.

TAKEAWAYS—SHOWING THE STANDARDS

- *In complex cases, the standards provide background information that helps the jury understand the story.*

- *Simplify the standards so they are easy for the jury to understand.*

- *Use the standards portion of the opening to keep the jury focused on the defendant.*

- *Showing the standards visually helps the jury to later see the relationship between the defendant's choice to deviate from the standards and the plaintiff's being harmed.*

- *Providing the standards visually enables the jury to see why the defendant is liable for harming the plaintiff.*

- *Showing the standards visually anchors the expert's opinion in the minds of the jury.*

9

IDENTIFYING CHARACTER CHOICES AND ACTIONS

What is evident in a character's external behavior begins on the inside with the character's internal values and decisions.

—Stanley D. Williams

Directors know that the characters in a story reveal themselves to the audience through their words, decisions, choices, and actions. They also know that these elements are all closely related to the theme that the story is communicating. Let's look at how the decisions and actions of Luke Skywalker reveal his character in a scene from *Star Wars IV: A New Hope*.

Luke Skywalker is flying his fighter and attempting to launch a missile at the only vulnerable point of the Death Star. All the other fighter pilots have failed to destroy it, and many of them have already died. Luke is making one more pass over the Death Star in an attempt to reach his target. As Luke looks at his radar and sets his sights on the target, he hears the voice of Obi-Wan Kenobi reminding him to trust the Force. With lasers blasting all about him, Luke's life as well as the Galaxy's hangs in the balance.

At this point Luke makes a decision that changes not only his life but also the lives of others. The decision is this: to rely upon his own inner voice instead of relying upon the ship's radar. As a result of this decision, Luke removes the ship's radar screen from view and trusts himself to know the appropriate moment to fire the missile. In doing so, Luke succeeds where all his fellow pilots have failed. He relies upon his own intuition and fires the missile at the exact moment needed to destroy the Death Star. It is at this point in the story that Luke reveals himself to be the true Jedi knight that he always dreamed of being. He earns this title because he trusts not only the Force but also himself. The audience understands and experiences the magnitude of this decision because it has been set up by other elements in the story and by the development of Luke's character in prior scenes.

Like a well-developed character in a film, the "characters" in a trial story are also revealed through their decisions and actions. When presenting a case from the plaintiff's point of view, it is essential to show the jury the moments when the defendant decides to break the rules. It is also critical that they *see* the moments when the defendant's actions break the rules. By presenting the story in this way, you can embed the essential facts of a case into the decisions and actions of the characters, making it easier for the jury to understand and remember.

Let's see how this was done in the cases we've been following.

> You can embed the essential facts of a case into the decisions and actions of the characters, making it easier for the jury to understand and remember.

Case Story: *Mason*

On June 16, 20XX, as city contract supervisor Brenda Archer begins her meeting with truck driver John Logan, she knows there are important city rules she must follow prior to renewing the annual contracts for this driver and his truck.

City supervisor Brenda Archer knows that before she renews Mr. Logan's driving contract, she must first review his driving record over the previous twelve months.

The supervisor knows there are important rules that must be followed.

But on this day in June, Ms. Archer chooses not to review or else ignores Mr. Logan's driving record. *[pause]* Instead, she signs his contract and renews his permission to drive for the city for one more year.

Without reviewing the driver's record, the supervisor renews his contract.

Had Ms. Archer glanced through Mr. Logan's file, she would have noted that he had a history of three collisions in the previous three years.

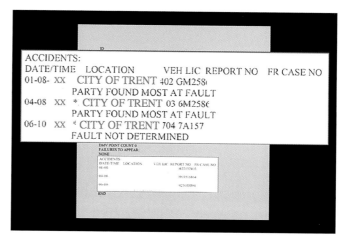

She would have also noted that fourteen months earlier Mr. Logan had been involved in a collision that caused substantial injuries.

The driver has a history of three collisions in the past three years.

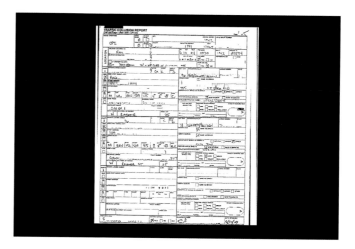

Presentation Strategy: Defendant City's Choices

The visual presentation of these facts creates juror interest in this story because the defendant does something that is not expected: she chooses not to review this driver's driving history. This creates interest in the story because the jury knows that this driver has a bad driving record with multiple violations and injuries to others.

Each new visual escalates the tension of this story and allows the jurors to see for themselves "who" breaks the rule, "where" the rule is broken, and "when" the rule is broken. Let's see how this defendant makes other decisions that put the public at risk.

On this same day in June, as Mr. Logan sits in her office, Ms. Brenda Archer also knows that the contract for Mr. Logan's truck is due for renewal.

She knows that before renewing the truck's contract, city rules require that she make sure that within the previous ninety days the truck's brakes have been inspected and found to be in compliance by the highway patrol.

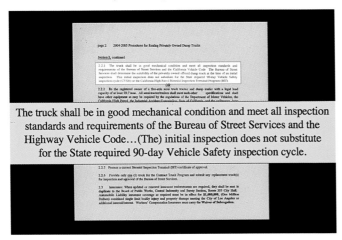

The truck shall be in good mechanical condition and meet all inspection standards and requirements of the Bureau of Street Services and the Highway Vehicle Code…(The) initial inspection does not substitute for the State required 90-day Vehicle Safety inspection cycle.

Ms. Archer knows that this means she must check the truck's paperwork and Commercial Vehicle Safety Association (CVSA) sticker. *[pause]*

The supervisor knows she must review the vehicle's paperwork.

Ms. Archer knows that there are no exceptions to this policy.

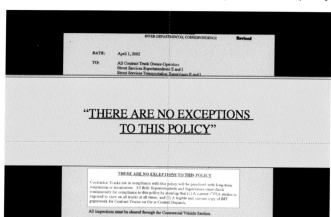

But on this summer day in June, Ms. Archer chooses not to review or else ignores the truck's paperwork and CVSA inspection sticker.

Instead, she signs the truck's contract and renews its use by the city for one more year. *[pause]*

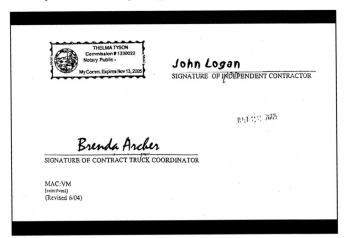

The supervisor renews the contract without checking the paperwork.

If Ms. Archer had inspected Mr. Logan's truck, she would have known that the truck was not in compliance and did not have a current sticker showing that it had been inspected by the highway patrol.

If Ms. Archer had required that the truck be inspected, she would have also learned that the front steering brake on Mr. Logan's truck had been illegally removed.

The front steering brake has been illegally removed.

But city supervisor Archer did not do any of these things, and so on a summer day in June 20XX, truck driver John Logan walks out of the city's office with the renewed authority to drive his truck for the city one more year.

Presentation Strategy: Defendant City's Choices

This portion of the story introduces the violation of another rule and shows the jury another choice that the city made that put the public at risk. The jury again sees "who" breaks the rule, "what" rule is broken, and "where" the rule is broken. The defendant city's choice is visually anchored, as before, by showing the jury the city supervisor's signature on the contract. At this point in the opening, the story has clearly set up that the city has made two choices that violated their own rules.

> The story shows that the city has made two choices that violated its own rules.

Summary of Defendant City's Choices

◆ CHOICE 1: The defendant city makes the choice to sign the driver's annual contract without reviewing his driving record.

◆ CHOICE 2: The defendant city makes the choice to sign the truck's annual contract without reviewing its safety inspections and current CVSA sticker.

These choices are visually anchored by using these exhibits:

> The defendant's choices are anchored with visual images.

City Choice 1   *City Choice 2*

Presentation Strategy: Defendant Driver's Choices

Continuing with our story, let's now look at how visuals are used to show the choices that the defendant driver makes.

> On the morning of October 13, 20XX, approximately four months after the city renewed the yearly contracts for driver

John Logan and his truck, Mr. Logan walks out of his house to get in his truck and begin another day of work for the city.

During the past four months, the city has continued to ignore another of its safety rules that says every ninety days, the city is supposed to receive documentation from the contracted owner-driver that his truck's braking system has been inspected and approved by the highway patrol.

The defendant ignores another policy rule.

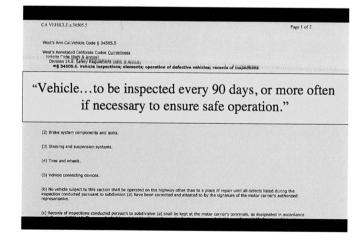

It is the city's written policy that if the owner-driver does not present this documentation to the city, the driver and his truck will not be permitted to work.

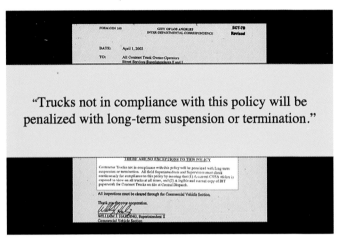

During the past ninety days, Mr. Logan has not submitted documentation of a brake inspection to the city, but the city, in violation of its own rules, has continued to allow Mr. Logan to operate his truck.

The truck is now twenty-seven years old, and it has over 900,000 miles. *[pause]* The front steering brake has been illegally removed, and the brakes are not in compliance with the vehicle code. *[pause]* By law, this truck should not be in service. *[pause]*

As Mr. Logan climbs into the cab and prepares to begin work for the city, he looks at his dashboard and sees that the gauge for his brakes indicates zero air pressure. Without pressure, the brakes of his truck will not work properly.

Without pressure, the brakes of his truck will not work properly.

Mr. Logan pumps the pressure back to normal and then starts down the road.

Mr. Logan arrives at an asphalt plant and picks up a load for the city. He then makes a delivery and returns to the plant to pick up another load of asphalt. After dropping this load, he begins driving back to the plant again. The street he is traveling on is called Valden Avenue.

There is a stop sign with a painted limit line at the intersection.

Mr. Logan approaches the intersection of Valden and Wibur avenues, where there is a stop sign with a limit line painted on the street.

As Mr. Logan approaches the stop line, he violates the public-safety rule to watch where he is going. Mr. Logan makes the choice not to look out his left cab window to see if there is any oncoming traffic on Wibur Avenue.

The driver violates the public safety rule to watch for oncoming traffic.

He also makes the choice not to stop for either the limit line or the stop sign.

Presentation Strategy: Defendant Driver's Choices

The truck-driver defendant has now made a series of choices that are about to cause serious harm.

- ◆ CHOICE 1: Mr. Logan has chosen not to have his truck's brakes inspected for safety nor have a current CVSA sticker.

- ◆ CHOICE 2: Mr. Logan has chosen to drive with the truck's front steering brakes illegally removed.

- ◆ CHOICE 3: Mr. Logan has chosen to drive his truck, knowing he has had air pressure issues with his brakes earlier that morning.

- ◆ CHOICE 4: Mr. Logan has chosen not to look left out his window to see if there is oncoming traffic.

- ◆ CHOICE 5: Mr. Logan has chosen to drive through the stop limit line and stop sign.

The defendant has now made a series of choices that are about to cause serious harm.

Summary: Defendant Driver's Choices

The visual panels that reflect these choices, when combined, look like this:

Driver Choice 1

Driver Choice 2

Driver Choice 3

Driver Choice 4

Driver Choice 5

Presentation Strategy: Defendant City's Choices

We have also introduced two new choices that the defendant city made. (These are in addition to the two choices previously identified.)

♦ CHOICE 3: The defendant city makes the choice not to request that Mr. Logan provide documentation that his truck's brakes have been inspected.

♦ CHOICE 4: The defendant city makes the choice to continue allowing Mr. Logan to operate a truck that has not been inspected.

Summary: Defendant City's Choices

If the visual panels that reflect these new choices are placed together with the city's previous choices to sign the contracts, they look like this:

City Choice 1

City Choice 2

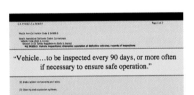

City Choice 3

City Choice 4

When we combine the choices of the defendant city with the choices of the defendant driver, we now have a visual story that shows nine choices these defendants have made that violate the standards and rules that were previously established.

Now that we have seen how the defendants' choices are visually anchored in *Mason,* let's look at this visual process in *Tucker.*

CASE STORY: *TUCKER*

In *Tucker,* a tdoctor and medical team make a series of choices that cause catastrophic injuries. These decisions begin on day two when no ENT sees the plaintiff to monitor his severe throat swelling. By day three of the story, when the defendant ENT examines Mr. Tucker for the first time and sees that his throat is almost completely blocked due to the swelling, the jury already knows that this patient may need an emergency airway procedure performed in his room.

Let's look at how this portion of the story is visually presented to accentuate the choices and actions of the defendants.

> Dr. Sienna sees that Ricky's throat is swollen to the point of being almost completely blocked. He then leaves the room to make a call on a house phone just outside of Ricky's room. When he returns, he sees that Ricky is turning blue. Dr. Sienna yells out, "The patient is crashing!" and code is called.

Dr. Sienna yells out, "The patient is crashing!"

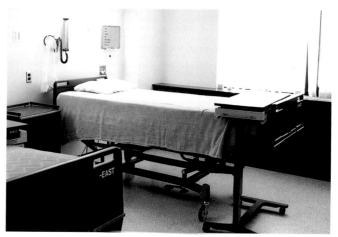

Ricky Tucker needs an immediate emergency airway puncture in order to breathe.

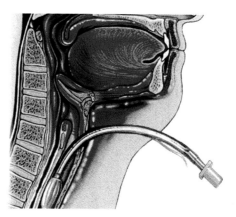

Instead of doing this immediately in the patient's room with a nearby instrument, Dr. Sienna makes the choice to take Mr. Tucker down to the operating room five floors below to perform the emergency airway procedure.

The medical team transfers Ricky to a gurney, and they begin pushing him out of his room. *[pause]* They push him down the hall and toward the elevators. *[pause]*

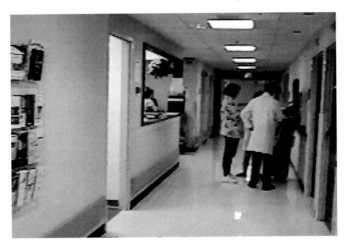

The team begins pushing the patient down the hall.

They push his gurney past a critical-care unit where scalpels and emergency airway equipment are located, but no one stops to get a sharp instrument to perform the emergency airway procedure. *[pause]*

Ricky is pushed to the elevator, where the medical team presses the button and waits. It is the lunch hour and the elevator is in use. The team waits thirty to forty-five seconds before the elevator arrives.

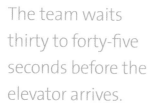

The team waits thirty to forty-five seconds before the elevator arrives.

Presentation Strategy: Defendant Doctor and Medical Team Choices

The ENT needlessly adds minutes of life-threatening delay by choosing to take Ricky Tucker down to the basement operating room. The photographs of the patient's hospital room, the hallway, and the elevator doors all allow the jury to see the pathway that the ENT and medical team chooses to take. The delay at the elevator continues to build the story's tension and focuses the jury's attention on the decisions of the defendants. Instead of immediately performing an emergency airway procedure on Ricky, the defendant medical team continues to choose the lengthy journey of taking him down to the operating room before they perform the procedure. These choices are not consistent with the standard of care, and they unnecessarily endanger the patient. At this point in the story, the medical team has made at least two choices that conflict with the standards and may cause unnecessary harm to this patient:

> The delay at the elevator continues to build the story's tension and focuses the jury's attention on the decisions of the defendants.

Summary: Defendant Doctor and Medical Team Choices

- ◆ CHOICE 1: Transport the patient five floors down to the basement operating room instead of performing the procedure in his room.

- ◆ CHOICE 2: Push the patient past the critical-care unit without stopping to get a sharp instrument that could be used to perform the procedure in the hall or elevator.

These are the two visuals used in this portion of the story to show where the defendant medical team makes choices that violated the rules:

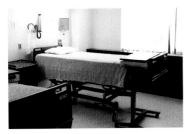

Medical Team Choice 1

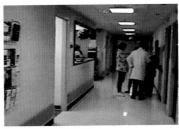

Medical Team Choice 2

Using visuals to show the places where the defendants make critical choices has the same effect as a television news broadcast or live-streaming video that allows an audience to see events as they are happening.

In summary, no matter what type of case is being tried, an essential part of the opening involves showing the defendant's choices. Next we'll look at how visuals are used to show the results of these choices.

TAKEAWAYS—IDENTIFYING CHARACTER CHOICES AND ACTIONS

- *Show the jury the critical decisions of each defendant.*

- *Visually establish the settings where each defendant makes these decisions.*

- *Show the corresponding actions that occur as a result of each defendant's decisions.*

- *Visually establish the settings where these actions occur. (Sometimes these settings are the same and sometimes they are different.)*

10

RE-CREATING CLIMACTIC MOMENTS

People don't remember what you say, they remember how you make them feel.

—Warren Beatty

Toward the end of a film, a director builds the conflict between one or more of the story's characters and a final crisis occurs. This final crisis is usually the most challenging event a character experiences in the story. All the decisions and actions that have led a character to this crisis reach their peak during the climactic moments of this event. That is why these moments are particularly memorable: they move the story toward its resolution and solidify its theme.

In *Casablanca,* toward the end of the film, Rick Blaine is at the fog-covered airport, helping Laszlo and Ilsa escape. Laszlo and Ilsa have just boarded a small plane that will take them to Lisbon, when Nazi officer Major Strasser arrives. Strasser talks with Rick and is about to inform the authorities that Laszlo is on the plane, when Rick makes the decision to protect Laszlo and Ilsa. Rick pulls out a revolver and shoots the Nazi officer.

This final crisis is usually the most challenging event a character experiences in the story.

These are the climactic moments of this film, and the entire story has led up to this point in time. Rick's decision to protect Ilsa and Laszlo signifies that he has moved beyond the self-centeredness that limited him earlier in the story. In the final minutes of the film, the audience sees that he is now willing to risk his life to protect those he cares for and loves. It is through these climactic moments that the story's theme is fully communicated: sometimes the most formidable enemies in life are not just the external ones but also the internal ones (such as the fear of loving, once one has been hurt).

Just as films have climactic moments, so do opening statements. The events that occur during these moments are the result of the decisions and actions that one or more of the characters have made. As in a good film, it is through these climactic moments that the opening's theme (as well as the trial's theme) is fully communicated. In a tort case, re-creating these climactic moments allows jurors to see the harm that results from the defendant's decisions and actions. These moments also make the story's theme real by showing jurors the causal relationship between the rules being broken and the plaintiff's being harmed. Let's look at how this was done in *Mason*.

CASE STORY: *MASON*

As we know from previous chapters, the events leading up to the climactic moments of this story have revealed that the defendants violated rules that say a city and its employees should not endanger the public. As a result of these decisions, the defendants have put the public at risk. In this portion of the story, we want to think like a film director and re-create the climactic moments so the jury can see them.

Presentation Strategy: Re-creating Climactic Moments

The climactic moments of a story show the jury what happens to the plaintiff as a result of the defendant's decisions to break rules and violate basic safety standards. The entire story leading up to this point has set up the events that are about to occur

> Just as films have climactic moments, so do opening statements.

as a result of the defendant's decisions and actions. We resume this story as a witness observes the truck driver rolling through a stop sign.

Witness Brett Layland, who is walking along the sidewalk on Valden, observes Mr. Logan's truck rolling through the stop sign. According to Layland, the truck looks like it is going to stop but then continues rolling into the intersection.

A witness observes the truck driver rolling through a stop sign.

As Mr. Logan proceeds into the intersection, he does not see out of his left cab window a fifty-two-year-old physician who is returning home on his motorcycle.

The physician is traveling in the lane by the curb at thirty to thirty-five miles per hour, well under the posted speed limit of forty miles per hour.

As Mr. Logan rolls into the intersection without stopping, the physician, who is wearing a helmet, swerves to the left to try and avoid colliding with the truck.

The truck's front left fender collides with the motorcycle.

The truck continues rolling forward after impact, dragging the motorcycle and leaving twenty-eight feet of gouge marks on the pavement before coming to rest.

There are twenty-eight feet of gouge marks on the pavement.

When the truck finally stops, the physician is unconscious. He is lying on the road with the motorcycle on top of his leg. He is almost decapitated. One carotid artery is severed. He has compound fractures throughout his body. He has a serious brain injury.

The injured physician has a serious brain injury.

Passing motorists stop their cars and try to help. During this time, Mr. Logan remains in his truck. After a while, he gets out of his truck and just stands there.

One of the citizens calls to Mr. Logan for help. The hot exhaust muffler of the six-hundred-pound motorcycle is lying on top of the physician's fractured right leg and burning his skin.

The exhaust muffler is burning the physician's fractured leg.

Mr. Logan ignores these pleas for help. Instead, he climbs back into his truck, gets his camera, and begins taking pictures of the scene for insurance purposes.

Paramedics eventually arrive on the scene and rush the physician, who is still unconscious, to River View Hospital. The physician's name is Dr. Gary Mason.

The physician is
still unconscious.

The police arrive and interview Mr. Logan, who tells them the motorcycle "came out of nowhere."

Summary: Re-creating Climactic Moments

The climactic moments of this story are presented using twelve photographs. These images orient the jury to the scene; they include the stop sign, truck's cab, intersection, point of impact, pavement markings, final resting place, and witnesses attending the injured physician.

If these images are placed together they look like this:

Moment 1

Moment 2

Moment 3

Moment 4

Moment 5

Moment 6

Moment 7

Moment 8

Moment 9

Moment 10

Moment 11

Moment 12

This documentary style of presentation takes the jury to the intersection and re-creates the climactic moments of the crash. The images show the place where the injury occurs, the mechanism of injury, the defendant's actions, and the results of the defendant's choices and rule violations.

Now that we have seen how to make the climactic moments in *Mason* visual, let's look at how to re-create them in *Tucker*.

CASE STORY: *TUCKER*

As we discussed in the previous chapter, the defendant doctor in this case makes two risky decisions with regard to patient Ricky Tucker. The first decision is to take the patient to the operating room five floors below rather than perform an emergency airway procedure immediately in the patient's room. The doctor's second decision is to push the patient past the critical-care unit without stopping to get a sharp instrument that could be used to perform the procedure in the hallway or elevator. Both of these decisions are in conflict with the standards that require the immediate performance of an emergency airway procedure when a patient's airway is blocked. Let's continue with this story.

> The elevator arrives and the doors open. As the team starts to push Ricky Tucker inside the elevator, he starts to have seizures from the lack of oxygen. The elevator doors have not yet closed. There are scalpels only a few feet away that can be used to immediately open his airway, but the medical team chooses to close the elevator doors and start their descent to the basement.

Floor four is passed. Floor three is passed. Floor two. Ricky's skin is blue. He continues to have big seizures from the lack of oxygen.

The elevator reaches the basement and the doors open. Ricky is now lifeless on the gurney. The medical team pushes him out of the elevator and into the hallway. They push him through the sliding doors leading to the operating rooms.

The elevator reaches the basement and the doors open. Ricky is now lifeless on the gurney.

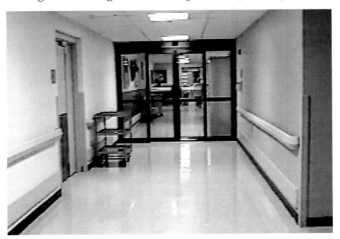

Presentation Strategy: Re-creating Climactic Moments

The emotional tension of these climactic moments continues building through the use of these documentary-style photographs. The jury knows that time is of the essence, because

Will he make it? Will he survive? The jurors want to know.

Ricky can't breathe and is having big seizures from the lack of oxygen. Will he make it? Will he survive? The jurors want to know the answers to these questions, and so their involvement with the story remains high. Continuing with the story:

The medical team pushes Ricky through the doors of Operating Room #6. Instead of making an immediate incision, Dr. Sienna and the medical team begin preparing the surgical suite, while the patient lies unconscious on the table.

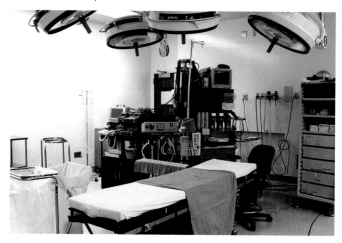

Approximately twelve minutes later, Dr. Sienna makes a simple incision below the airway block, which takes less than ten seconds. Thirty seconds later, an oxygen tube is placed in the patient's trachea.

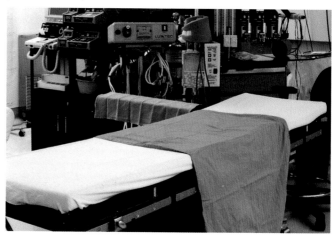

The patient has now gone without oxygen for approximately fourteen minutes.

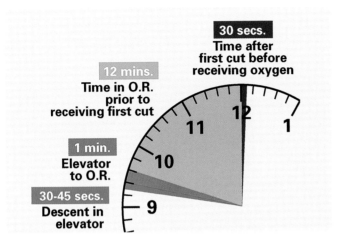

The patient is revived and begins breathing again, but neurological testing later determines that he has severe brain damage.

The patient has now gone without oxygen for approximately fourteen minutes.

In the days that follow, it is determined that patient Ricky Tucker can no longer do anything for himself. He will require assisted living for the rest of his life.

He will require assisted living for the rest of his life.

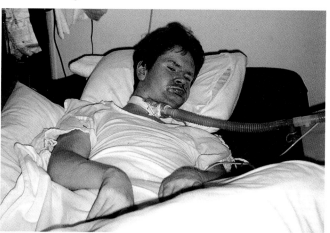

Summary: Re-creating Climactic Moments

The climactic moments for this story are presented using seven images that orient the jury to this scene. These include the elevator, an exterior of the hospital, the basement hallway, the basement operating room, the operating room table, a graphic, and a photograph of the plaintiff after the injury. If these images are placed together, the visual story looks like this:

Moment 1

Moment 2

Moment 3

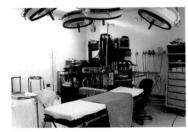

Moment 4

Moment 5

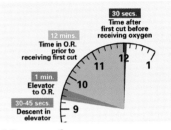

Moment 6

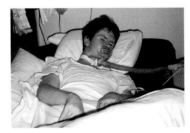

Moment 7

Like the previous example, this documentary style of presentation takes the jury through the hallways of the defendant hospital and shows the places where the defendants make decisions, the defendants' actions, and the injury to the plaintiff.

In summary, this visual story shows the climactic moments of this case and allows the jury to see for themselves the moment-by-moment events that unnecessarily endanger a patient and cause catastrophic injury.

TAKEAWAYS—RE-CREATING CLIMACTIC MOMENTS

♦ When presenting the opening, re-create the climactic moments visually.

♦ Show the places where the defendant makes risky decisions.

♦ Use images to show the place where the injury occurs.

♦ Use images to show the mechanism of injury.

♦ Show the defendant's actions in a moment-by-moment documentary style.

♦ Use the climactic moments to anchor the opening's theme.

11

SEEING THE BIG PICTURE

Design is a plan for arranging elements in such a way as best to accomplish a particular purpose.

—Charles Eames

In previous chapters we have discussed how a film direc-tor introduces characters, sets up the story's conflict, shows the characters' decisions and actions, and portrays climactic moments. These and other visual elements all work together to communicate the theme to the audience. You can use these same techniques to communicate the theme of a case in the opening (and throughout the trial). With this in mind, let's look at the big picture and see how the visual elements we have discussed work synergistically to deliver the thematic message.

The visual elements all work together to communicate the theme.

CASE STORY: *MASON*

In *Mason,* the rule or theme states a city and its employees are not allowed to needlessly endanger the public, and if they do, they are responsible for the harm.

Rule or Theme

At the beginning of the opening, the rule or theme establishes the story's subject.

Panel 1: Rule or Theme

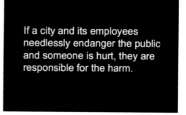

Panel 2: Rule or Theme

Inciting Incident

The inciting incident focuses the jury's attention on a defendant's choice or action to violate the rules. In *Mason,* a truck driver did not tell the supervisor that his truck's brakes had not been inspected and the truck's contract got renewed. Facts like these have a direct relationship to the theme because they involve a defendant's decision to break rules.

Panel 3: Incident

Panel 4: Incident

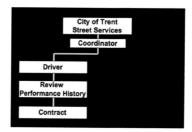

Panel 5: Incident

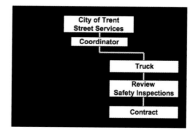

Panel 6: Incident

Panel 7: Incident

Panel 8: Incident

Panel 9: Incident

Standards

The standards educate jurors about the rules and the risks involved in breaking them. In *Mason*, the jury was sensitized to several city rules.

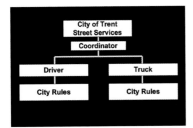

Panel 10: Standards

Panel 11: Standards

Panel 12: Standards

Panel 13: Standards

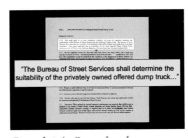

Panel 14: Standards

Panel 15: Standards

Panel 16: Standards

Panel 17: Standards

Panel 18: Standards

Choices and Actions

The defendant's choices and actions develop the conflict in the story and communicate the plaintiff's theory of liability. In *Mason,* the defendant city renewed the driver's contract without reviewing his driving record. The city also renewed the truck's contract without confirming if its safety inspections were current. These actions set up the story's conflict and communicated the theme of needless endangerment.

Panel 19: Choice

Panel 20: Choice

Later in the story, the decisions and actions of the defendant driver showed how he made the decision not to look out his left cab window, did not yield to oncoming traffic, and chose to drive through the stop limit line and stop sign. This portion of the story also communicated the theme of rules being broken and public endangerment.

Panel 21: Choice

Panel 22: Choice

Panel 23: Choice

Climactic Moments

The climactic moments show the harms caused by the defendants as a result of their decisions and actions to break the rules. During this portion of the story, the jury saw how the driver caused a serious injury. Facts like these all reinforced the case theme of a city and its employees being responsible for the harm they caused if someone was needlessly endangered.

Panel 24: Moment

Panel 25: Moment

Panel 26: Moment

Panel 27: Moment

Panel 28: Moment

Panel 29: Moment

Panel 30: Moment

Panel 31: Moment

Using cinematic techniques like these strengthened the jury's understanding of the case theme and visually reinforced the meaning of the story's message. It also provided a visual explanation of the *who, what, where, when,* and *why.* Jurors saw for themselves the needless harm that resulted from the defendants' risky actions. All this played an important part in winning a substantial verdict for the plaintiff. This successful outcome was directly related to the process of thinking like a film director and showing the story as presented above.

CASE STORY: *TUCKER*

The same types of visual elements used in *Mason* were also used to communicate the theme or big picture in *Tucker*. In this case, the theme involved the needless endangerment of a patient's safety.

Rule or Theme

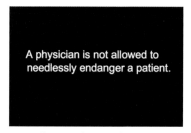

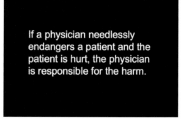

Panel 1: Rule or Theme   *Panel 2: Rule or Theme*

Inciting Incident

Following the introduction of the rule or theme, the inciting incident focused the jury's attention on a life-threatening situation involving a hospitalized patient who couldn't breathe. This incident accentuated the need for an immediate surgical procedure to help the patient breathe.

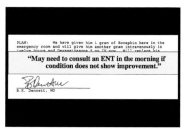

Panel 3: Incident   *Panel 4: Incident*

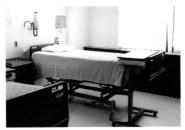

Panel 5: Incident

Panel 6: Incident

Standards

The standards then oriented the jury to a normal airway in the mouth and informed them about the emergency airway procedure that needs to be performed when a patient's airway is blocked and they can't breathe. These visuals kept the jurors focused on how a physician should act so a patient is not needlessly endangered. The risks of delaying this procedure were also presented to reinforce the story's theme.

Panel 7: Standards

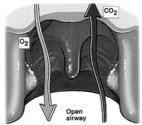

Panel 8: Standards

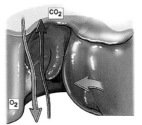

Panel 9: Standards

Panel 10: Standards

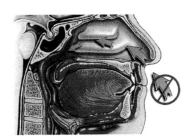

Panel 11: Standards

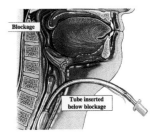

Panel 12: Standards

Panel 13: Standards

Panel 14: Standards

Panel 15: Standards

Choices and Actions

The story of the defendant's choices and actions were then shown, allowing the jury to see how those decisions and actions needlessly endangered the patient, thus setting up the story's conflict and communicating the theme.

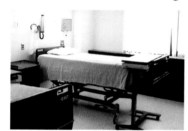

Panel 16: Choice

Panel 17: Choice

Panel 18: Choice

Panel 19: Choice

Climactic Moments

The climactic moments showed the plaintiff being catastrophically harmed as a result of the defendant's decisions and actions. These facts all reinforced the case theme.

Panel 20: Moment

Panel 21: Moment

Panel 22: Moment

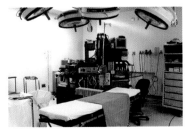

Panel 23: Moment

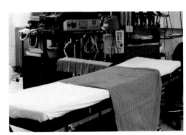

Panel 24: Moment

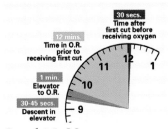

Panel 25: Moment

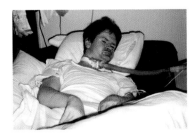

Panel 26: Moment

Summary: The Big Picture

Show the story. The way you present a story, both orally and visually, has an enormous impact on how jurors process information. The same fact pattern sequenced in a different way can produce an entirely different result. That is why it is so important to think like a film director and give careful consideration to how you develop the story, establish the settings, introduce characters, set up the conflict, show the standards, reveal character choices, re-create climactic moments, and weave the theme. Using cinematic techniques like these will make you a better communicator and improve your ability to both educate and persuade.

In the next section we will look at how specific graphic tools and techniques can be incorporated into the story to visualize facts.

Takeaways—Seeing the Big Picture

- Establish the rule or theme.

- Show a decision the defendant makes that breaks a rule and endangers the plaintiff.

- Establish the standards and explain the risks if they are not followed.

- Show the defendant's decisions *that break rules.*

- Show the defendant's actions *that break rules.*

- Re-create the harms that result when rules are broken.

PART
THREE

Visual Tools
and Techniques

12

MAKING YOUR CASE STICK

I'm not sure that the world always makes as much sense to us as we would hope.

—Malcolm Gladwell

Effectively communicating the facts and the law to both the judge and the jury requires a verbal and visual presentation. You want your message to resonate with the audience long after you finish presenting it. Combining words and images is the best way to make this happen. Just how much better is a multimedia presentation compared to words alone? A pioneering

You want your message to resonate with the audience long after you finish presenting it.

1986 study led by Professor Douglas R. Vogel at the Management Information Systems Research Center at the University of Minnesota[1] sought to answer this question and revealed dramatic differences when visuals were added to a sales presentation:

- Speakers were 43 percent more persuasive.

- Audience attention and comprehension increased over time.

- Speakers with only average skills were seen by the audience as much better when using visuals.

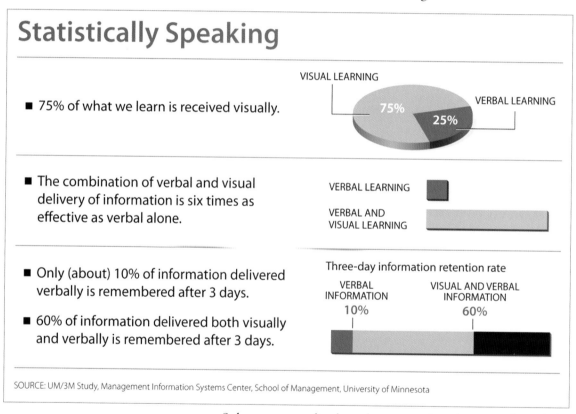

Statistically Speaking

- 75% of what we learn is received visually.

VISUAL LEARNING 75%
VERBAL LEARNING 25%

- The combination of verbal and visual delivery of information is six times as effective as verbal alone.

VERBAL LEARNING
VERBAL AND VISUAL LEARNING

- Only (about) 10% of information delivered verbally is remembered after 3 days.

- 60% of information delivered both visually and verbally is remembered after 3 days.

Three-day information retention rate
VERBAL INFORMATION 10%
VISUAL AND VERBAL INFORMATION 60%

SOURCE: UM/3M Study, Management Information Systems Center, School of Management, University of Minnesota

Subsequent studies by other researchers have confirmed the basic conclusions of the University of Minnesota study.

---

1. Douglas R. Vogel, Gary W. Dickson, and John A. Lehman, "Persuasion and the Role of Visual Presentation Support" (June 1986).

THE RELATIONSHIP BETWEEN WORKING AND LONG-TERM MEMORY

The explanation of why visuals improve retention resides within the limitations of human memory. Even with intelligent people, the brain works like a leaky bucket, hampered by limited storage capacity. New information is quickly lost if not presented in a memorable way, as the brain only "retains the new information for . . . a few seconds."[2]

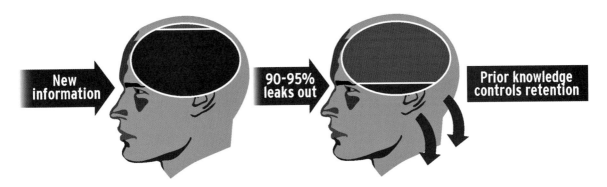

Our brains are not tape recorders. New information has to make sense to us in light of what we already know. Our long-term memory is the gatekeeper to what stays and what goes. Lawyers long have realized this at some level, using appeals to common sense in jury arguments, a classic method of tying the old to the new.

An attrition rate of 90–95 percent of what a juror hears is rather startling and presents you with a stiff challenge. Research shows that the multimedia effect plays an important role in helping jurors overcome these memory limitations. A message containing both words and pictures leads to deeper understanding and better recall by the audience.

---

2. Richard E. Mayer, ed., *The Cambridge Handbook of Multimedia Learning* (New York: Cambridge University Press, 2005), 22.

DIFFERENT LEARNING STYLES

Beyond memory considerations, you need to be aware of differences in individual learning styles. Some people are very literal engineering types, while others are more impressionistic and emotional. Different people will interpret the same presentation in different ways, based on factors unique to each.[3] While fine-tuning and applying this concept goes beyond the purposes of this book, it is important that you be aware of these fundamental distinctions in audience members and that you raise them with your experts and media consultants as your case comes together. Consultant Jay Syverson is well aware of the need for diverse visual presentation strategies in legal cases, trying to appeal to all the basic learning styles:

> It is always a challenge. If your images appeal more to one learning style, those who are excluded will say, "I don't get this." There must be something for everyone.[4]

THE CRITICAL ROLE OF STORIES

Stories in any form—visual, verbal, or both—are powerful tools. More than just entertainment, stories provide one of the most effective means of overcoming the limitations of working memory:

> The human brain has a natural affinity for narrative construction. People tend to remember facts more accurately if they encounter them in a story rather than in a list.[5]

Stories both inform and shape human perception:

> These narratives guide behavior in every moment, and frame not only how we see the past but how we see ourselves in the future.[6]

People tend to remember facts more accurately if they encounter them in a story rather than in a list.

---

3. Mayer, *Cambridge Handbook*, 13.
4. Jay Syverson, interview with William S. Bailey, September 5, 2008.
5. Benedict Carey, "This Is Your Life," *New York Times,* May 22, 2007, 5.
6. Carey, "This Is Your Life," 5.

THE ROLE OF GRAPHICS

Graphics are an important tool in helping an audience to get a point quickly, overcoming both perception and memory problems:

> When problems are translated into . . . graphic forms, it is often easier to solve them. . . . Simply by presenting problems as diagrams often lets us quickly "see" the solution.[7]

By simplifying complex ideas, graphics prevent the working memory from being overwhelmed. Graphic forms also can eliminate the irrelevant detail often found in photographs,[8] making the intended message easier to see. Graphics can make use of unifying symbols that tie one idea to another, improving audience comprehension.

BASIC COMMUNICATION RULES

To overcome the brain's leaky bucket, you have to use proven techniques to help audiences remember information. Research supports the following basic rules for using visuals in your presentations:

1. Use words and pictures rather than words alone.

> By simplifying complex ideas, graphics prevent the working memory from being overwhelmed.

---

7. William Winn, *The Design & Use of Instructional Graphics,* in Heinz Mandl and Joel R. Levin, eds., *Knowledge Acquisition from Text and Pictures* (New York: Elsevier Science, 1989), 134.

8. William Winn, *The Design & Use of Instructional Graphics,* 127–8.

2. Present words and pictures simultaneously, near one another on the page or the screen, rather than successively or split apart.

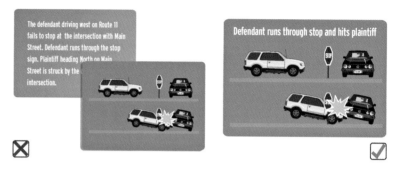

Don't talk over a PowerPoint slide that has words on it, because it will divide attention and reduce learning.

3. Don't talk over a PowerPoint slide that has words on it, because it will divide attention and reduce learning.

4. Prune extraneous words and pictures from your presentation. Too much information is a real negative. Stick to what is most essential to explain your points, and leave out the rest.

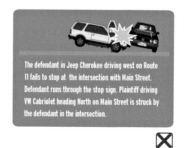

5. Draw upon the prior understandings and experience of the audience, connecting new information to what is already in their long-term memory.

6. Encourage group learning where members of the audience get perspectives other than their own.

7. Provide an opportunity for the audience to get feedback about their thinking, with an opportunity for revision.

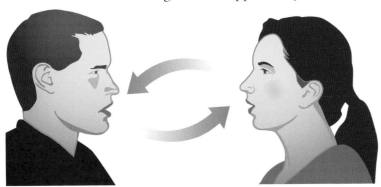

8. Be mindful of the fleeting nature of animation images, extracting still pictures that preserve the most essential elements of the animation.

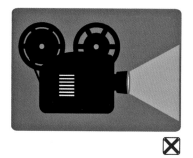 

9. Design images that are consistent with the words used, reinforcing the message.

Cell phones distract drivers

10. Sequence the information so it moves from the simple to the complex.

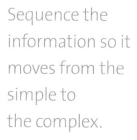

Sequence the information so it moves from the simple to the complex.

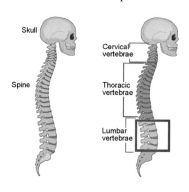 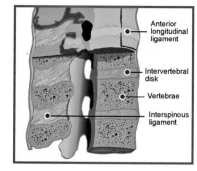

11. Present the information in a conversational, less formal style, as it is easier to retain.

Present the information in a conversational, less formal style, as it is easier to retain.

12. Use graphic devices such as circles, arrows, close-ups, or highlights, drawing attention to what is most important.

13. Regulate the pace at which the new information is presented, tracking the audience's ability to absorb it.

14. Use site maps, timelines, or visual tables of contents to orient people to the overall structure and content of the information.

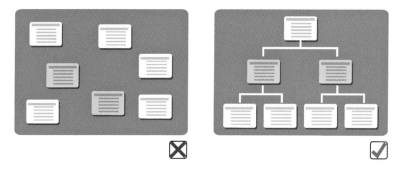

15. Use words and pictures in a way that will allow people to construct a mental model of the information in their own minds.

16. Use pictures that provide perceptual information about already-learned concepts (size, shape, color, movement).

17. Try to simplify the complex through pictures, making the abstract more concrete.

Basic photosynthesis

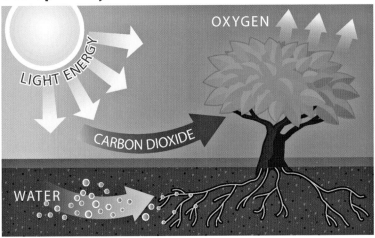

18. Use graphic symbols on a visual to make it more memorable than just using dots or squares.

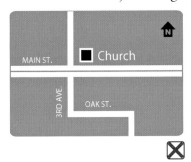

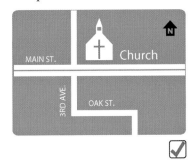

19. Present problems as diagrams, allowing people to "see" the solution.

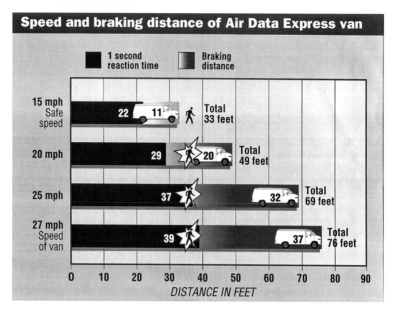

TAKEAWAYS—MAKING YOUR CASE STICK

- *Using words and pictures dramatically improves the memory and comprehension of the audience.*

- *The working memory of normal human beings is like a leaky bucket.*

- *New information must fit into the structure of what people already know in order to be retained.*

- *Learning styles vary from one person to another, requiring presentations that take these differences into account.*

- *People remember facts much better if they hear them in stories.*

- *Graphics make problems easier to understand and solve.*

- *Research has identified a number of techniques to make presentations more memorable and persuasive.*

13

How Tech Savvy Should I Be?

I think it's fair to say that personal computers have become the most empowering tool we've ever created. They are tools of communication, they are tools of creativity, and they can be shaped by their user.

—Bill Gates

An important consideration to keep in mind is the optimum balance of low-tech and high-tech evidence. While physical exhibits, such as models, often are low tech, this is counterbalanced by their "high touch" aspect. When I[1] started out as a public defender in the 1970s, many misdemeanor courts had toy cars set up next to the bench to help motorists explain their versions of the events to the judge. The time-honored method of butcher paper and Magic Markers never has gone out of style, ready to be used in every courtroom at any moment to help explain or preserve testimony. Bone and joint models give

---

1. Here and elsewhere in the book, "I" refers to coauthor William Bailey, unless the "I" is part of quoted material.

Jurors like things
that they can hold
and examine.

an immediacy to medical testimony that high-resolution imaging studies still can't achieve.

Jurors like things that they can hold and examine. While low in technology, such exhibits are high in credibility, as we have seen them before and can evaluate them on our own. All of us remember the skeleton models from junior-high and high-school science classes. Added to the greater familiarity and trust of low-tech exhibits is the fact that high-tech evidence can restrict your presentation style.

Kathy Cochran of Wilson, Smith, Cochran and Dickerson in Seattle is aware of the downside of too much high-tech evidence, and emphasizes the importance of a blend in the courtroom:

> I use both low-tech and high-tech exhibits. Too much media either will put the jury to sleep or lose impact because it's too repetitive. It is important for you to get physically active. Write something up on the butcher paper so the jury is not just lulled into looking at the screen like they do television. One of the disadvantages of PowerPoint is you become a little more dependent on it than you should. Your next question is driven by your next slide. It's a bad syndrome. You don't move around the courtroom as much.[2]

Do I Need to Be Able to Do All This Myself?

Beyond these considerations of the optimum mix of low-tech and high-tech evidence, the sheer mass of hardware and software products requires you to ask, "How much of this do I really need to know?" Products go through upgrades very quickly, making past understandings and working methods obsolete. How much of this is really necessary to your work?

Once again, think like a film director. While a director has to know about the available tools for the creation of special effects, he or she doesn't have to be able to create those effects personally. The director brings in others more proficient and

2. Kathy Cochran, interview with William S. Bailey, October 28, 2009.

skilled in the technical aspects to accomplish the task. However, the director must guide these technical consultants, keeping in mind what the end result should look like.

HIRING CREATIVE CONSULTANTS—COST, COMPATIBILITY, AND SKILL CONSIDERATIONS

Where do you find creative consultants, and what do they cost? There is a wide range in sophistication, depth, and cost among vendors to the legal community. Lawyer magazines, seminar materials, and Internet marketing are common sources of information on creative consultants, as is word of mouth. Some are limited to more generic clip-art images for simple PowerPoint presentations, while others do sophisticated custom images.

Use the same methods as when you check out any other kind of expert. Take the time to look at the consultants' work, ask for references, find out what other cases they have been involved with and what they charged. Look for a consultant who is a good fit with your philosophy and approach. Is the consultant a good collaborator who enhances your own creativity? If not, keep looking.

The cost of creative talent not only varies by the hour, but also by the job. Images for a major products liability or intellectual-property case will cost much more than a simple rear-end auto collision graphic. Factor in the inevitable revisions and changes in the images as the case evolves. While the price of graphics and artwork has steadily come down, a series of images in any case will likely run at least several thousand dollars by the end. A computer animation can easily cost five thousand dollars or more, depending on how demanding and intricate the foundation. There always are alternative approaches, so you should discuss the art budget openly, just as with a home remodel.

Where do you find creative consultants, and what do they cost?

DEFINING THE WORKING RELATIONSHIP— WHO DOES WHAT?

Once you identify compatible visual consultants, long-term working relationships tend to develop, just as in the film industry, where a director prefers a familiar cameraman or editor. While you may not need to know how to work with Adobe Illustrator, Photoshop, or any other computer-graphics software, like a film director, you do need to know what visuals will best convey the theory of the case. You then can collaborate with and direct an illustrator or an animator skilled in the use of computer-graphic tools to achieve these results.

Your sound judgment will provide valuable guidance to the illustrator or animator in creating credible evidence that will be admitted at trial. Even though artists are adept at creating and manipulating images, they cannot appreciate what details are most important in the proof of a legal case. With knowledge of the basic tools available, working with able computer-graphics specialists, you can get the job done.

Michael Reiss of the Seattle office of Davis Wright Tremaine models the hands-on concept of a film director in working with multimedia consultants, staying involved in the process throughout:

> Visuals always start with the question, "What are we trying to show here?" You can't just turn it over to your graphics people. And you can't think that it can happen in one iteration. Where lawyers make mistakes in conceptualizing their cases is either they don't think about visuals at all or just turn it over to some graphics person. What you get back is not good. Graphics illustrators aren't lawyers. They either make mistakes in translating legal theories into images or the pictures don't convey what you want them to.
>
> Stay involved and say, "That's not right, do it again." Then, finally, you get something that is better.[3]

Your sound judgment will provide valuable guidance to the illustrator or animator in creating credible evidence that will be admitted at trial.

---

3. Michael Reiss, interview with William S. Bailey, October 29, 2009.

BEING ABLE TO EXPLAIN THE FOUNDATION WHEN THE EVIDENCE IS CHALLENGED

Beyond knowing the possible technological tools that can be used in any given case, you have to understand the basic principles of computer technology well enough to explain them to the judge in the process of laying the foundation for admitting any visual evidence. The more effective any computer-generated image is, the more determined the effort by the opposing counsel will be to keep it out. Arguments to keep out high-tech evidence will call it unreliable, a product of the imagination, a cartoon. Educate the judge on how it was created and why the process used was reliable.

Arguments to keep out high-tech evidence will call it unreliable, a product of the imagination, a cartoon.

DIGITAL PHOTOGRAPHY

The use of digital photography is the easiest sell to a judge, as nearly everybody has a digital camera and appreciates the ease it affords in the display, printing, storage, manipulation, transmission, and archiving of images. The troublesome evidentiary issues come with the manipulation aspects of digital photography, raising the question of whether any changes are fair and appropriate.

Some of the main advantages of digital photography are:

◆ IMMEDIACY. A photo can be reviewed as soon as it is taken to determine if it is adequate. No need to scan the image before viewing it on a larger computer screen.

◆ PORTABILITY. The images are easily stored on a computer.

◆ REPRODUCIBILITY. Photos may be copied from one digital medium to another without any degradation.

◆ PLUG-INS. Many digital cameras have an AV-out connector to allow reviewing of photographs by an audience, using a television.

WORKING WITH DIGITAL IMAGES

Image quality needs to be a constant concern, particularly since it is highly likely that any courtroom display will require projection of images onto a screen. The greater the degree of enlargement, the more obvious the underlying flaws of the image. If you are working with a photographer, make sure the person knows the size of screen on which you plan to display the image. This can help the photographer choose appropriate camera settings.

WHAT IS RENDERING?

Rendering is the process of generating an image from a model by means of a computer program. Adobe Illustrator is an important rendering tool. It has uses in architecture, video games, simulators, and special effects. The best way to understand the potential application of Adobe Illustrator is to do a step-by-step analysis of how it can transform a photograph into a graphic illustration.

Example: We Want to Show a Man Hit by a Vehicle

STEP 1: Get the desired photo reference by posing a model in the position needed or from a suitable Internet photo.

STEP 2: Import the scanned or digital-camera photo into the Adobe Illustrator program and lock it into the background. The pen tool is used to trace different areas of the photo. The red line is used for contrast.

STEP 3: Continue with the pen tool until there is sufficient detail in the areas of interest. This example is a fairly simple one.

STEP 4: Unlock the photo from the background and move it to the side for comparison. The areas outlined in red are filled in with the appropriate color.

STEP 5: Once the necessary detail for a simple sketch is achieved, move the legs, arms, and head a bit if the pose needs to be adjusted.

STEP 6: The right hand and right arm positions have been changed from the original photo, bringing in a drawing of

a vehicle previously created from a photo reference. Adjust the size of the man's image to scale and move it into position on top of the vehicle graphic.

WHY MIGHT I NEED TO USE ILLUSTRATIONS LIKE THIS?

The manipulation of the simple image above demonstrates the versatility of computer graphics. While photographs are inexpensive and easy to get, they also are limited. For example, in the pedestrian–motor vehicle collision above, it would be difficult, dangerous, and expensive to use photographs to re-create what happened. Using a stunt person to take the risk of injury just to get a "real" photo is unnecessary and ill-advised.

The most practical way to approach visuals where photographs are not suitable is to use illustrations. These often start with a photograph of some element, which then is manipulated to conform with what happened in the case. Your job is to guide the illustrator in this process. Also, since it is not unusual for the facts of a case to evolve as the discovery process goes forward, the illustrator can modify the images whenever changes in position or detail are indicated by new information.

Your job is to guide the illustrator in this process.

TAKEAWAYS—HOW TECH SAVVY SHOULD I BE?

♦ *You don't need to know how to use all the forms of computer-graphics technology personally. Like a film director, you only have to be aware of the visual tools available and their potential applications.*

♦ *High-tech exhibits have not made their low-tech predecessors obsolete. Jurors often like the interactive high-touch aspects of low-tech exhibits.*

♦ *Mix up presentation media—include the low-tech exhibits that require you to get up and move around. Don't lull jurors to sleep by restricting your presentation to images on a screen.*

♦ *You cannot simply delegate the creation of exhibits and images to a graphics specialist. This is a collaborative process that requires multiple drafts. Keep an eye on foundation and accuracy throughout.*

♦ *Digital photographs are inexpensive and versatile, but they have limitations. Go the next step and use software that can change or adapt a photo.*

♦ *Rendering allows you to change the position of objects and people in a scene to reflect your foundation and case theory. As discovery proceeds and facts change, the illustrations can be modified to reflect these changes.*

♦ *If the judge rules that visuals need to be modified, it is easier to change an illustration than a photograph.*

♦ *Stay involved in the image-creation process. You need to be able to explain to the judge the foundational basis for all the assumptions that go into an illustration and be prepared for skepticism that an illustration is a mere cartoon that came out of some artist's imagination.*

14

EMPLOYING THE
LOCUS IN QUO

All our knowledge has its origins in our perceptions.

—Leonardo da Vinci

While we may prefer the safe, secure, and predictable environment of our offices, sometimes we need to get out of them to develop the best ideas for our cases. The importance of personal field investigation in a case has been well understood for many years. In the first edition of *Trial Tactics and Methods,* Robert Keaton advised:

> Personally observe . . . physical objects and scenes that are material to the case. . . . Go to the scene of the accident yourself and study it thoroughly. [This] not only increases your own understanding of the facts . . . but also may provide you with new ideas and leads for investigation.[1]

---

1. Robert Keaton, *Trial Tactics and Methods* (New York: Prentice-Hall, 1954), 303–4.

The creative stimulus of a scene visit is reinforced by lawyers in literature. Author John Mortimer uses his fictitious alter ego, Horace Rumpole, to expound upon the value of going to the *locus in quo.*[2] In "Rumpole and the Bubble Reputation," Rumpole delivers an impromptu lecture on the subject at Pommeroy's Wine Bar to his stodgy colleague, Claude Erskine-Brown:

Erskine-Brown: I have to ask you for a few tips on a tray.

Rumpole: Visit the *locus in quo!*

Erskine-Brown: The what?

Rumpole: Go to the scene of the crime. Inspect the geography of the place.[3]

In "Rumpole and the Sporting Life," Rumpole follows this advice when his client is accused of having shot her husband

Go to the scene of the crime. Inspect the geography of the place.

---

2. The scene of the event, in British common law. The phrase comes from Latin, "the place in which."

3. John Mortimer, "Rumpole and the Bubble Reputation," in *Rumpole and the Golden Thread* (London: Penguin, 1983).

on the grounds of their estate. Jeremy, the young local solicitor, asks Rumpole for an explanation of what he is trying to accomplish as they view the scene:

JEREMY: What are you looking at?

RUMPOLE: The scene of the crime. The *locus in quo*.

JEREMY: What do you do now? . . . Crawl about on your hands and knees collecting bits of cigarette ash in an old envelope?

RUMPOLE: Not exactly.[4]

Instead, Rumpole turns his attention to a nearby cottage, its windows visible above an adjacent hedge. Rumpole notices that these upper windows are in a direct sight line to the spot where the victim was shot. He learns that the old man who lives

4. John Mortimer, "Rumpole and the Sporting Life," in *Rumpole and the Golden Thread* (London: Penguin, 1984), 191.

in the cottage, Figgis, has a habit of shooting out this window at game birds on his property.

The *locus in quo* provides Rumpole with the visual strategy that he later uses in court. He calls Figgis to the stand, implicating him as the source of a fatal shot—he missed his aim and hit the victim instead:

RUMPOLE: That afternoon . . . you were doing a bit of shooting, were you?

FIGGIS: I may have been . . .

RUMPOLE: And your cottage is not more than fifteen yards from the scene of this alleged crime?[5]

Combining this with a devastating cross-examination of the prosecution's forensic medical witness, Rumpole wins an acquittal. His strategy was based on spatial relationships he noted at the scene.

His strategy was based on spatial relationships he noted at the scene.

---

5. Transcribed from the script of the television episode "Rumpole and the Sporting Life."

Going to a scene feeds your instincts, leading to powerful common-sense strategies. Rumpole is exactly right: the geography of the place shows you things that may not be evident from behind your desk.

GEORGE VANDERVEER—A LAWYER BEFORE HIS TIME

George Vanderveer was a lawyer ahead of his time. Like Rumpole, he believed in going to the scene to build his strategy in a case. A tireless defender of the working class, he was once described by a peer as:

> A man nobody quite understood . . . in continual revolt against orthodoxy, cynical, contemptuous, dour and always spectacular.[6]

George Vanderveer

In April of 1917, he took up the challenge of his professional life: using the *locus in quo* method to win a very difficult murder case with class-struggle implications. The year before, the Industrial Workers of the World (IWW), a radical labor organization popularly known as the "Wobblies," organized a mass demonstration in the lumber-mill town of Everett, Washington. To get all the demonstrators to Everett, the IWW used the regular passenger ferry service, a ship called the *Verona*. A small army of heavily armed deputies and citizen vigilantes was waiting for them at the dock, with a hail of gunfire breaking out soon after the *Verona* arrived.

The deckhand had only been able to tie off the bow when the shooting started and the stern drifted out to a nearly ninety-degree angle. Mostly unarmed, the IWWs forced the ship to return to Seattle when the gunfire from the dock continued.

In the end, five IWW members were killed on the ship, along with two of the deputies. Dozens more were wounded on each side.

The Everett authorities brought murder charges against seventy-four IWW members, targeting Tom Tracy as the leadoff

---

6. Douglas Welch, *Seattle Post-Intelligencer,* July 2, 1976.

Pilot house of the 'Verona' riddled with rifle bullets at EVERETT

defendant. He was charged with conspiracy to commit the murder of Everett sheriff's deputy Jefferson Beard, though the prosecution conceded it could not prove that Tracy fired the fatal shot. The case consisted of law enforcement testifying that Tracy was seen firing a weapon out a portside window.

Prior to trial, Vanderveer thoroughly immersed himself in all the details of the scene, spending many days there, taking multiple measurements and drawing sketches. He spoke with eyewitnesses and determined their vantage points, relentlessly seeking any physical evidence not collected by the authorities, including from local boys who had combed the dock afterward.

Vanderveer also spent many hours on the *Verona* itself, noting where the bullet holes were, grouping them into patterns.

He also established where law-enforcement personnel were positioned on the dock before the shooting started. He was interested particularly in the window placements on the boat. The critical angle of the boat in relation to the dock is re-created in the diagram below, which Vanderveer replicated in his scene visits.

He stood on the dock and determined what could be reasonably seen on the boat, and then the other way around.

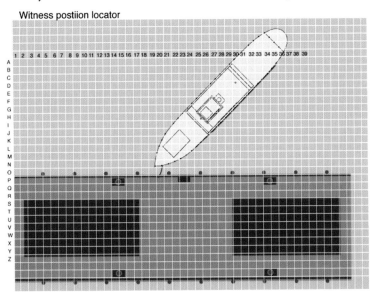

At the end of his pretrial investigation, Vanderveer knew everything about the Everett city dock and the sight lines available from any part of it. He instantly could size up the credibility of any claim by a prosecution witness.

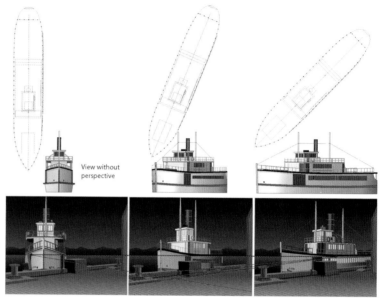

View without perspective

Red perspective lines apply to center view only. Perspective on dock difficult to translate to boat changing angle.

In the end, the key to his strategy was the angle of the boat. The sudden outbreak of shooting had disrupted normal docking procedures. The stern went untied, causing it to drift away from the dock.

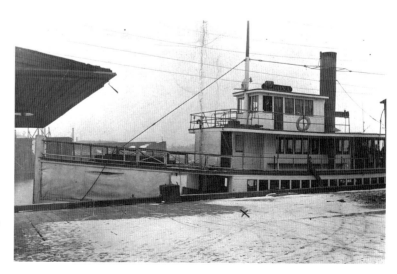

Verona photo used later in wrongful death civil case.

Going to the scene and experimenting with the visibility of the boat from various locations gave Vanderveer everything he would need to take on the law-enforcement witnesses.

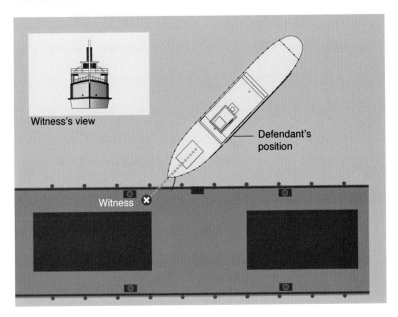

Despite claims to the contrary, the angle of the boat blocked their views of it from the dock.

When the trial began, one after another prosecution witness got on the stand and identified Tom Tracy as having fired a gun from a window on the port side of the *Verona*. Sheriff McRae was first up, and Vanderveer eagerly pounced on him when it came time for cross-examination. He staged the scene in the courtroom with a physical demonstration showing that the sheriff's view was completely cut off. Confidence shaken, backpedaling, Sheriff McRae left the stand with his credibility in ruins.

Deputy sheriffs William Bridge and "Honest" John Hogan did no better than their boss. Using a scale model of the *Verona*, Vanderveer proved that it would have been physically impossible for either deputy to have seen the defendant's face.

The jury later went up for a scene view of the Everett city dock. When the captain swung the boat out to the same angle as it had been on November 5, the jury confirmed that it was impossible to see a face in the window where Tracy was supposed to have been.

A photograph proving this was taken at the scene and introduced into evidence.

Vanderveer hammered away at the *locus in quo* evidence in his closing argument:

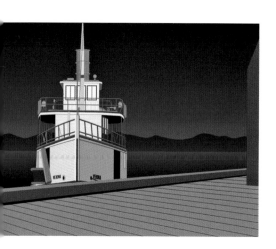

> [the prosecution witnesses] did not see this man at all. . . .
> You know it because you went there to the dock and
> you saw the boat lined up to a mathematical certainty.[7]

The day following closing argument, the jury returned a not-guilty verdict to a stunned courtroom.[8] The *locus in quo* and the superior advocacy skills of George Vanderveer had carried the day.

---

7. Walker Smith, *The Everett Massacre* (Chicago: I.W.W. Publishing, 1917), 250–51.
8. Lowell S. Hawley and Ralph Bushnell Potts, *Counsel for the Damned*, (Philadelphia and New York: Lippincott, 1952), 207.

Twenty-First-Century Applications of the *Locus in Quo*

The advantages that come with your mastery of the scene are not limited to historical or literary cases. This technique of George Vanderveer and Horace Rumpole continues to be a winning strategy in modern trials.

Case Study: Premises Liability—*Simmons v. Celebrity Hotels*[9]

In *Simmons v. Celebrity Hotels,* the plaintiff was on his way to a business conference when he had a serious fall at the front entrance of the defendant's hotel. Although he sustained multiple fractures in his right leg, premises liability cases often are difficult for plaintiffs to win.

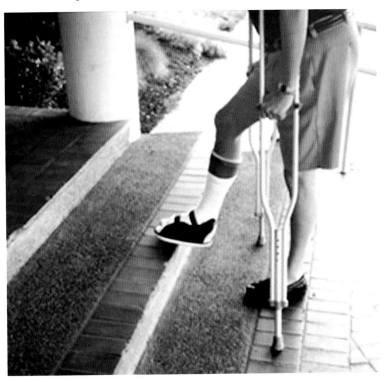

---

9. A pseudonym of the real case name.

Jurors seem quick to blame the injured person under these circumstances, presumably on the theory that he or she should have seen the hazard and avoided it. Looking for a winning theory in the same way as Rumpole and George Vanderveer, I met with my client at the *locus in quo,* retracing all the events leading up to his fall on the front steps of the hotel. What immediately grabbed my attention were the multiple chips out of the leading edges of the brick steps.

I met with my client at the *locus in quo,* retracing all the events leading up to his fall on the front steps of the hotel.

The defense questioned the plaintiff at great length at his deposition on this hazard's being open and obvious, suggesting that he should have placed his feet more carefully. I was worried about a big reduction in damages for comparative fault.

Fighting back with the deferred-maintenance theme, I focused on violations of the defendant hotel chain's corporate brand standards for safety and appearance. Maintenance records showed that needed work had not been done due to cash-flow problems. The yearly inspection reports by the parent corporation contained multiple failing grades.

But was this enough to eliminate comparative fault of the plaintiff as an issue? My continuing worry about this led to a visual strategy to dramatize the deferred maintenance. I decided to combine a video deposition of the hotel manager with an inspection of the premises, using two civil rules simultaneously. The defense fought this, bringing a motion to strike, but the judge allowed the deposition to proceed. It would include an examination of the manager on camera on the front steps where my client fell.

Oct-25-04 12:26:41

In the week prior to the deposition, I made several visits to the scene, carefully noting all the defects, just like George Vanderveer would have.

The hotel manager was glib and well spoken, adroitly dodging the thrust of my questions during the first part of the deposition in the hotel conference room. But the game changed when I dragged him out to the front steps. Surrounded by the obvious deferred maintenance on camera, he became ill at ease. It did not matter what answers he gave, as it was obvious that the hotel had gambled with the safety of the guests:

Q: Mr. Fugleman, we're now out in front of your hotel. Do you recognize this area?

A: Yes, I do.

Q: And this is the general area where Mr. Simmons fell?

A: Yes.

Q: Do you see the damaged areas of your front steps?

A: Well, I see that there are some chips in the leading edge of some of the bricks, yes.

Q: Right behind you there are some rather significant areas of damage.

A: Uh-huh.

Q: Would you describe this as deferred maintenance?

A: As deferred maintenance? No, not necessarily.

Q: This is right on traffic pattern towards the front entrance to the hotel; isn't it?

A: Yes.

Q: And you've been aware of this maintenance problem for a long time?

A: Yes.

Q: You had a bid to fix this for $4,000, correct?

A: Well, the one bid that we looked at was $4,800 for one solution and more for another.

Q: And this was a violation of corporate safety standards?

A: Well, it was showing up on the inspections, absolutely.

Would you describe this as deferred maintenance?

Oct-25-04 12:28:26

Q: I'm going to take off my shoe. Do you see how it makes contact with the edge?

A: I see your shoe does that.

Q: And this presents a hazard to secure footing?

OPPOSING COUNSEL: Objection, relevance, lack of foundation. Calls for speculation.

A: You know, there would be some hazard . . .

The case settled shortly after this deposition was concluded, a tribute to the value of a visit to the *locus in quo*.

Case Study: Wrongful Death—*Constantine v. Prince*[10]

In *Constantine v. Prince* the defendant driver struck and killed the decedent bicyclist in a marked crosswalk. The key issue was the visibility of the bicyclist in the crosswalk.

The defense theory was that the motorist could not have seen the bicyclist and that it was unsafe for the bicyclist to have entered the crosswalk.

---

10. Pseudonym.

The police department had done a very thorough investigation of this accident, taking several hundred photographs. I studied these with great care, supplemented with multiple visits to the scene. After multiple drive-throughs of the intersection, I confirmed that the defendant's visibility of the bicyclist was unobstructed. Even if there were cars in the right-turn lane as he claimed, the defendant still could see the bicyclist.

After multiple drive-throughs of the intersection, I confirmed that the defendant's visibility of the bicyclist was unobstructed.

Q: Okay. Let's go to the photo of the SUV you were driving on the day that you hit the bicyclist.

A: Yes.

Q: Do you see that the police have put Mr. Constantine's bicycle in front of the SUV?

A: Yes.

Q: And do you see that the seat comes over the top of the headlight?

A: I do see that.

Q: If a man over six feet two inches tall is riding this bike, he's going to be visible to you driving this SUV, isn't he?

A: Yes.

The second photograph was used to rebut the defendant's excuse that his view of the bicyclist was blocked by cars in the right-turn lane.

Q: Mr. Prince, this is a photograph taken by the police department. Are you looking at it now?

A: Yes.

Q: Even though that police car is parked there in the right-turn lane, you can still see the bicyclist, can't you?

A: On the picture I can.

Q: As you approached this intersection that day of the collision, where were you looking?

A: I don't recollect.

Q: At some point you would have gone past any car turning right at that intersection, wouldn't you?

A: Correct.

Q: Looking at this photo, you should have been able to see the bicyclist in the crosswalk then if you were looking, right?

A: Presumably.

In this chapter, we have seen the importance of getting out of your office and going to the *locus in quo* to see the "geography of the place." At the scene, you can see for yourself what

At the scene, you can see for yourself what makes sense.

makes sense. Scene visits stimulate your thought process and creativity, leading to good visual ideas, the stuff that powerful arguments are made of.

TAKEAWAYS—EMPLOYING THE LOCUS IN QUO

◆ *Go to the scene or scenes where the key events in a case occurred.*

◆ *A scene visit will deepen your understanding of the case and lead to visual ideas.*

◆ *Witnesses frequently can be mistaken about what they were able to see. Scene visits allow you to double-check their claims.*

◆ *Judges generally do not like to take the time and trouble to take jurors to the scene. If you develop a promising angle from your visit, think of a way to memorialize it.*

◆ *Do not hesitate to combine discovery rules in pursuit of a case theory. Rule 34 inspections of the land can be joined with Rule 30 video depositions.*

◆ *Entire cross-examinations can be created out of what you learn by going to the scene.*

15

BUILDING THE THEME

A trial lawyer without a theme is a warrior without a weapon.

—Charles L. Becton

A good theme is critical to the success of your story, providing the basic structure for the words and images presented. A theme is to a story as architectural plans are to a building. While possible to construct a house without a plan, it is not likely to be one that you would want to live in. The same goes for a story without a theme. As Dr. Amy Singer observes:

> You can't . . . communicate in any meaningful way—in court or out—without a compelling theme . . . [jurors] look for evidence that supports the theme while ignoring evidence that doesn't.[1]

The purpose of this chapter is to help you develop your story's theme.

---

1. Amy Singer, *Focusing on Jury Focus Group*, 19 *Trial Diplomacy Journal* 326 (1996).

WHAT IS A THEME?

We all have themes running through our lives, including the search for love, personal happiness, and meaning. In a story, a theme is the central idea that you want the characters and events to convey, providing narrative structure and guidance on what to include and exclude. In J. D. Salinger's *The Catcher in the Rye,* the themes of refusal to grow up and clinging to childhood innocence define Holden Caulfield's three drunken, lonely days in New York City after being kicked out of prep school. In Ernest Hemingway's *The Old Man and the Sea,* the themes of grace under pressure and refusal to give up frame the story of simple fisherman Santiago's struggle against the open sea to bring home a giant, powerful fish in a small boat.

Classic stories involve two forces locked in conflict. Some well-known examples include:

- STAR WARS. The struggle between the good Luke Skywalker and the evil Darth Vader in a futuristic sci-fi setting.

- THE SOPRANOS. The contradictions between a New Jersey mob boss's violent career and his life as a husband and father.

- OTHELLO. The tragic hero's conflict between jealousy and love.

Legal cases fit right into this story structure, as there are at least two opposing parties, sometimes more. Your theme should build your client in a positive light and the opponent's in a negative one, though not in an obvious or mean-spirited way. The best themes are subtle.

STRUCTURE OF A THEME—STERN'S PRINCIPLE OF THE WHOLE

In his book *Trying Cases to Win,*[2] Judge Herbert J. Stern advises lawyers to pose three questions when considering potential themes:

1. What do jurors need to make a decision?

2. What will jurors believe after hearing everything?

3. What best reconciles discrepancies in the facts?

Take the facts of your case and organize them into "Jurors Need" and "Jurors Will Believe" columns. What theme best ties these together? Don't expect to find the best theme quickly, as it is a process of trial and error, requiring great thought.

HOW CAN YOU IDENTIFY AND BUILD A THEME?

Here are some ideas to help you in indentifying and building a theme:

- ◆ Who in the story do you want the audience to like and dislike?

- ◆ What behaviors support this?

- ◆ What is the conflict or struggle in this story about?

- ◆ Who is to blame for what happened, and why?

Answering these questions will move you steadily closer to finding a theme that presents your client's behavior in a positive light and the opposing party's in a negative one. For example, plaintiffs suing corporations will use themes like "people over profits" or "they just didn't care." Corporations defending such cases counter with themes like "everything in life has risks" or "people always want to blame somebody else."

> Don't expect to find the best theme quickly, as it is a process of trial and error, requiring great thought.

---

2. Herbert J. Stern and Stephen A. Saltzberg, *Trying Cases to Win, Anatomy of a Trial* (Aspen Law and Business: Gaithersburg & New York, 1999), 7–36.

Throughout the process of theme selection, you must keep careful focus on the emotional appeal of a story to the audience. Your choices as the director of the story can invoke hope, inspiration, fear, or simple escape. Though most of us do not realize it, given a choice between reason and emotion, emotion often wins. There is no question that the appeal of a story largely is determined by the hearts of the audience, not their heads.

Throughout the process of theme selection, you must keep careful focus on the emotional appeal of a story to the audience.

FINDING THE RIGHT THEME: *CHAPMAN V. PROGRESSIVE HEALTH*[3]

The medical-malpractice case of *Chapman v. Progressive Health* illustrates both the difficulty of finding a good theme and the power shift that occurs in the trial story with the right one.

Chapman involved a patient whose colon was perforated and then sutured during routine hernia surgery. Lack of communication afterward between members of the hospital's health-care team led to peritonitis and a near fatality.

I struggled to find the right theme for my client, the plaintiff, that reflected the hospital's negligence. I considered and rejected many possibilities, including:

- Communication breakdown

- Black hole

- Dropped the ball

- We don't care; we don't have to

- The right hand doesn't know what the left hand is doing

None of these potential liability themes really worked with the facts. This became evident when I considered sample visuals for each theme. For example, a clip-art photo of a baseball player dropping a ball not only did not track with the medical errors, it trivialized them. If none of these themes worked, what

---

3. Pseudonym.

would? All the good liability facts for the plaintiff just didn't come together without the right theme.

In the Loop, Out of the Loop

I consulted with my brother Robert.[4] Together, we identified the powerful twin themes of "in the loop" and "out of the loop," perfectly capturing the communication failures within the defendant hospital. Robert explained his reasoning to me over the phone:

> You are either in the loop or out of the loop, just like you are either on the bus or off the bus. This turned a routine procedure into a life-threatening ordeal.

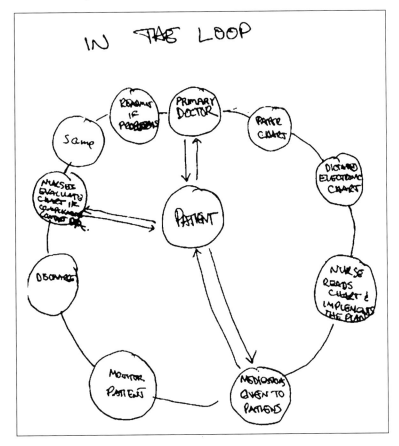

---

4. Coauthor Robert Bailey.

The "loop" imagery themes matched the looping configuration of the plaintiff's damaged intestine. When the intestine was obstructed, the process broke down. In the same way, the lack of information in this health-care system caused the quality of this patient's care to break down.

The arrows going in and out in the "loop" diagrams matched the function of the intestine, a permeable membrane. The simplicity of his "loop" diagrams also eliminated any medical complexities.

The jury would get a vivid sense from these themes of how the care Mr. Chapman received was different from what he had a right to expect. The steps that his caregivers should have taken to protect this patient disappeared into dotted lines in the "out of the loop" diagram.

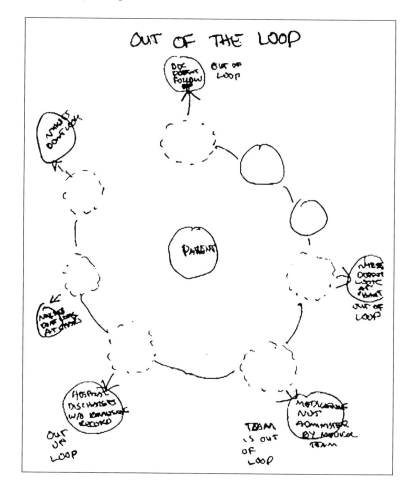

I gave the rough drawings of the theme Robert drew to an artist to put into more polished form.

The result was an iconic symbol that visualized the theme and created strong feelings about the defendant's conduct in the case. It achieved the same effect that marketing consultants strive for in creating a brand image for a company or a product.

It achieved the same effect that marketing consultants strive for in creating a brand image for a company or a product.

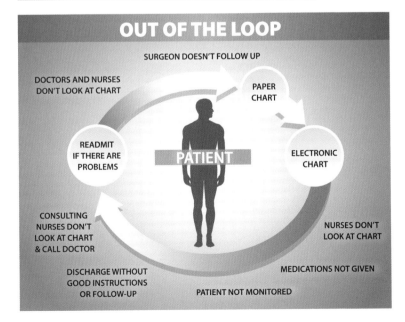

Themes that Enhance the Client's Character: *Moore v. Rufus County*[5]

In the battle for credibility with the jury, it is important to develop themes that build your client up as they tear down the other side. The case of *Moore v. Rufus County* demonstrates how this is done. While on his lunch hour, plaintiff Ray Moore was run down by a van driven by a careless fellow employee, resulting in significant injuries. The employer denied workers' compensation coverage on technical grounds and later moved to dismiss the plaintiff when his injuries limited his ability to work as a bus mechanic.

One of the plaintiff's liability themes was that the defendant was unfair. This was visualized by a faceless man with hostile body language.

> One of the plaintiff's liability themes was that the defendant was unfair.

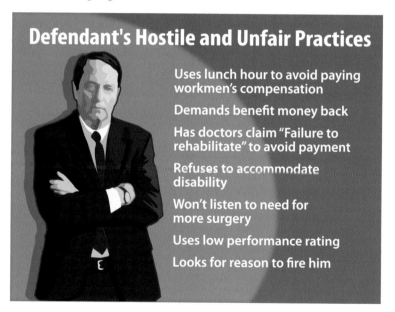

Of equal or greater importance were the damages themes that presented the plaintiff as deserving and worthy. These emphasized the plaintiff's:

---

5. Pseudonym.

- Prior level of physical activity

- Strong work ethic

The trial story centered on these themes, building up the plaintiff's character while tearing the defendant's down.

Ray loved sports, fishing, waterskiing, hiking

Ray is family oriented and loves his wife and children

He was physically active and still loved the outdoors

TAKEAWAYS—BUILDING THE THEME

- *Identifying the right theme(s) is critical to the success of a trial story.*

- *The theme is the central idea that drives the story.*

- *The most powerful themes involve opposing forces, one good and the other evil.*

- *What theme(s) best reconcile discrepancies in the facts, while pointing in your client's favor?*

- *What theme(s) emphasize the important information that the jury needs to make a decision?*

- *Who in the story do you want the jury to like, and why?*

- *What is the conflict in the story about?*

- *Who is to blame for what happened, and why?*

- *Finding the right theme can present a real challenge as a case progresses and information accumulates.*

♦ *The more complicated and detailed the facts, the more important the theme becomes.*

♦ *Themes that take the moral high ground and enhance your client's character are the strongest.*

16

CREATING COMPUTER ILLUSTRATIONS AND ANIMATIONS

Reality is a sliding door.

—Ralph Waldo Emerson

This chapter will take you from the known world of photographs, which we all use, to the less familiar terrain of computer images. Though few of us could explain the scientific principles on which digital photography is based, we are comfortable with it. Everybody knows how to hold a camera, point, and shoot.

Digital photography makes the process virtually idiot proof, with no need to wait for prints from the photo lab. If the shot doesn't come out, we know it right away and can take another one.

Lawyers have used photos in their cases since the early twentieth century. We either get them from other sources, including the opposing counsel in discovery, or generate them ourselves.

The right photos can help support our client's position and weaken our opponent's. For example, the night photo below was taken at the scene where my client was struck by a courier van in the crosswalk. It established that the area was well lit, leaving the defendant driver in a poor position to claim that she could not have seen him.

After photos are created or gathered, all lawyers understand that a foundation must be laid for the fairness and accuracy of each one before it can be used at trial. The foundation script is a tightly defined staple of law-school trial-advocacy training, used regularly in both depositions and trials.

"Ms. Witness, are you familiar with the scene where my client was hit in the crosswalk?"

"Yes."

"How?"

"I drive through there every night on my way to work."

"Were you an eyewitness on the night my client was hit in the crosswalk?"

"Yes."

"Can you please look at the photo and tell the court if it fairly and accurately represents the way this area looks at night?"

"Yes, it does."

Many photographs can be easily verified. For example, we can physically go to an accident scene and compare the conditions to a photo.

The availability of real world reference opportunities is helpful to us when disputes are raised over lighting conditions, distances, and the location of objects in a photo.

Laying the foundation for a photo often is a rubber-stamp proposition. The witness is asked, "Does the photo fairly and accurately represent what is shown?" If the answer is "No," typically, it doesn't come into evidence. If the photo is largely accurate, indicated with a "Yes, but" answer, any discrepancies between the facts and the image typically go to the weight of the photograph, not its admissibility.

Even though the courts put photos and computer images in the same category of evidence, they are different. Though fixtures on our desks, most of us do not have the training or

Even though the courts put photos and computer images in the same category of evidence, they are different.

experience to understand computers, particularly the graphics they generate.

If our use of the computer is limited primarily to e-mail, research, and surfing the Internet, there is no real need for any deeper understanding of how it works. But this all shifts when you start using computer graphics in your cases. The creation of computer graphics is a more complicated process, based on verbal and visual input from multiple sources. The "point and shoot" simplicity of a photo is missing. All of this has implications for foundation and admissibility issues.

Computer images are more complicated.

THE DIFFICULTY OF USING WORDS AND MEMORIES TO CREATE IMAGES

Turning the words of witnesses or experts into precise computer-graphics images presents a fundamental challenge. The imprecision of words and the variability of human perception create obstacles to computer-generated visuals that accurately reflect the actions, events, or processes at issue.

Information also degrades as it passes from person to person. Remember the grade-school game of "telephone." A secret whispered from one person to another around a circle ends up very different than when it started.

Whenever words are the primary basis for telling a story, the pictures formed in the minds of the audience will vary according to individual values, experiences, and personalities. Just as no two sets of fingerprints are alike, the unique qualities of each person will cause them to visualize the spoken word in different ways.

If you read facts to a group of people whose eyes are closed, asking them to create pictures in their heads, each person will come up with a different image. It doesn't matter that they all heard the same facts. When they open their eyes and look at the photograph or illustration of the scene described in words, the vision in their heads won't match. This variability in human perception can cause problems when re-creating a scene for a legal case with a computer illustration.

In *Searching for Memory,* Daniel L. Schacter summarizes the basic fragility, vulnerability, and distortion in both storing and retrieving events from memory. One of the most powerful influences in this process is preexisting knowledge, which determines "how we encode and store new memories . . .

contributing to the nature, texture and quality of what we will recall of the moment."[1]

Memory depends on existing knowledge.

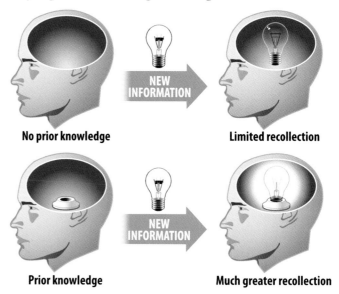

No prior knowledge   **Limited recollection**

Prior knowledge   **Much greater recollection**

Perception and communication are not purely objective; they combine present sense information with past experience and emotional content. The content of memory is shaped by whether a person is an observer or a participant in an event, the circumstances in which an event is recalled, and the motivation of the individual.

It is obvious that the human brain does not record visual information with photographic accuracy. While there is a wide range in the capacity to retain and recollect detail, the memory of all people is fragmentary in relation to the actual event or object on which it is based. Schacter describes an experiment by French artist Sophie Calle in which viewers familiar with a Magritte painting at the Museum of Modern Art were asked to describe it from memory. The level of variation was stunning, ranging from "It's just a murder scene" to an intricate

> Perception and communication are not purely objective; they combine present sense information with past experience and emotional content.

1. Daniel L. Schacter, *Searching for Memory* (New York: Basic Books, 1996), 6.

re-creation of the clothes, body positions, facial expressions, and colors in the painting.

Schacter summarizes this maddening variability of human perception, which is a constant challenge to creating images based on memory:

> We remember only what we have encoded, and what we encode depends on who we are—our past experiences, knowledge and needs all have a powerful influence on what we retain. This is one reason why two different people can sometimes have radically divergent recollections of the same event.[2]

HOW DO COMPUTER IMAGES HELP ADDRESS THE VARIABILITY OF HUMAN MEMORY?

Though computer images require more sustained effort to create than point-and-shoot photography, the potential benefits make the effort worthwhile:

1. Like puzzle pieces, the memory fragments from multiple witnesses can be blended into one whole image that is greater than the sum of its parts.

---

2. Schacter, *Searching for Memory*, 52.

2. The memory of a witness often becomes more precise when the illustrator presents him or her with a draft image for discussion; for example, "No, it wasn't like that, you need to move the position of this to here."

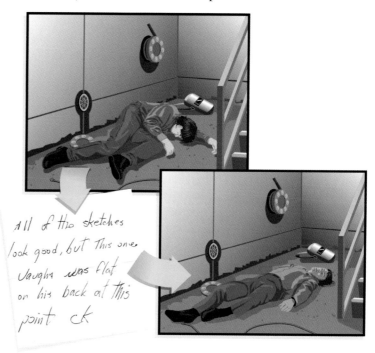

All of the sketches look good, but This one, Vaughn was flat on his back at This point ck

3. Having the witnesses' memories illustrated in a scene avoids the vagaries of a verbal description from a photo, which will trigger variable responses from the jury. A computer graphic allows the jurors to see exactly what the witnesses meant, rather than hearing it and creating their own individual interpretations.

Photos can often contain unnecessary and distracting details.

4. Photos can often contain unnecessary and distracting details. A computer illustration can eliminate those, focusing on only what really matters to the case.

5. An effective computer graphic illustrating an expert's testimony will make it more vivid, simultaneously increasing the expert's level of conviction, enthusiasm, and confidence.

WHAT IS THE INTENDED USE OF THE ILLUSTRATION?

Early on, you have to figure out how you intend to use an illustration. Is it just a demonstrative aid, or is it the cornerstone of your case? Defining this in advance can save you money and time. There is no need to go through multiple drafts for a simple demonstrative aid. If, on the other hand, an illustration is critical to the case, backed up by expert testimony, you'll likely need multiple drafts to create a solid foundation.

In this process, it is important to keep your terms straight, as lawyers often confuse "illustration" and "animation." Though both refer to visuals created by a computer, they are not interchangeable. An illustration is a single image and does not move. An animation is a collection of illustrations put together resulting in movement.

It's important to start creating your visuals early, particularly when you are trying to find out the whole story of what

Illustrations don't move, animations do.

happened. Doing so will provide a reference point for witnesses as well as an analytical tool for you.

Don't worry about spending too much money on graphics up front, as you will get good value from these during discovery, particularly in depositions. Even though visuals likely will change some as discovery proceeds and more facts become known, even draft images allow you to work from a common point of view, giving witnesses and experts the same starting point.

THE BOTTOM LINE: IS IT ACCURATE?

Computer graphics and animations now are seen with greater frequency by the general public—in films, on television, in newspapers, and in magazines. The dividing line between fact and imagination in these visuals becomes ever more hazy.

However, when computer graphics and animations appear in legal cases, it is no longer enough that they merely be visually interesting. You must use all of your training in the principles of foundation to make sure that they are accurate too.

As gatekeepers, judges have to be sure that your visuals accurately represent what you claim. It is up to you to convincingly explain why they are fair and accurate.

The lack of understanding in the legal community on just how computer images are created leads to a certain amount of skepticism among judges. Some jurists regard these as Disney cartoons, products of the imagination, not fact. The reality is

very different among professional computer-graphics and animation artists, who hold themselves to a very high standard of accuracy. Professionals do not just make things up; they review the foundation with care, trying to make sure that what they create on the screen is supportable. One such artist, Jay Syverson, explains the standard to which he holds himself:

> We are technicians, responsible for the literal translation of the information given to us by witnesses, turning this knowledge into visual images.
>
> The end product must be an accurate presentation of the information given to us.
>
> Whether the scene is depicted in a photo, video, or animation, the foundation involves the same process.[3]

Jay Syverson

At the end of the day, the accuracy of an illustrator's or animator's work is judged by the answer to the following question to the expert witness:

Is this an accurate representation of your opinions?

The same goes for fact witnesses:

Is this an accurate representation of what you saw that day?

TAKEAWAYS—CREATING COMPUTER ILLUSTRATIONS AND ANIMATIONS

- *While you may be more comfortable with photography, the computer is more versatile in creating images to fit the needs of a case.*

- *Words and human perception are imprecise, making it a challenge to reconstruct computer images from the memory of witnesses.*

- *Information degrades as it passes from person to person.*

---

3. Jay Syverson, interview with William S. Bailey, March 20, 2008.

- *The picture created in the mind of an individual from words alone is based on the values, experiences, and personality of that audience member.*

- *Human memory is fragmentary, prone to vulnerability and distortion in storing and retrieving events.*

- *Preexisting knowledge determines how we encode and store new memories.*

- *Past experience and emotions affect perception and communication.*

- *Computer images allow for the blending of memory fragments from multiple witnesses into one image.*

- *Computer graphics enable a witness to be more precise, unlike with words alone, allowing jurors to see exactly what the witness means.*

- *Photos can contain unnecessary and distracting details not present in computer graphics.*

- *Expert testimony is more effective when key points are visualized with the computer.*

- *You must think about the intended purpose and use of all illustrations in a case.*

- *It is critical to strive for a high standard of accuracy in computer graphics, based on the evidence.*

- *Computer-graphics specialists are technicians, translating the knowledge of witnesses into visual images.*

- *When asked about the foundation of computer graphics, witnesses with knowledge have to be able to agree they are fair and accurate.*

17

WORKING WITH COMPUTER-GRAPHICS SPECIALISTS

If you have a strong foundation . . . you can build or rebuild anything on it. But if you've got a weak foundation, you can't build anything.

—Jack Scalia

The overall goal of collaborating with a graphics specialist is to develop computer images that are not only effective, but admissible in evidence. The basic message is foundation, foundation, foundation. The steps in creating a solid foundation are universal for all types of computer visuals. While the end product may be different, the process in getting there is the same.

KNOW YOUR CASE BEFORE INVOLVING AN ILLUSTRATOR

You need to be on top of the facts of your case before involving an illustrator. It is not the illustrator's job to sort through piles of paper and make command decisions or to develop the

Patrick O'Neill

It is a basic fact of
litigation that the
more effective the
computer images are,
the higher the stakes,
with correspondingly
more effort by the
opposing counsel
to keep them out of
evidence.

theory of the case. That is strictly your role, though the process of working with an illustrator often results in a heightened understanding of your case.

In order to explain your case to another, you need to know it very well. This is particularly true in working with an illustrator or animator, who will require a detailed foundation to come up with a finished product. Forensic computer-graphic specialist Patrick O'Neill describes the two-way benefit of this process as a "reality test":

> The process of explaining the case to me is a reality test for the lawyer. Does it add up? It is not uncommon for me to see a big flaw in an attorney's theory. This discussion can produce an important piece of the puzzle just from the questions I ask. I'll go, "Huh? How did you get from there to there? You have to either explain it to me in a way that I can understand or change the theory." The attorney typically responds, "Oh, I didn't think of that. I'll have to investigate and get back to you."[1]

HOW COMFORTABLE ARE YOU WITH THE FOUNDATION?

It is a basic fact of litigation that the more effective the computer images are, the higher the stakes, with correspondingly more effort by the opposing counsel to keep them out of evidence. The challenge to your partnership with an illustrator or animator is matching on the screen what happened in real life. In some circumstances, for example, with lighting issues, this can be difficult.

A deposition is always an important information source in any case because it is sworn testimony. Witnesses can say one thing to you off the record and then change it when placed under oath. Any changes in the facts leads to changes in a visual based on these facts.

---

1. Patrick O'Neill, interview with William S. Bailey, July 20, 2008.

After all the depositions are concluded, you will generally have a pretty good idea what your images need to portray. If the illustrator or animator does finished work before the witnesses are deposed, revisions are almost inevitable. But having a working image of an important fact for a witness to comment on at a deposition can help make the final image more accurate. An illustration or an animation is no different than writing a brief or a speech. With each draft, a written document or speech gets better. The same with an illustration or an animation.

THE ONE-MINUTE RULE

A basic rule of thumb is, if you can't explain what happened to the illustrator or animator in one minute or less, you are not ready to proceed.

PREPARING FOR THE FIRST MEETING WITH AN ILLUSTRATOR OR ANIMATOR

There are a number of steps you should follow prior to the first meeting with an illustrator or animator. Following these will save time and money and make admission of the final product into evidence more likely.

Step 1: Develop Your Story's Bullet Points

Ideally, you should be able to reduce the entire liability case to three to five bullet points prior to beginning any computer visuals. A common response computer-graphics consultants get from attorneys to this approach is, "That's impossible."

Often, lawyers are so caught up in the minutiae of law and procedure that they can't focus on telling a coherent story. But that's what the jury is interested in, the story, not legalese. It is those three to five bullets that summarize your case story.

Step 2: Ask "What Do You Need?"

The most efficient way to do your first in-person meeting with the computer-graphics or animation team is to discuss the case

A basic rule of thumb is, if you can't explain what happened to the illustrator or animator in one minute or less, you are not ready to proceed.

and allow them to ask questions. Brainstorm for possible solutions. An in-person meeting like this doesn't create a paper trail for the opposing counsel to use later on. Ask the illustrator or animator, "Here is what I have. What else do you need?" After the meeting, gather and send requested follow-up information.

Step 3: Have All Your Facts in Place

You have to make a determination, "How comfortable am I with the information from the expert or fact witnesses?" If any of it is shaky, so will the computer-generated evidence on which it is built be shaky.

A lawsuit is an evolutionary process. Facts change as discovery proceeds. Wait until the basic facts of your case are well understood before handing the project to your computer-graphics specialist.

Step 4: Think It Through to the End

Working with an illustrator or animator requires you to really dig into the facts early on, a process of forced learning. Always keep your eye on the foundation required to support your images. This requires you to look at your goals. Where do you want to end up? These goals direct you to the steps you need to take. This is a tough concept for most of us to grasp, but it is the key to developing effective computer images. Once we know what we want, our creative consultants can focus on how to get us there.

THE CREATIVE PROCESS

How do computer-graphics consultants turn our ideas into images? There is a bit of a "finding a needle in a haystack" flavor to this. A huge volume of pretrial discovery may result in no more than three or four visuals.

The creative process starts with the initial meeting between you and the artist. The challenge is to see the big picture of the trial story and its underlying theme without getting lost in boxes of documents.

A twenty-five-year veteran of helping lawyers to visualize their cases, Aaron Weholt describes the process this way:

> Usually what I want to know about the case at the first meeting is what most jurors would also want to know. As I ask those questions and paraphrase back to my lawyer clients what I think they are trying to say, I begin to apply my toolbox of graphic techniques. This usually boils down to:
>
> 1. A background that presents the theme of the story in a clean, simple, effective way.
>
> 2. Looking for materials in the file that will best illustrate the story.
>
> 3. Filling in objects, texture, and color.
>
> 4. Adding only enough visual detail to tell the story.
>
> 5. Simplify, simplify, simplify.[2]

Aaron Weholt

Of necessity, the creation of images for legal cases is an incremental process, requiring input from multiple sources. The ever-present background concern is, "Will this meet the foundational tests of fairness and accuracy?"

CONTINUED INVOLVEMENT IN THE DRAFTING PROCESS

Expect to direct the artist in revising the drafts. Your voluminous knowledge of the details of a case is quite useful, typically superior to your artist's knowledge. Spot mistakes and have them corrected, anticipating the challenges that are sure to come from the opposing counsel.

Once the artist has all the pieces of the scene and the sequence right, your legal analysis needs to shape the visualization, emphasizing the strengths of your story. Collaborate with the artist to

---

2. Aaron Weholt, interview with William S. Bailey, August 23, 2008.

figure out how to best accomplish this. Beyond editorial decisions on telling the trial story, sequencing also demands your attention. What is the best order to put the images in, flowing from one to the next in a crescendo? You don't want to repeat yourself or peak too soon. These sequencing decisions don't happen until the end, when the pieces are done.

With animations, be aware of the timing of the actions and events in the story. Does this match what would have happened in real life, or is it either too long or not long enough? Where do you start or stop the story? You have to make those decisions jointly with the artist. "Do we play it through or hit pause? If so, for how long? What text do we put in?" The artist can't decide this without your input.

Other issues also require your attention, such as putting explanatory text in an animation. Text gives the jury information, but it also stretches and delays the time sequence. The slower the sequence, the less powerful. Using labels on the screen is a trade-off, explaining things but reducing the dramatic impact. You have to make this judgment call.

Each camera movement and camera angle in a computer illustration or animation requires planning and analysis. You must decide camera placement and perspective questions: "Why is the camera over there rather than here?" "What side of the action do we want to put the camera on?" "What are we trying to see?" For every camera angle, high or low, there is an accompanying psychology, imparting a definite feeling to the audience. Many times, the only way to figure out the right approach is to try out several until you see one that feels right.

Framing is a major design consideration in this process:

> Framing is the use of images, words, and context to manipulate how people think about something. . . . [It] can . . . emphasize the positive (e.g., glass is half-full) or the negative (e.g., glass is half-empty).[3]

> Text gives the jury information, but it also stretches and delays the time sequence.

---

3. William Lidwell, Kristina Holden, and Jill Butler, *Universal Principles of Design* (Gloucester, MA: Rockport, 2003), 92.

The type of frame you use to present the information in your illustrations and animations will have a direct effect on how the jury reacts to it. Positive frames move people to take action (for example, make a decision in your client's favor), while negative frames move people toward inaction (for example, deny the remedy sought by your opponent). Typically, similar to a political campaign, your case will be a blend of positive and negative frames, with your client in a positive one and your opposing side in a negative.

Deciding What Image to Use

The artist can walk you through various options for telling the story. Be involved and ask questions: "Why don't we try this?" "Is there any problem with doing that visually?"

In your collaborations with the artist, ask, "What are the repercussions of that image in the case?" Focused on telling the story, the artist oftentimes doesn't have all the background facts. You do, and are better able to make judgment calls as issues come up.

Computer animations have different levels of cost and quality. Simple can be effective, and embellished as time goes on, like buying a basic economy car, then adding leather seats and a better sound system later.

Throughout the image-creation process, keep your broad range of choices in mind, exploring options, thinking of when, where, and how visuals can be used, as well as in what form. Michael Reiss maintains a keen awareness of his options throughout the process:

> A lawyer always has choices. You can turn a video into freeze-frames or photographs. Will you have voiceover or silence? Do you turn an animation into slides or stills? Do you ever pass these out? I want evidence in a form that the jurors can take back with them to the jury room.
>
> I try to think of as many visuals as I can. If this doesn't work, what will? My goal is to convey my client's

I always have at least one backup plan for each point I am trying to communicate visually.

story at different times in the trial—opening statement, witness on the stand, cross-examination, and closing argument.

I always have at least one backup plan for each point I am trying to communicate visually. What are the alternatives if the first plan doesn't work? I usually do the videos two ways, with and without a soundtrack. I can't be sure what a judge is going to do. I can use the silent version in opening statement. When a key witness takes the stand, I can run the tape a little bit, stop it, and ask, "What are we seeing here?" I always want to have the option of my witnesses talking directly to the jury with media, as it is more personal and immediate.

I also want to have a number of still photographs from a video so my witnesses can describe the scene at different points.[4]

GETTING INPUT ON DRAFT IMAGES AFTER THEY ARE FAIRLY ACCURATE

Since computer images often are drawn from multiple sources, figure out when to present them to witnesses or experts for review, ideally when you have a relatively high degree of confidence in their accuracy. Don't give the opposing counsel any impeachment opportunities if you can help it. Changes, sometimes many, in the draft images are inevitable. That, in and of itself, is not a bad thing, as it shows effort to get all the details right. But take the lead in the drafting process, getting visuals in the best shape you can before circulating them.

---

4. Michael Reiss, interview with William S. Bailey, October 29, 2009.

TAKEAWAYS—WORKING WITH COMPUTER-GRAPHICS SPECIALISTS

- *Your constant focus must be on foundation, foundation, foundation.*

- *Know your case before involving an illustrator.*

- *You must be able to pass the one-minute rule, explaining your case to the illustrator in that amount of time in a way that makes sense.*

- *Develop your story's bullet points.*

- *Ask the illustrator or animator, "What do you need?"*

- *Have all your facts in place.*

- *Think through to the end what you are trying to achieve.*

- *Decide what image to use.*

- *Get input on draft images after they are fairly accurate.*

- *Continue to stay involved throughout the drafting process, making strategic and tactical decisions.*

18

AVOIDING THE PITFALLS

In this business, by the time you realize you are in trouble,
it's too late to save yourself.

—Bill Gates

Many of us are fearful of computer-generated images. We don't know how to lay the foundation, and then we get panicky as the case proceeds. This is based both on ignorance of the process and fear of the opposing counsel's using any changes in the images for impeachment. A paranoid "Attack of the Outtakes" vision lurks in the backs of our minds during the creation of images: "Can what I am doing here be used by the opposing counsel to get me later on?" In the adversary system, such fears are healthy, as they really are out to get you.

A good bit of the fear factor revolves around questions of your work-product. How much of your preparation can be kept from the opposing counsel? It doesn't help that the reported cases on this point are somewhat inconsistent, leading to more uncertainty and fear.[1]

This chapter, when combined with chapter 23, "Dealing with Evidentiary and Ethical Issues," will help you develop a protocol for the image and animation drafting process. Like everything else in life, if you know the process, there is less to be afraid of. Above all else, be careful about what you put in writing and send out of your office. We'll cover the reasons for this in this chapter as well as in chapter 23.

One of the biggest risks you take in the computer-image drafting process is putting your thoughts in writing and sending them to your experts or creative team. E-mail is a wonderful convenience, both quick and easy. But it also is forever and may come back to haunt you. Before you hit Send or sign a letter, ask "Would anything in here really hurt me if the opposing counsel got it?" If the answer is yes, don't send it; use the telephone instead.

> Above all else, be careful about what you put in writing and send out of your office.

Quantity over Quality

Many lawyers have the mistaken notion that foundation is a matter of quantity over quality. An illustrator or animator likely will not want anything beyond the basic factual documents, such as police reports in an auto accident, or the depositions of key fact witnesses. Sending more than that, at least initially, only makes the work more difficult for him or her, as the paper has to be sorted, reviewed, and retained, even if of little value.

A huge volume of paper from the attorney also makes the deposition of the illustrator or animator more burdensome. The opposing counsel typically subpoenas his or her entire file, asking about each document at the deposition: "Did you use

---

1. For an excellent overview of attorney work-product, foundation, and admissibility issues, see Hon. James P. Flannery Jr., "Using Videos at Trial: The Big Picture," Ill. B. J. 95, no. 12 (December, 2007): 642. Cases discussed in Judge Flannery's article are worth looking at, including *Cisarik v. Palos Community Hospital*, 579 NE 2d 873 (1991) and *Neuswanger v. Ikegai America Corp.*, 582 NE 2d 192 (3rd D 1991).

this in any way?" A quantity-over-quality approach to foundation means that the deposition likely will be spent discussing paperwork of no value. This makes it look as if the illustrator or animator did not use all the information available, cherry-picking to support a narrow, skewed point of view.

THE DRIBBLE EFFECT

The dribble effect drives computer-graphics artists crazy. In this scenario, a package of information arrives from you with the message, "This is all there is." The artist then relies on this representation. If the facts change later, this often requires revision of the images, resulting in much more expense than if you had waited until the facts were reasonably clear.

This dribble effect, where you send incremental waves of information, is very wasteful. It often occurs either because you haven't thought through your case well enough or didn't wait until discovery resolved major factual disputes.

This dribble effect, where you send incremental waves of information, is very wasteful.

OVERPROMISING WHAT IT SHOWS

Lawyers get into foundation trouble when they overpromise what a computer illustration or animation shows to a judge or a jury. Don't call an animation an accident reconstruction when it is not based on expert testimony and is really only an illustration of the client's testimony. For example, in the multi-defendant intersection-collision case of *T. H. v. D. M.*,[2] one defendant turned left in front of a speeding car driven by the other defendant, causing serious injury to the plaintiff passenger. In representing the plaintiff, T. H., I elected to do a filmed re-creation of the view of the oncoming car by the left-turning defendant. Since there were a number of disputed facts, I called the resulting video a "visibility study," not an "accident reconstruction." The only purpose of the video was to show the jury the view of the left-turning driver. The trial judge admitted it

2. Pseudonym.

on this basis. Many of the technical foundation challenges to the video were avoided when I did not overpromise that it was a precise re-creation of what had happened that night.

THE SHOTGUN METHOD

Another problem is the shotgun method, where you ask the illustrator or animator to create many alternative scenarios. Subliminally, this says, "We don't know what works, so we're going to try everything." Just as a student has to commit to one answer to a multiple-choice question, so must you in a theory of the case. Without the foundation of three to five bullet points defining what a case is all about, the computer images that result often suggest weakness or confusion.

Explore the possibilities in your head and then pick one. It is much better to think through the strategic visual alternatives first and decide which one best explains your theory of the case. Don't turn the illustrations into a multiple-choice scenario for the judge or jury.

Build your visuals around facts that will hold up in discovery, based on real evidence, such as photos and measurements. The basic facts you use need to be consistent, so get them nailed down. Some attorneys go to the scene and experiment, saying, "Let's try this." Thinking out loud at the scene in the presence of others is a bad idea. You run the risk that the opposing counsel will find out and use it to attack your exhibits. Discretion in image creation is hugely important.

TOO MANY COOKS

The old saying "Too many cooks spoil the stew" applies to computer graphics. There should only be one contact in the law firm per project. Information from different, uncoordinated sources results in garbled, conflicting foundation. Difficulties arise when one lawyer spreads a computer illustration or image around the law firm, with multiple lawyers, legal assistants, and staff looking at it. This often leads to e-mails critiquing what is

Don't turn the illustrations into a multiple-choice scenario for the judge or jury.

in the draft and offering conflicting directions, compounded by telephone calls that do much the same.

THE MORE REMOVED THE INFORMATION, THE FUZZIER THE IMAGE

Secondhand information results in fuzzier images. Although you should play a key role in the early stages of image creation because of your superior knowledge of the case, the creative team will need some direct input on the draft from the client, experts, and other witnesses by the end of the process. As we will present, keeping the client and the expert out of the loop at early stages reduces the potential for impeachment by the opposing counsel if mistakes in the foundation are identified. But when the deposition of your artist is taken by the opposing counsel, the accusation is often made, "You did just what the lawyer that hired you told you to do, didn't you?" If the computer-graphics consultant has spoken directly with the client, eyewitnesses, or experts, the reply to this question can be, "No, I did what the eyewitnesses or experts said happened. I didn't just rely on the lawyer for the facts." If the information supplied was only from secondary sources, the foundation is shakier.

EXPERT TROUBLE

If the expert is impeached during the deposition, so that the opposing counsel can argue, "The expert doesn't know what he's talking about," any computer images based on that expert's testimony also suffer. The best approach here is to spend enough time discussing the potential problems, issues, and responses by the opposing counsel with your expert before creating images based on the expert's opinion.

Hold off until enough information has come out in discovery that you are sure of the expert's foundation.

TAKEAWAYS—AVOIDING THE PITFALLS

- *Many lawyers don't have a clear sense of the foundation required for computer images and worry about it.*

- *Use discretion in what you put in writing and send out of your office.*

- *The information you send to the creative team should not be considered work-product. Your opponent can ask for it prior to a deposition.*

- *Don't send the computer-graphics specialists more paperwork than is necessary.*

- *After image creation has started, changes make it necessary to start over.*

- *Don't overpromise what a computer animation or illustration shows.*

- *Create your animations or illustrations on solid evidence, based on direct input from your client, experts, and other fact witnesses.*

- *Don't create multiple-choice visual scenarios. Stick to the one that best explains your theory of the case.*

- *Input from multiple lawyers leads to confusion.*

19

Examining Computer-Illustration Case Studies

An inner process stands in need of outward criteria.

—Ludwig Wittgenstein

The challenges of creating computer illustrations are best understood in the context of actual cases.

MABREY V. WIZARD[1]—EVEN SIMPLE THINGS CAN BE HARD

In examining *Mabrey v. Wizard,* a simple fall-on-a-stairway case, we will go from start to finish, step by step, showing how hard even a simple fact pattern can be to illustrate. *Mabrey* required multiple conferences and corrections in order to get all the details correct, illustrating that human beings fill in the gaps of fragmentary information from their own experience.

---

1. *Mabrey v. Wizard,* Cause Number 2:05-cv 01499-RSL. Filed 8/31/05. Disposition date 8/30/07. Bench trial with judgment entered in favor of plaintiff.

This may not match what really happened. The drafting process requires a back-and-forth dialog between illustrator, attorney, and client until all the details are finally right.

The initial e-mail description in *Mabrey* from plaintiff's counsel, Mike Myers, to the illustrator, Patrick O'Neill, seemed straightforward enough, focusing on the construction of the stairs:

> The stairs are something between stairs and a ladder. They are steep, with handrails. The treads are made of steel diamond plate. It was slippery on the date our client fell.[2]

Mr. Myers didn't mention anything in the e-mail about how the fall occurred, or the client's body position.

The drafting process requires a back-and-forth dialog between illustrator, attorney, and client until all the details are finally right.

Scene photo from lawyer

THE QUEST TO FIND THE MISSING DETAILS

A person in motion has a number of distinct body movements that combine to form the overall action. Illustrators have to identify at least some of those in a case involving a physical

---

2. E-mail from Myers & Company to Patrick O'Neill, May 11, 2007.

event. The client's deposition in *Mabrey* described some aspects of the event, but a number of details were missing.

Illustrator Patrick O'Neill described all the choices that initially faced him in doing even this simple illustration.

> Everybody in this case knew the plaintiff had fallen down the stairs. But in what manner? Words are imprecise. I have to make definite decisions on the client's movements. What is the environment, lighting, wall color, and floor texture?[3]

When Mr. O'Neill finished reading the material Mr. Myers furnished, his mental picture was that the client must have tumbled down the stairs, head over heels. After the first draft, O'Neill found out that the client's feet had shot out from underneath him.

Everybody in this case knew the plaintiff had fallen down the stairs. But in what manner?

None of the foundation information specified whether it was a slip, trip, or tumble. It was only when the client saw the first draft that he cleared this up—his feet had slipped out from

---

3. Patrick O'Neill, interview with William S. Bailey, July 25, 2008.

underneath him. O'Neill prepared a second draft with the new information but still had a number of questions.

> I still did not understand completely the mechanism of the fall. In a conversation with the lawyer, I learned that the rocking boat was a key factor. Suddenly a lightbulb went on, "Now I get it."
>
> Another question that kept coming up was, "Where exactly were his feet on the stairs?" This had to be straightened out in order to do a close-up.[4]

This lack of clarity continued to play out in the drafting process. Drafts showed the client with his hands on the wrong rails, facing in the wrong direction, and not using his shoulder enough on the door. The client's body also was steadily spun clockwise on an axis to its proper position. As the process unfolded, Mr. Myers and Mr. O'Neill corrected all these mistakes.

Axis Rotation Changes in Client Body Position during the Drafting Process

Draft 1

---

4. O'Neill, interview.

This lack of clarity continued to play out in the drafting process.

Draft 2

Draft 3

THE ILLUSTRATOR FINALLY MEETS THE CLIENT IN PERSON

After the second draft was completed, the attorney allowed his client to speak directly to the illustrator, which was critical for foundation purposes.

> Everything was cleared up. The client's body language was so helpful, "Now I know what you are talking about." Some of this information is intuitive, based on instinct. You can't express it in an e-mail or over the phone.[5]

Client photo of body position as he begins descent

PHOTOGRAPHS

In addition to the personal contact, photographs of the client modeling the body positions were helpful:

> These told me right where he was, eliminating the guesswork. I could see the rotation of his body as he went down the stairs, and which rail he grabbed with his right hand.[6]

> In Draft #1, I incorrectly had the client grab the right rail with his right hand. The photos showed me how it really happened.[7]

LAWYER AS INTERMEDIARY, FILTERING INFORMATION

At the beginning of this whole process, the attorney provided information about the client's actions and body positions, based on his client's answers. Plaintiff's attorney, Michael D. Myers, did not want to leave a paper trail for the opposing counsel to use for impeachment.

---

5. O'Neill, interview.
6. O'Neill, interview.
7. O'Neill, interview.

Our case theory was based on reverse engineering. Clients don't usually know split second by split second what their body was doing. It all goes by very quickly. We piece things together by working with our experts.[8]

Mr. Myers was wary of doing anything that could be construed as waiver of either the attorney-client privilege or attorney work-product protection.

Michael D. Myers

When you create a diagram of a scene, it becomes the physical reality of a case. I want to be a filter, an intermediary, which allows for work-product and attorney-client privilege. I don't want the lawyers on the other side to be able to use this for impeachment. The client doesn't always know what happened. This can end up undermining the case.

When I talk with my client about the scene, I have become personally familiar with it. I will run my theories by the client as possibilities.

I am in a lot better shape for getting rid of an animator's draft that I don't like if the client is not involved with it. That is attorney work-product. If the client meets directly with the animator, that protection may not apply.[9]

Mr. Myers also was concerned about the effect of litigation pressure on his client. As the case proceeded, the client became increasingly aware of the claims and tactics of the opposing counsel and felt pressured to arrange the facts in the best possible light. Mr. Myers was well aware of this problem and kept tight control over his client:

The aggressive defense tactics threw my client off balance, making him want vigorously to dispute everything. We had to calm him down and tell him that

---

8. Michael D. Myers, interview with William S. Bailey, July 25, 2008.
9. Myers, interview.

I have to keep the big picture in mind: what is going to present our theory visually to best advantage?

the law would support a finding of liability against the defendant just the way it happened.

If I had let him meet with the illustrator early on, he would have probably told him what he thought would help his case. Because I served as an intermediary, this wasn't a problem.

I have to keep the big picture in mind: what is going to present our theory visually to best advantage? It is better to have the illustrations or animations 90 percent done and then bring the client in for an in-person meeting with the animator to fine-tune them.[10]

Mabrey v. Wizard—Lessons Learned

◆ It is very difficult to translate words into accurate images. Be prepared to go through multiple drafts before a computer graphic reflects what really happened. Even with sworn testimony and photographs as an initial foundation, illustrators are likely to get some parts wrong.

◆ Until the images are in a more finished state, a lawyer should be the primary contact.

◆ A single computer graphic can be based on multiple sources of information. A client cannot be expected to have complete details on location and body position.

Moore v. Rufus County[11]—The Risk of Impeachment

The concern of counsel in *Mabrey* for potential impeachment of the client on inaccurate foundation details was borne out in *Moore v. Rufus County.* A meeting between the client and the illustrator too early in the process ended up giving an impeachment opportunity to the opposing counsel.

10. Myers, interview.
11. Pseudonym.

The plaintiff, Ray Moore, was run down by a van as he stood next to his pickup truck while on his lunch hour. He suffered injuries to his right shoulder and arm as well as his chest. Taken from the scene to the hospital, Mr. Moore did not have the opportunity to inspect the damage to his truck, not seeing it again until after it had been repaired.

Following the state civil equivalent of an FRCP 34 inspection of the accident scene, I provided photos and information to the animator about the events leading up to the collision.

The client had broken glass in his hair and on his clothing after being struck. He presumed from this that his head had broken the driver's side window. Photographs taken by the body shop prior to the repairs were ambiguous, showing broken glass all over the cab. Considerable repairs had been made to the driver's side door. All of this made the client's description of the injury seem correct.

Based on this information, the computer animation showed the client's head hitting and breaking the window. Feeling on solid foundation, I provided the animation and stills taken from it to the opposing counsel.

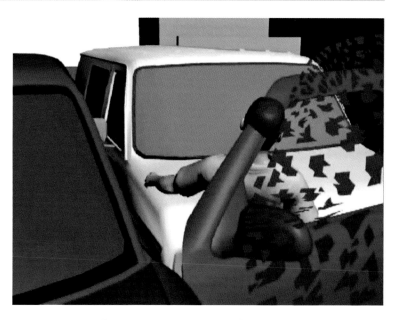

Later on, the opposing counsel found additional photos of the accident investigation. These revealed that the driver's side window had not in fact been broken in the collision. This formed the basis of the opposing counsel's efforts to discredit the

plaintiff. By this point, his deposition already had been taken. He had testified that the animation and the illustration stills showing his head breaking the window were fair and accurate:

Q: What parts of your body impacted the driver's side door of your vehicle?

A: My right ribs, my shoulder, elbow, and then my head went through the driver's window.

Q: And your head?

A: Yeah, went through the driver's window on the door.

Q: Did it break the glass?

A: Yes.

Q: I want to show you what's marked as Defendant's Exhibit 1.

[Computer animation still marked for identification]

Q: Do you recognize this?

A: Yes, it was prepared by my attorney.

Q: Is this a fair and accurate representation of your head getting hit in the accident?

A: Yes, my head hit the window of my truck door, breaking the glass.

Once the photo of the truck was produced showing that the window was not broken, a follow-up deposition of the plaintiff was taken by the opposing counsel on this issue. My client was questioned very aggressively about his mistake:

Q: Do you remember the prior occasion when I took your deposition?

A: Yes.

Q: You testified under oath that your head shattered the glass of your truck window?

My client was questioned very aggressively about his mistake.

A: Yes.

Q: And you said that this computer illustration was accurate?

A: Yes.

Q: But looking at this photo of your truck, we now know that the window didn't break.

A: That's right.

Ultimately, Mr. Moore's mistake on the broken glass did not seriously impeach his credibility when the case went to trial. The bump on the back of his head noted in the emergency room report, broken glass all over the scene, and a specific item in the truck repair bill to "clean up broken glass," made this an understandable mistake.

However, a mistake on the basic facts of an occurrence has the potential to damage the credibility of you and your client. It is best not to have the client speak directly with the illustrator until the discovery process is further along. Any mistake in a visual that is attributable to a client allows the opposing counsel to ask the jury, "What else was he wrong about?"

A mistake on the basic facts of an occurrence has the potential to damage the credibility of you and your client.

MOORE V. RUFUS COUNTY—LESSONS LEARNED

- Wait until you are confident of the essential details of what happened before starting computer visuals.

- Initial contacts with the computer-graphics person should be with the lawyer, not the client.

- Take plenty of photographs of the area involved.

- You, not the client, should review the preliminary computer-graphics work.

Takeaways—Examining Computer-Illustration Case Studies

- ◆ *Accurate and detailed communication for the foundation is a challenge due to the frailty of human memory and perception.*

- ◆ *Necessary details are often missing, requiring the illustrator to guess about some parts.*

- ◆ *Depositions tend to mush visual information together in an indistinct way.*

- ◆ *It often takes multiple drafts to get all the details right.*

- ◆ *In the early stages, the attorney should act as the primary conduit for information to the illustrator.*

- ◆ *Photographs are a valuable source of information for illustrators.*

- ◆ *Attorneys often have to piece together what happened through a process of reverse engineering.*

- ◆ *It is easier for an attorney to claim an illustration as workproduct if the client is not directly involved with the creation of it.*

- ◆ *The pressures of litigation can cause clients to distort facts.*

- ◆ *The attorney needs to stay involved throughout the process of exhibit creation, keeping in mind the big picture of what is going to drive the case forward.*

- ◆ *Vouching for incorrect details in a computer illustration can damage client credibility.*

20

CREATING ILLUSTRATIONS FROM SOURCE MATERIAL

Details create the big picture.

—Sanford I. Weill

This chapter starts by describing the process by which computer graphics are created, then showing examples of different legal cases in which the graphics were used. Duane Hoffmann of Seattle, Washington, applied his fine arts degree to illustrating front-page newspaper stories shortly after graduation. The skills required for this proved adaptable to legal cases. In the section below, Mr. Hoffmann explains his basic procedure in creating computer graphics.

BASIC THOUGHTS FROM AN ILLUSTRATOR

My philosophy is to make everything as accurate as possible, best representing what the attorney wants to show. The more realistic a graphic is, the more accurate it is expected to be. There is more leeway on a simpler graphic.

Duane Hoffmann

1. GRAPHICS CHOICES

- Chart, graph, or illustration of information
- Map or overview of a scene
- Timeline of events
- Series of illustrations to show a sequence of events

It can save a great deal of time and money if the attorney/client can refer to something similar that I have done before or show me an example of something to adapt from elsewhere.

2. REFERENCE MATERIAL

I look over the information provided and determine what is most important for the graphic. Photos are extremely helpful in this effort—the more the better. The Internet has opened up a great deal of quick reference material too. Site visits are very helpful, giving me a much better idea of what happened and allowing me to take my own photos. Any reference material or photos can be scanned into my computer and then adapted.

Photos are extremely helpful in this effort—the more the better.

3. DIGITAL COMPUTER GRAPHICS

I do almost all my work in computer graphics. Digital images allow me to e-mail graphics to the client and adapt them to various forms of presentation—posters, displays, or screen.

4. PRESENTATION CHOICES

While displays can be printed and mounted at almost any size, many attorneys now prefer to use a digital projector:

- Less lead time and no printer
- Less cost
- Easy and cheap to adapt to PowerPoint, animation, or video

◆ If necessary, last-minute fixes are easy. [1]

The remainder of this chapter describes some representative cases where computer illustrations played a significant role.

MALKOW V. COURIER EXPRESS[2]

FACTS: A commercial fisherman was hit by a courier van in a crosswalk at night.

EXHIBIT ISSUES:

1. Show the path taken by the van and the pedestrian.

2. Show operation of traffic and pedestrian crosswalk signals.

3. Show the nighttime lighting conditions accurately.

4. Visually re-create key moments of eyewitness testimony.

Approach to Exhibit Issues

1. Get police report and hire accident reconstruction expert.

2. Go to the scene at night, under similar lighting conditions.

3. Hire forensic photographer to take panoramic night photo of scene.

4. Meet with illustrator to discuss exhibits.

5. Provide photo of plaintiff to establish his height, weight, and build.

6. Provide plaintiff's actual clothing worn that night.

7. Combine all events into a single image, used as a courtroom billboard.

---

1. E-mail from Duane Hoffmann to William S. Bailey of June 9, 2009, answering a series of questions submitted to him on June 2, 2009, on how he goes about his work as an illustrator.
2. Pseudonym.

Reducing a Case to One Image

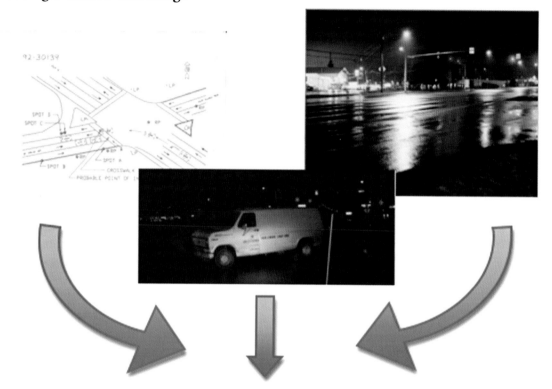

Police Diagram and Photos merged into 3-D image of intersection.

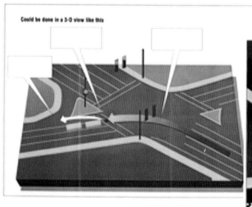

Facts of the case fill the dialog boxes, explaining all key events in one *USA Today* style image.

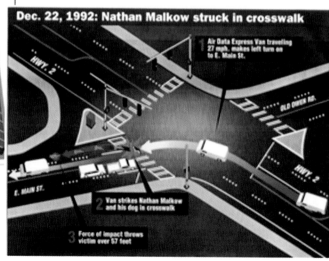

Re-creating Key Scenes

1. Photo of plaintiff used to establish height, weight and build.

2. Night photo of scene to establish lighting, signs and objects.

3. Police survey of Scene

4. Police photo of van

VAUGHN V. GOLDEN GARBAGE RECYCLERS[3]

FACTS: A welder is dropped on his head from a height of thirty feet when a mobile hydraulic crane malfunctions.

EXHIBIT ISSUES:

A construction site is
a scene in transition.

1. A construction site is a scene in transition. Conditions had changed since the time of the accident, but investigation photos had been taken.

2. Show the complete path of the plaintiff's body and the falling man basket, incorporating the vantage point of the key eyewitness.

Approach to Exhibit Issues

1. Review accident report and photos.

2. Visit scene to get a general sense of space and distance.

3. Collect online information about the mobile hydraulic crane.

4. Interview eyewitnesses.

5. Meet with the illustrator to discuss background information and possible exhibits.

6. Illustrator re-creates each stage of the plaintiff's fall.

Putting the Puzzle Pieces Together: Use Only Photos to Re-create a Scene

Less is more in this circumstance. It is important to keep the illustration as simple as possible, consistent with the known details.

---

3. Pseudonym.

1. The photo of the mobile hydraulic crane at the scene becomes the single most important reference.

It is important to keep the illustration as simple as possible, consistent with the known details.

2. The background reference photo of the catwalk is scanned and adjusted.

3. The damaged railing is below grade level, requiring a cut-away view.

4. The man basket is a basic geometric-shape box, which makes it easier to manipulate.

5. The final illustration combines what the witnesses saw with all known scene details.

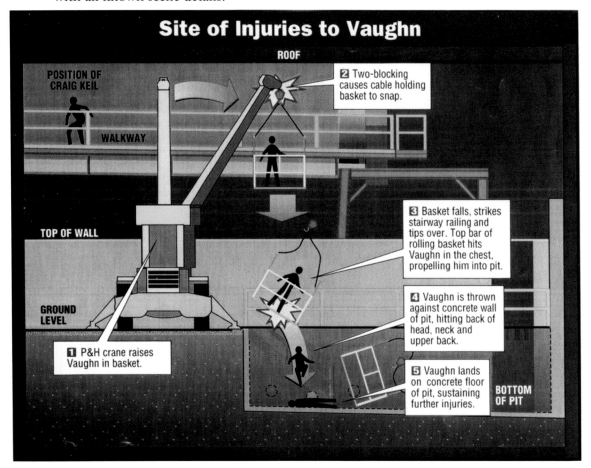

GRANT V. FOAM MATTRESSES, INC.[4]

FACTS: A five-year-old girl was facially disfigured by the intense radiant heat from her untreated foam mattress when she accidentally ignited it with a cigarette lighter.

EXHIBIT ISSUES: It was very important to eliminate every other potential fuel source. The photos taken by the fire investigator were too small to give the viewer a sense of the room.

The photos taken by the fire investigator were too small to give the viewer a sense of the room.

4. Pseudonym.

Approach to Exhibit Issues

1. Review fire investigation report and photos.

2. Get dimensions of apartment bedroom from landlord.

3. Provide illustrator with photos and floor plan of the room, meeting to discuss graphics.

Re-creating a 3-D Image of a Room from a Floor Plan and Photos

1. The main reference for the illustrator was the floor plan.

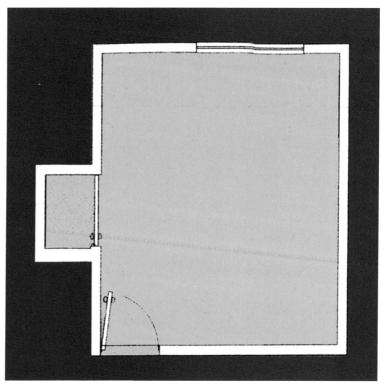

Assembling the Puzzle Pieces

2. Using a room diagram and measurement grid, the illustrator placed the objects.

3. Use standard dimensions for the furniture from the Internet.

4. Apply the size of common objects for correct proportion—for example, the width of a door.

5. Rotate floor plan for greater visual interest.

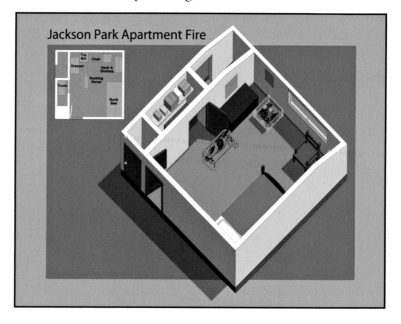

6. Different views are easy to create once the scene is done.

Jackson Park Apartment Fire

(Bedroom door and wall removed)

The ground-level perspective the audience is used to in everyday life has more immediacy. Removing the bedroom door and wall is just a matter of manipulating the information already in the computer.

QUALITY SAND & GRAVEL V. HIGHWAY DEPARTMENT[5]

FACTS: The state condemned a portion of property owned by a sand and gravel company to expand a highway. This will block two of the three existing entrances.

The ground-level perspective the audience is used to in everyday life has more immediacy.

The state's offer of compensation is far below the plaintiff's estimate.

EXHIBIT ISSUES:

    1. Show day-to-day operations.

    2. Demonstrate future impact on use of the property.

Approach to Exhibit Issues

    1. Retain experts.

---

5. Pseudonym.

2. Show dramatic change in "before" and "after" views of property.

3. Artist works with all the other experts, doing his own site investigations too.

4. Create a series of fully animated sequences to show vehicles entering and exiting the site from the perspective of a driver.

5. Distill the commercial real-estate appraiser's detailed report showing the loss of value into a short PowerPoint presentation.

Create a series of fully animated sequences to show vehicles entering and exiting the site from the perspective of a driver.

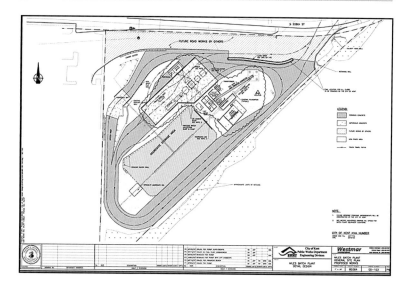

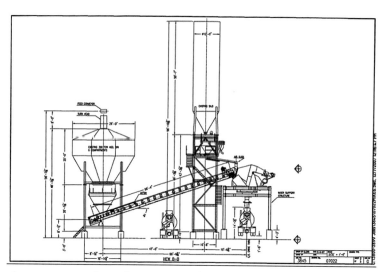

Accurate site plans drawn to scale.

"Before" and "after" images from multiple perspectives

Joiner v. Property Developers[6]

Facts: A carpenter's head is caught between a freight-elevator platform and a safety gate during an extensive remodel of an older building, causing serious injury.

Existing photographs of the freight elevator lacked detail.

Exhibit Issues:

1. The freight elevator had been removed prior to counsel's getting the case.

2. Existing photographs of the freight elevator lacked detail.

---

6. Pseudonym. An animation used in this case is included on the DVD that accompanies this book.

3. Documentation of interior lighting at the time of injury would be difficult.

4. Many changes had been made in the building.

5. Justify why the plaintiff's actions were reasonable, eliminating or reducing comparative fault.

6. Make the elevator expert's opinions more real and powerful by visualizing them.

Approach to Exhibit Issues

1. Collect project information from defendant developer, subcontractors, and government agencies.

2. Interview eyewitnesses.

3. Retain elevator expert.

4. Have client draw stick figures, mark up photos and plans, and model body positions.

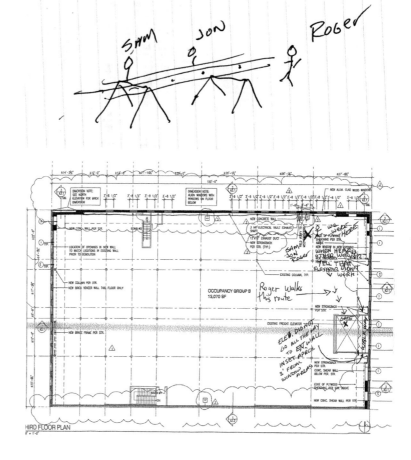

5. Retain a computer animator and provide all the information.

6. The animator creates a succession of drafts, which are reviewed first by the attorney and then by the client and the expert.

The liability
expert, client, and
eyewitnesses
are key players in
establishing the
foundation of the
expert.

7. The DVD animation that accompanies this book shows the hazards and the importance of the missing safety measures.

Basic Approach

The liability expert, client, and eyewitnesses are key players in establishing the foundation of the expert.

The final version of the computer animation from the *Joiner* case is included in the DVD for this book.

TAKEAWAYS—CREATING ILLUSTRATIONS FROM SOURCE MATERIAL

- ◆ *Computer illustrations are effective, versatile, and relatively low-cost tools to assist you in visualizing your case themes.*

- ◆ *Professional illustrators seek to make their graphics as accurate as possible.*

- ◆ *The more realistic a graphic purports to be, the greater the expectation that it is accurate.*

◆ *More leeway is given on simple graphics.*

◆ *A wide variety of graphic choices exists.*

◆ *You can save time and money by providing an illustrator with images that you have seen somewhere else, which might be adaptable to your case.*

◆ *Background reference material for the graphic is important.*

◆ *Photos, Internet resources, and scene visits all are helpful.*

◆ *Digital computer graphics are easy to work with and easily adaptable.*

◆ *Using digital projectors to show computer illustrations saves money and time.*

21

USING GOOGLE EARTH

We ought to fly away from Earth to Heaven as quickly as we can; and to fly away is to become like God, as far as this is possible.

—Plato

Most people have had the experience of looking at the ground from an airplane. Everything looks totally different from the air, even terrain we are well familiar with. Aloft, we are able to better understand proximity, relative size, and contrasts. From the air, an interstate highway is a much more dramatic concrete-covered slice in the landscape than a winding rural road. Satellite-generated photography has accustomed audiences to seeing images of the earth from outer space.

THE NEW VIEW FROM ABOVE—GOOGLE EARTH

Google Earth displays the new view from above, a virtual globe that takes the user on a magic-carpet ride to nearly any location in the world, allowing the flexibility of zooming down as close as necessary to pick up fine details. This program maps the earth by superimposition of a combination of satellite imagery, aerial photography, and other technology. The large amount of media attention devoted to the release of Google Earth in June 2005 stimulated significant public interest in all its applications.

While at present the image quality is variable, depending on location, Google Earth can show both the geography and buildings of many urban areas in a high-quality 3-D format. Starting in 2008, Google Street View allows viewers to get a virtual tour of many cities at ground level. Users also can overlay their own data from other sources onto Google Earth images, creating a customized, focused look. It is inevitable that Google will continue to upgrade the quality and versatility of this program.

How Google Earth Can Make Cases Come Alive

As members of the audience, we all want to go to the scene of any story. Google Earth gives you the opportunity to make this happen for the judge and jury. Google Earth gives an immediacy and excitement to this that cannot be achieved by other means. Just as an aerial-establishing shot gives an audience a strong sense of place in a movie, so does a Google Earth image in a case.

The events of every legal case play out in a specific location or locations. Like a film director, it is your job to make those events vivid and real and bring a sense of place to the courtroom. Google Earth empowers you to anchor the testimony of a witness by providing visuals of the scene of an incident. The several examples that follow will give you an idea of some basic ways that you can use Google Earth to achieve this.

In *D. C. v. Ski Boats, Inc.,*[1] a twenty-one-year-old woman was overcome and killed by carbon monoxide fumes from a motorboat. The law-enforcement incident report described the basic setup verbally—the decedent was out with friends on a

Like a film director, it is your job to make those events vivid and real and bring a sense of place to the courtroom.

---

1. Pseudonym.

ski boat and decided to swim approximately thirty feet to shore with a friend.

Narratives
Dispatched for a water rescue near Interlake Island. While enroute, FireComm advised that a 21 y/o female was swimming with a group of friends and never returned to the dock. FireComm also advised that approximately 10 people were swimming in the water attempting to locate the girl. E44 responded to station 4-6 for Marine 4-6, E42 moved up to station 4-1.
Auburn Fire Department dive team was requested and on arrival helped coordinate search patterns with EPFR and PCSO. It was determined that all three teams would dive simultaneously in different areas. It was also decided that the incident would transition to a recovery mode. Once daylight came all dive teams began searching. Auburn FD located the victim approximately 30' from the dock in twelve and a half feet of water. She was brought to the surface and transported via N46 to the shore where she was then loaded into M41 and transported to station 4-1 to await the Medical Examiner.

The words of the incident report alone do not translate into a crisp image of the scene. A marked Google Earth overhead view of the location does.

Many cases involve a series of events occurring at multiple locations. Google Earth allows you to combine all of these into a single overhead view, giving the audience a global sense of where everything occurred.

Google Earth can also be used to create emotion and perspective about a scene, institution, or individual human being.

Google Earth is not limited to mapping and geography functions. It can also be used to create emotion and perspective about a scene, institution, or individual human being. In *Chapman v. Progressive Health,* described in chapter 15, I used Google Earth to create a feeling about the defendant, Progressive Health, in this medical-malpractice case. One of the themes in *Chapman* was that the defendant HMO was too big, inefficient, and uncaring. I reinforced this by collecting a series of Google Earth images of the various hospitals, clinics, and administrative offices of Progressive Health throughout an entire geographic region.

The overhead views of the defendant's various facilities then were combined in one exhibit, intended to create the feeling that the defendant was an unwieldy health-care octopus. This

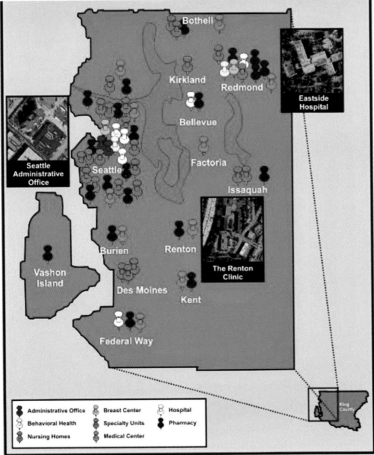

fit nicely with plaintiff's theory that the surgical complications and problematic aftercare that endangered the plaintiff's life were the result of a bloated medical bureaucracy where nobody really talked to one another.

You can use screenshot software[2] to enhance and adapt Google Earth images to the needs of any particular case. A simple automobile case illustrates how you can use images from Google Street View and screenshot software to create a much more effective exhibit. In this fact pattern, the defendant driver hit the plaintiff after making a right turn too fast, spinning out of control.

The plaintiff's attorney, Mimy A. Bailey of Seattle, Washington, had the challenge of creating an exhibit that would give the audience the sense that the turning driver:

1. Had a clear view of the plaintiff as she approached the intersection.

2. Knew the conditions were icy.

3. Knew that, as she made the turn, centrifugal force would push her car outward.

4. Knew if this happened, she would hit the plaintiff.

Using Google Street View and screenshot software, Ms. Bailey came up with a series of scene photos to support her case of negligence against the oncoming driver. She customized these to emphasize the defendant's unobstructed view of the intersection, with arrows for the path of travel and the point of impact. This not only illustrated all of the plaintiff's liability arguments, but also effectively undermined the defendant's assertion that she could not have anticipated this collision.

Mimy A. Bailey

---

2. One example is Snagit, created by TechSmith.

She customized these to emphasize the defendant's unobstructed view of the intersection, with arrows for the path of travel and the point of impact.

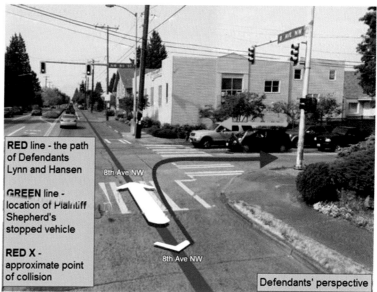

RED line - the path of Defendants Lynn and Hansen

GREEN line - location of Plaintiff Shepherd's stopped vehicle

RED X - approximate point of collision

Defendants' perspective

TAKEAWAYS—USING GOOGLE EARTH

◆ *Audiences understand and retain information better when they are anchored visually in the place where events occurred. This is why television news reporters broadcast live from the scene.*

◆ *The view from the air above is very different from the one on the ground, allowing us to distinguish patterns, spatial relationships, and relative size.*

◆ *Through the influences of film, television, and satellite photography, modern audiences are used to aerial views. They expect lawyers to use them in the courtroom.*

◆ *Google Earth allows you to create custom views of a case scene without even leaving the office.*

◆ *Information in police reports, witness statements, and other documents can be translated into Google Earth images, eliminating the randomness that comes with describing physical locations with words. Instead of each audience member's having a different mental picture from the words, the whole audience is working from the same image.*

◆ *Besides geographical orientation, aerial views also can create feelings about places and people that reinforce case themes.*

◆ *Software editing programs allow for the addition of graphic elements to Google Street View images, building a customized look that incorporates other information from the trial story.*

Visual Foundation

EXHIBIT

FILED

22

HEARING A JUDGE'S PERSPECTIVE

Leaders have to act much more quickly today. The pressure comes much faster.

—Andy Grove

If any jurist knows the shape of the past, present, and future use of technology in our court system, it is U.S. District Court Judge Marsha J. Pechman.

Judge Pechman has presided over cases of great public interest with significant electronic discovery and computer-generated evidentiary issues in a federal court system that is embracing technology and making the procedural changes necessary to accommodate it.

As a former professor of trial advocacy and clinical faculty for the National Institute for Trial Advocacy (NITA), Judge Pechman is a trained, sophisticated observer of trial techniques. In this interview, Judge Pechman offers guidance on how you

Judge Marsha J. Pechman

can best incorporate high-tech visual evidence into the mix of traditional advocacy tools.[1]

TOPICS COVERED

- Advocacy skills in decline
- The main problems with lawyers' media presentations
- What makes skilled lawyers stand out
- Evidentiary and logistics problems created by electronic exhibits
- Video evidence at trial
- Computer animations
- Foundation for electronic evidence
- Deposition video for impeachment
- Mixing old and new communication techniques
- The need to think critically

ADVOCACY SKILLS IN DECLINE

WILLIAM BAILEY: Many lawyers have appeared before you as judge, in both state and federal court. How well have they done? Is there any general trend you can report?

MARSHA PECHMAN: I wish this weren't the case, but I think that the level of trial skills I'm seeing is deteriorating, primarily because so many lawyers never get to trial. I often don't see highly polished or well-thought-out presentations.

In large cases, the big firms want to reward their lawyers with a part. So they will give one lawyer one witness, another lawyer another witness, and a third lawyer gets

---

1. Marsha J. Pechman, interview with William S. Bailey, November 6, 2008.

another witness. You wind up with a fairly disjointed presentation. There needs to be a captain of the ship, marshaling resources and making it coherent.

THE MAIN PROBLEMS WITH LAWYERS' MEDIA PRESENTATIONS

WB: If you were to make a list of the main problem areas with the visual presentation skills of the lawyers appearing before you, what comes to mind?

MP: It all has to do with the lawyers' lack of familiarity with their equipment. They may have put together a fine PowerPoint presentation, but then when they get in here, they can't push the right buttons. And they haven't thought out a backup plan if equipment failure strikes.

Most lawyers haven't practiced enough with their equipment. It is not unusual to see the lawyers out of sync with their visual aids. They will be talking when the slides behind them say something totally different.

Very few lawyers can pull off a fine media presentation. It takes a lot of time, effort, and practice.

WB: Many PowerPoints I have seen are all text, lots of words on the screen. Are you seeing this kind of thing?

MP: Yes, lawyers often do put too many words on the screen. Lawyers come in with their PowerPoint slides for me to look at. Many times these haven't been well thought out. For example, I can't read the copy of the contract on the screen. They don't think about, "Can the judge read this from twenty-five feet away?"

Color is another issue. Whoever thought that purple backgrounds with red lettering was a good idea? They try to get too fancy with all these gimmicky ways of having words pop up on the screen too. Lawyers try to get too cute with this, and it makes no sense.

Color is another issue. Whoever thought that purple backgrounds with red lettering was a good idea?

It doesn't work for lawyers to sit at their desks and look at the presentation on their computers. They've got to go sit in a room that's big enough, like a courtroom, and then see what it looks like.

Lawyers also have to think about the limitations of the actual courtroom where the presentation will take place. In many courtrooms, the lights are either on or off. If people can't see your slides except with the lights off, count on having at least a few go to sleep on you.

All that being said, I've seen a few people who do it really, really well too.

JUDGE PECHMAN'S TAKEAWAYS—THE MAIN PROBLEMS WITH LAWYERS' MEDIA PRESENTATIONS

♦ *Always have a backup plan in case of equipment failure.*

♦ *Take time to practice your media presentation in advance.*

♦ *Limit the amount of text in your PowerPoint slides.*

♦ *Consider whether the judge or jury can read your slides when they're on the screen.*

♦ *Give the judge a hard copy of your slides in advance.*

♦ *Minimize gimmicky backgrounds and presentation effects.*

♦ *Don't just look at the media presentation on your desktop computer. Go to the actual courtroom and view it there.*

♦ *Take note of any lighting and architectural limitations of the courtroom.*

♦ *Don't turn all the lights off for your media presentation or jurors will go to sleep.*

WHAT MAKES SKILLED LAWYERS STAND OUT

WB: What distinguishes the performances of lawyers who do presentations with technology well?

MP: For starters, simply practicing with their material ahead of time and having a competent tech person on hand.

One particular lawyer who appears before me prepares his cases the same way. He brings it all together. It's as if he's putting out a constant underlying message of "He knows what he's doing."

WB: So you have a certain expectation when you see his name as counsel on a case?

MP: It's going to be a good show, to the point where I say to myself, *I cannot let him manipulate my impartiality.*

WB: Whether it's a trial to the court or the jury, should a lawyer's approach really be that different?

MP: It shouldn't be that different, except a little more sophisticated in front of a judge. But it shouldn't be different. I appreciate a visual timeline. I appreciate seeing a chart on how the witnesses fit into the case. I appreciate having the elements of the cause of action.

WB: If you could put together the prototype of a lawyer you would like to see in your courtroom, what would this person be like?

MP: Every successful trial lawyer takes complicated facts and puts them into a simple story that people can understand and identify with.

For starters, it doesn't have to be high tech to be effective. Good lawyers know how to use simple photos well. For example, in a *Worldwide Enterprises*[2] employment-discrimination case, the defense counsel took pictures of the various

> Every successful trial lawyer takes complicated facts and puts them into a simple story that people can understand and identify with.

2. Pseudonym.

The whole idea of coming in and trying to ambush somebody with a surprise media presentation, forget it. You've got to lay this out ahead of time.

plaintiffs at their depositions. He put these up in the trial when he was talking about them. He put the defendant's picture up too. He didn't try and make anybody look bad in the photos. You've got to be fair about it. When he was pulling up pieces of testimony from their depositions, the witnesses' pictures were right next to the words. This lawyer's use of simple photos was a big help.

WB: As a judge, does it give you any courtroom-management concern when a lawyer is whipping things onto a screen during a presentation?

MP: Not if the lawyer tells me what he or she is going to do ahead of time. It's all a matter of educating the judge about what you're going to do and showing your opponent what you're going to do. The whole idea of coming in and trying to ambush somebody with a surprise media presentation, forget it. You've got to lay this out ahead of time.

In the *Worldwide Enterprises* case I just mentioned, the defense counsel introduced pictures of each plaintiff, using the same ones again later in the trial. Everybody knew what was coming.

JUDGE PFCHMAN'S TAKEAWAYS—WHAT MAKES SKILLED LAWYERS STAND OUT

- *Have a competent technology person on hand who knows the equipment, the case, and what to do.*

- *Develop a comprehensive game plan that brings the case together.*

- *Think through your case, both on paper and visually.*

- *Orient the judge and jury with a visual timeline of events, a witness chart, and a chart listing the elements of the cause of action.*

- *Reduce your case to a simple story that people can understand.*

◆ *Know how to use simple photos effectively.*

◆ *Educate the judge in advance about your media presentation.*

EVIDENTIARY AND LOGISTICS PROBLEMS CREATED BY ELECTRONIC EXHIBITS

MP: Another problem with some electronic evidence is making the trial record complete. If an electronic diagram is used and the witness is asked to point to the screen during testimony, no markings are created for the record. As soon as you take that digital picture off the screen, the record of where the witness pointed is gone.

WB: Yes, that is a real problem. One possible solution is to have a hard copy printed out, which the witness also marks.

MP: Most lawyers haven't thought these kinds of issues through. There is a good bit of utility to the standard butcher-paper approach of the cop's marking the location of the car in the intersection. Then the next witness comes and puts an X where he or she was.

WB: Have you raised that with lawyers in your court?

MP: Oh yes. But they don't seem to know what to do about it.

WB: It's easy enough to take a screen shot of everything for the record. Anything that appears on a computer screen can be preserved, if lawyers know what program to use.

MP: That's one of the main problems: lawyers don't practice with the technology and don't really know how to use it.

We plan for computers in the jury room, and most of the data and materials used are in electronic format. Exhibits come up on the screens during testimony, and everybody looks at them. And then we get all ready for jury deliberations and get the exhibits to go back. These are still in paper notebooks. The jury balks and says, "Now wait

That's one of the main problems: lawyers don't practice with the technology and don't really know how to use it.

a second—you expect us to thumb through these twelve binders of stuff and find what you guys were working with? Where's the disc?"

WB: And what's the answer?

MP: Some judges have computers available that can't access the Internet. Inevitably you've got to find somebody on the jury who is tech savvy or you do a tutorial with court staff to show them how to call up material. You give the jury an index with the numbers of the exhibits, and you let them have the kind of electronics they need to call these up on demand. But there's the whole issue of who supplies the computer. I haven't got an extra one just sitting around.

WB: Well, how about the lawyers on the case?

All the fancy arguments and pictures don't do any good unless they are in a format that the jury can use later on.

MP: Astonishingly, the current lawyer mentality says if they put the show on out in front, they don't have to worry about the show in the back. All the fancy arguments and pictures don't do any good unless they are in a format that the jury can use later on.

WB: Have you suggested to lawyers in document-heavy cases, "I think it would be good for you to put this on a disc and then have a computer available for the jurors"?

MP: Yes, we actually did that in one case. Part of the issue, too, becomes, What happens when some evidence doesn't get in? Who is going to burn the ultimate disc with only the trial exhibits on it that were admitted? How do I ensure that the disc that goes back there only has what actually got admitted?

That is a real logistics problem. Do the lawyers trust one another?

WB: How do you work that out?

MP: I've only done it once. Basically, I just said, "Okay at the end of the day here is what will be admitted. You burn these onto your disc each night, so that at the end, all we've got on the disc are the edited documents."

WB: Makes sense.

MP: The courts don't have the resources to be able to do that. It is the lawyers' job.

The federal courts are in the best position here. If we have an IT problem, I've got the staff to handle it. But I don't know that this really is the courts' obligation. It's our obligation to keep the record and preserve it. But if the lawyers want it presented in a particular way, then the lawyers have got to think that through.

The other thing is that we don't want to generate higher court costs with higher-tech presentations. People are already complaining that we're too expensive.

JUDGE PECHMAN'S TAKEAWAYS—EVIDENTIARY AND LOGISTICS PROBLEMS CREATED BY ELECTRONIC EXHIBITS

- *Preserve any electronic evidence used with the witness for the record. If the witness points to a screen, have him mark up a hard copy too, referencing what he is saying.*

- *Don't overlook simple visual approaches like props or making butcher-paper lists. They still work well.*

- *Think of the show in the front of the house as well as the show in the back of the house—the jury room. Put the exhibits in a convenient form for the jury to use later on.*

- *Put all the exhibits that are admitted each day into an electronic file that can be combined to create the ultimate disc, with every exhibit.*

- *Make arrangements for burning the ultimate disc for the jury with only those exhibits that were admitted.*

VIDEO EVIDENCE AT TRIAL

MP: The *Mass Civil Disturbance*[3] trial was amazing because we actually could watch the events happen.

WB: Was this news footage?

MP: There was news footage, private camera footage, and surveillance footage. It was a very unique case. You didn't have to talk about the events; you could just roll the tape. All the witnesses were pointing at the television screens and saying, "See that guy sitting over there, two from the center with the backpack on his back? That's me."

But then we didn't do a very good job of thinking through what it would mean to jury deliberations to have the evidence in this form. We sat and watched the tape during the trial. So what am I going to do during deliberations if they want to review the tapes?

WB: You mean the tape that was played during the trial?

MP: Right.

WB: And how was that handled?

MP: I adapted a "read back" procedure that is commonly used in federal trials in California.

I anticipated that the jury might want to review portions of the video and came up with a "video on demand" protocol to accommodate this. After the lawyers completed their final arguments and the jury retired, I got the lawyers to agree to this protocol before they left the courtroom.

If the jury requested to see any portion of the video, they came back into the courtroom and my clerk played the relevant portion. While all counsel were informed of the content of the jury's video request, no lawyers were present in court for the playing of the video. After the jurors saw

I anticipated that the jury might want to review portions of the video and came up with a "video on demand" protocol to accommodate this.

3. Pseudonym.

the footage they wanted, they returned to the jury room and continued deliberations.

This protocol worked exactly as I'd hoped, with no problems.

The *Mass Civil Disturbance* trial raised logistical questions about what happens when the lawyers and the tech staff go away and the deliberations start. Have a plan for what happens with media-based evidence in the back of the house during deliberations. Who comes in, sets it up, plays the tapes?

WB: Are there other protections you would want to see placed around the deliberation process in these circumstances?

MP: I view that the same way as sending a stack of photographs. I don't feel we need protections to say how many times you can look at the photographs. I feel the same about videotapes.

Some of these other kinds of electronic images are logistically difficult to handle. If I'm not going to let the jury take evidence back to view it at will, then I have to provide a way for the jury to review it on demand.

WB: What other kinds of electronic images do you mean?

MP: Film clips, PowerPoints, animations, charts, and summaries, anything that's done visually.

WB: How much of the actual *Mass Civil Disturbance* trial was spent reviewing videotape?

MP: A huge amount. The trial essentially was just about watching tape.

WB: How was it to preside over a trial where the evidence was mainly electronic?

MP: It was fascinating. It was one thing to hear the recollections of the witnesses describing what was going on, and quite another to see it actually happening. The video exposed distortion on both sides. The protestors said, "Oh,

> Have a plan for what happens with media-based evidence in the back of the house during deliberations.

it was a peaceful protest." Then you see the clip where they were sitting on the ground, snarling, hurling verbal provocation and obscenities at the cops. On the other side, the police said, "We made sure that everyone was peacefully handcuffed and walked to the bus." Then you see the video where the police pick up a protestor by his FlexiCuff. Sure, they put on the FlexiCuff and walked him to the bus, but they practically broke his arms in the process.

COMPUTER ANIMATIONS

WB: How do you look upon computer animations?

MP: Anybody who has been to see *WALL-E* or any of the *Toy Story* or *Narnia* series of films knows that you can make images do anything.

Aside from convincing your judge that your animation is legitimate because you have based it upon appropriate data and foundation, I think a lawyer would do well to repeat this directly in front of a jury too. Unless you convince your jury that you built the animation accurately, you run the risk of having it discounted.

> Unless you convince your jury that you built the animation accurately, you run the risk of having it discounted.

FOUNDATION FOR ELECTRONIC EVIDENCE

WB: How well have lawyers laid a foundation for any higher-tech stuff, starting with simple e-mails?

MP: I haven't seen anybody do this right. They haven't thought about it in just a simple way. People don't think of laying the foundation for e-mails.

WB: So what do we need to be doing in this area of foundation for electronic evidence? Do we need to turn this over to the IT people?

MP: It may well be that your tech people hold the key here. They have the knowledge to say, "I can tell this is an e-mail from my company because it has the distinguishing characteristics of our digital stream."

But I don't think it has to be so difficult. Getting a picture into evidence is really pretty easy. All it has to be is a fair and accurate representation of what was there. So look at your e-mail and apply the fairness principles. "Who is it that could say this is what you see?"

WB: You could have the sender or the person that received the e-mail authenticate it, just like a letter.

MP: Or you could authenticate it as a business record. A computer is just like a file cabinet. Was the e-mail kept in the ordinary course of business?

WB: One difference I see between photographs and electronics is the ease of alteration. E-mails can be changed. How do we know the one in question has not been altered in some way?

MP: Sure. But obviously you can also tell who has had access and when those alterations came into play. The cases where people are actually altering documents and lying about it are rare. I have had only two cases where people tried to alter their electronic data.

WB: Was it discovered?

MP: Yes.

JUDGE PECHMAN'S TAKEAWAYS—VIDEOS, COMPUTER ANIMATIONS, AND FOUNDATION

- ◆ *Figure out a protocol for on-demand playback of any video evidence during jury deliberations.*

- ◆ *Anticipate any contamination issues when tech people have to play video for jurors during deliberations.*

- ◆ *Give every juror either a hard-copy set of the exhibits or the electronic means to view the evidence on demand.*

- *If using animations, you must convince the jury that you have created them accurately.*

- *Lay the proper foundation for electronic evidence. You must prove it is the real thing.*

DEPOSITION VIDEO FOR IMPEACHMENT

WB: Have you seen any effective impeachments in trial by video-deposition excerpts?

MP: Only one time, in a patent case. One of the key issues was who designed the invention first. At trial, the lawyer put up the video clip of the same question being asked in the deposition, along with the transcript. I got to see not only the words but, side by side, what the witness looked like the first time the question was posed.

WB: That must have been devastating.

MP: It was, absolutely convincing me that this witness was lying about when it was that he invented this thing. He was rolling back the clock to try and beat the other guy's invention.

WB: So there is a real premium then on having a focused deposition with clean, consistent questions. At trial, if the witness gives a different answer, it is huge if a lawyer can play you a clean video of the inconsistent deposition answer.

MIXING OLD AND NEW COMMUNICATION TECHNIQUES

WB: Why is the law lagging so far behind other professions in basic communication skills?

Is part of it that the legal academy resists teaching these new tools?

I got to see not only the words but, side by side, what the witness looked like the first time the question was posed.

MP: I don't think so. Lawyers just have lost sight of the principles of education in their approach to judges and juries. There are different kinds of learners. Lawyers must know how to appeal to the visual learner, the audio learner, and the kinetic learner.

WB: Are lawyers missing out on any basic communication and persuasion opportunities?

MP: Yes. Now that we've got everything available visually, I haven't seen anybody pass around an item to a jury in a long time.

WB: Why is that a loss?

MP: We've run amok with this glut of technology, forgetting some traditional principles that really worked. In a case recently, they had all sorts of charts and diagrams. But the most effective moment in the whole trial was in the middle of the examination, when a lawyer pulled out a piece of butcher paper as the witness was testifying. He just wrote the numbers up on it; he made it simple. It was the best part of the whole trial. High tech is not the whole show.

WB: Your point is well taken. So part of effective advocacy is the lawyer as director, asking, "What's my mix?"

MP: Yes. I did a patent case over basketballs. I had all these sophisticated pictures with dynamic images to visualize the core of the basketball. But these didn't give me the information I needed. I finally said, "Look, will somebody just bring a basketball in here and cut it open? Then I can see what you're talking about." I'm sure this lawyer spent thousands of dollars trying to visually demonstrate how this basketball was laminated. Yet, he could have done far better with a fifteen-dollar playground basketball.

WB: The person who has the biggest art budget doesn't necessarily win.

> There are different kinds of learners. Lawyers must know how to appeal to the visual learner, the audio learner, and the kinetic learner.

MP: Right. And many of these visual technology things are too expensive for the average case. You've got to have a million bucks at stake before you throw fifty thousand or more at the graphics.

WB: Yes, although graphics are a whole lot cheaper now. You can get many visuals for free or next to nothing on the Internet. Effective does not necessarily mean expensive.

MP: I remember one seaman's case. The liability issue centered on the tray that the buckets of oysters had to be dumped onto for shucking. The defense built out the shucking station. All my law clerks went out there during the lunch hour, stood there, picked up the buckets, and tried to heave them onto the thing. We became convinced that there was nothing wrong with this process. The same approach should be used for stairway cases. Any time you have a slip and fall on a stairway, bring it in.

JUDGE PECHMAN'S TAKEAWAYS—VIDEO IMPEACHMENT, AND MIXING TECHNIQUES

- *Lay your foundation at depositions carefully, knowing what you want, getting people pinned down.*

- *Use of deposition video clips for impeachment can be effective, but you must have a clear, clean inconsistency between what was said before and what was said at trial.*

- *Use the principles of education and be a good teacher. Judges and juries are your pupils.*

- *Appeal to all learning styles among the jurors—visual, audio, and kinesthetic.*

- *Pass around tactile exhibits to the jury once in a while.*

- *Use a mix of high- and low-tech exhibits. Expensive does not necessarily mean effective.*

THE NEED TO THINK CRITICALLY

WB: If the lawyers responsible for a case don't have command of the computer and don't know how to use it properly, it won't help.

MP: Right. You can't dump your case into a computer and expect it to be converted into something better than your own calculations. You've still got to think critically about how you're going to deal with your facts, evidence, and theory of the case.

WB: Lawyers aren't thinking it all the way through, developing a systematic way of using what the computer has to offer.

MP: Right. And then dumping all this volume of material on the jury with a thoughtless splat. You've got all your stuff on disc, you flashed it on the screen, and now you're going to give the jury the old black notebooks without an index. You're not thinking how anybody else can manipulate or observe this data.

WB: So it's an overkill phenomenon?

MP: Yes. Now that we can store so much paper on one tiny disc, there's a tendency by lawyers to want to saturation-bomb the jury with more. I see people coming in here with five hundred exhibits on this little disc.

WB: You do it just because you can?

MP: That's right.

WB: So an important concept for lawyers to know about electronic evidence is, How will the jurors or the judge be able to navigate through all the information on this disc? Is this just a haystack of information in disc form? It's deceiving. The haystack is smaller now, but it's still the same old difficult search for the needle.

MP: Yes, exactly.

> You can't dump your case into a computer and expect it to be converted into something better than your own calculations.

How will the jurors or the judge be able to navigate through all the information on this disc? Is this just a haystack of information in disc form?

WB: A lawyer's job doesn't end with using technology in a presentation. The strategic plan has to include the needs of the end users that you're trying to persuade, judge or jury. Have you made this navigation easy for them?

MP: Juries and judges are the pupils; lawyers are the teachers. It's not enough to stack up your evidence on the rail and assume that people will have learned it. If you don't build the case properly, they're not going to get it.

JUDGE PECHMAN'S TAKEAWAYS—THE NEED TO THINK CRITICALLY

- *Think critically in advance about how you are going to deal with your facts, evidence, and case theory.*

- *From the first interview on, think in terms of where and how the data pertinent to the case is stored, as well as how you will access it.*

- *Be sensitive to the jurors' ease of use. If they can't find it, forget it. Even a simple index is helpful.*

- *Be selective. Don't saturation-bomb the jury with information just because you can.*

23

DEALING WITH EVIDENTIARY
AND ETHICAL ISSUES

Nothing will ever be attempted if all possible objections must first be overcome.

—Samuel Johnson

As a policy matter, courts have encouraged the use of demonstrative evidence in trials, finding that it enlightens the jury, promoting a more intelligent consideration of the issues.[1]

Over time, the courts have sought to increase the resources available to the jury, allowing visual evidence in a wide range of circumstances.[2] For this reason, most trial-practice textbooks conclude that judges as a group will be reasonably sympathetic to the use of visuals:

---

1. See, e.g., *Campbell v. Menze Construction Co.*, 166 N.W. 2d 624, 626 (1969).
2. See, e.g., *State v. Tatum*, 58 Wn.2d 73, 360 P.2d 754 (1961); *Hardamon*, 29 Wn.2d 182, 186 P.2d 634 (1947); *Kellerher v. Porter*, 29 Wn.2d 650, 189 P.2d 223 (1948).

Most judges in exercising judicial discretion will permit the use of visual aids if it can be demonstrated in advance that these aids can properly be used.[3]

THE DISCOMFORT ZONE

Despite the solid case support for visual evidence, lawyers often feel anxious about foundational and ethical questions. The concerns and questions feeding this discomfort include the following:

1. Most lawyers have no training in creating exhibits.

2. Both court rules and case law don't specifically state how to create exhibits.

3. Does the doctrine of attorney work-product apply?

4. If so, can it be compromised or waived?

5. What category does this evidence fall in—real or demonstrative?

6. Widespread attorney ignorance of the technical details involved.

7. Will I have to provide embarrassing or compromising outtakes to the opposing counsel?

8. Is a media consultant subject to the same disclosure requirements as an expert?

9. What is the potential for impeachment over foundation details?

What category does this evidence fall in— real or demonstrative?

---

3. Alan E. Morrill, *Trial Diplomacy*, 2nd ed. (Chicago: Court Practice Institute, 1973), 26. Thomas Mauet is even more expansive and states, "If the exhibit is not in evidence, tell the judge you wish to use it during your opening statement and that you will establish a proper foundation for the exhibit during the trial. Today, almost all judges will allow the use of such exhibits under these circumstances." Thomas J. Mauet, *Fundamentals of Trial Techniques*, 3rd ed. (Boston: Little, Brown, 1992), 47.

10. Will this kind of evidence be perceived as too slick by a jury?

This chapter is intended to shrink the fear from these uncertainties, identifying trouble spots and providing guidance to help you when problems arise.

WORKING THROUGH THE DISCOMFORT ZONE— A CASE HISTORY

The process of preparing visuals on behalf of a badly injured five-year-old in *Scruggs v. Snyder*[4] illustrates the risk, unpredictability, and ethical issues that can arise in creating this kind of evidence. Sam Scruggs had been hit by a car while camping with his family at a state park. As Sam's counsel, I expected a series of photos and a video at the scene to show that the defendant driver should have noticed the child by the road. Instead, the photos and video actually proved that the child would have been hard to see; I experienced momentary panic and confusion. The story of what happened after that illustrates how you should handle such experiments gone wrong.

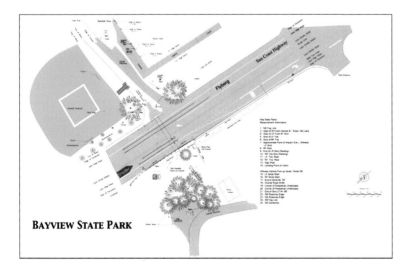

BAYVIEW STATE PARK

---

4. Pseudonym.

I had a cameraman shoot both video and still pictures through the windshield of a car with a shoulder-mounted camera . To simulate the boy's appearance by the road, I had my six-year-old daughter, approximately the same height and weight as Sam, stand at a safe distance back from the road.

My cameraman agreed that this plan would demonstrate that the defendant driver should have seen the child and braked in time. "Editing in the camera" is always a wise move though, testing reality before committing it to film. We did a preliminary series of test passes, as the cameraman looked through the viewfinder to confirm that the child was visible. After these test runs, the filming began. For the first few runs, the cameraman took sequential still photos at a rate of one per second. Then he switched to video, filming the driver's view through the windshield. As we wrapped up our day's work at the scene, all of us assumed that the still photos and video would prove the defendant's negligence.

When the courier package from the cameraman arrived at my office three days later, I eagerly opened it. My anticipation suddenly turned to fear when I looked at the photos—the child was barely visible!

I played the video, hoping for better, but it was worse. At least the still photos had stopped time, freezing the child in the moment, making her somewhat visible. With the motion of the video, it all went by too quickly. This experiment showed that the child was *not* visible until it was too late. I anticipated how jurors would react if they saw the video: "This was a driver's worst nightmare. The child came out of nowhere."

Now What?

I was squarely in the middle of the discomfort zone: "Now what? If the opposing counsel sees this, we're sunk. What have I done?" I sat down with my law partner Steve Fury to discuss the options.

Together, we watched the video over and over, trying to understand why it favored the defendant driver, simultaneously looking for a new angle. Why did this child seem invisible? Would any alternative yield a different result?

After repeated viewings, we better understood the combined effects of the passing road signs, vegetation, and moving cars. All of these played parts in making the child harder to see. More important, in the actual event, Sam had first run down the hill, paused, and fidgeted on the road's shoulder before making his dash across the highway. For obvious safety reasons, I had positioned my daughter much farther back than Sam had been before he crossed. I also didn't have her run toward the road like Sam did, for the same reason. These were big differences with a major effect on visibility.

Changing from Live Action to Animation

It took multiple viewings of the visibility study to put all of this together, understanding why this approach had not worked.

In the process, we decided an animation could re-create the actual placement and forward motion of Sam that day. Here are the conclusions that we reached:

Steve Fury and William Bailey

- ◆ The motion of the child is the critical visual cue, particularly in a place where a child is not supposed to be—by the side of a busy road. The child would only stand out when he is moving toward the road.

- The child was not the only visible cue to the driver. The truck coming from the opposite direction dynamited its brakes, creating smoke and a loud screeching noise.

- An animation would be much more flexible as to what could be shown.

- An animation could show our accident-reconstruction expert's calculations of how the defendant could have braked and avoided the accident.

- An animation could shift the camera angles and the points of view, giving the option of playing the event in real time or slowing it down.

- A computer animation could show exactly what the defendant could see at the time he should have put on his brakes to avoid the accident.

While the video had not worked, an animation of the event likely would. The drafting process of re-creating the visibility would continue in the new form of computer animation.

While the video had not worked, an animation of the event likely would.

THE REMAINING ETHICAL DILEMMA—HOW MUCH TO DISCLOSE TO THE OPPOSING COUNSEL?

Even with the new computer-animation plan, an ethical issue remained. Did I have to disclose or turn over copies of the failed visibility study to the opposing counsel? Could I shield or destroy this information? Did an attorney work-product discovery exemption apply to it?

What would have happened if the subsequent computer animation was successful? Would the prior video and still photographs need to be turned over to the opposing counsel as foundation?

Did I have to disclose or turn over copies of the failed visibility study to the opposing counsel?

WHEN IN DOUBT, CALL AN ETHICS EXPERT (OR TWO)

I needed guidance on how to handle the unsuccessful video issue and called two legal-ethics experts for advice: Professor Robert Aronson at the University of Washington School of Law and Professor David Boerner at Seattle University School of Law. My question to both was, "Do I have to either turn over this video or disclose anything about it?"

Both Professor Aronson and Professor Boerner independently agreed that I did not. Their reasons were:

1. This was attorney work-product, done at the attorney's direction to create demonstrative evidence supporting his theory of the case.

2. Lawyers use consulting experts all the time. There is no obligation to turn over information received from a consulting expert who is not called in the case. The cameraman was akin to an expert.

3. A lawyer has no ethical duty to preserve something that is not real evidence in the case.

4. This visibility study was not done to further a testifying expert's opinion. (If it had been, and was based on an expert's opinions, or the expert had relied on the video in any way, the answer would have been different.)

Both legal-ethics experts agreed that there would be one consequence of the failed visibility study—I could not continue to use the same cameraman without turning over copies of the disastrous first effort. Though this was a close call, Professor Aronson explained his rationale in the following terms:

Robert Aronson

> Lawyers shop around for experts all the time. If one expert isn't helpful, or comes at too great a cost, it is always within your power to drop the expert. You just didn't use them, end of story. Nobody expects you to tell who all the people are that you consulted with in preparing a case. However, if someone like the cameraman was identified as a witness, copies of all his work would have to be turned over, including things that did not turn out as planned.
>
> You have to make a choice. You can change the form of demonstrative evidence from video to computer animation with no problem. But, if you stick with video, trying other approaches, you can't bury the first attempt with this same cameraman.
>
> If you had kept the cameraman and instructed him prior to a deposition, "Don't mention the first video," —that would have been crossing over an ethical line.[5]

Admissibility battles over visual evidence, particularly the high-tech kind, tend to spotlight your role in creating it. The higher stakes involved cause the opposing counsel to argue that they should get everything. What will the trial judge do under these circumstances?

Federal Rule of Civil Procedure 26(b)(3)(A) itself is clear enough: an attorney's work-product is out-of-bounds under most circumstances.

These materials are only discoverable if:

The party shows that it has substantial need for the materials to prepare its case and cannot, without undue

---

5. Robert Aronson, interview with William Bailey, March 18, 2008.

hardship, obtain their substantial equivalent by other means.[6]

LESSONS LEARNED: HOW TO AVOID DISCLOSURE TROUBLE

All the anxiety over my failed visibility study in *Scruggs v. Snyder,* along with the ethics consultations, led to a number of lessons learned:

- Be careful about putting anything in writing that you don't want the other side to see.

- If you suggest changes of a visual evidence draft, use muted, bland language—for example, "This isn't accurate. The lighting is wrong. It wasn't like this at the time. It's from the wrong angle. It's not to scale."

- Don't involve an expert directly with the visual evidence creation process until it is closer to the version you expect to be able to use in court, something close to what you think actually happened.

- Assume that your e-mail instructions to media consultants are going to be admissible or discoverable, and write them accordingly.

- Delete prior, outmoded versions of visual evidence from your computer system if they are not relied upon by your experts, the same way you would delete a prior draft of a brief.

- While there are exceptions protecting the confidentiality of such communications, presume that any information you send to testifying experts will be discoverable.

Be careful about putting anything in writing that you don't want the other side to see.

---

6. Fed. R. Civ. P. 26(b)(3)(A)(ii).

ATTORNEY WORK-PRODUCT ISSUES

In nonvisual forms of trial advocacy, your thoughts go no further than your own mind. This is clear attorney work-product that no opposing counsel has the right to get. However, creating visual evidence can change this, putting your theories and stratagems in a glass house for the opposing counsel to see and then throw stones at.

The presence of expert witnesses further compromises the attorney work-product issue. A traditional part of the expert-engagement ritual is for you to send a package of material and a cover letter to an expert at the beginning of a case. This may include things such as your preliminary summary of the facts, possible legal theories, investigation reports, and scientific articles. This paper trail, containing artifacts of your thought processes, is deposited in the expert's file.

If you decide not to call an expert as a trial witness, it is clear that consulting experts are not available for a deposition by the opposing counsel, absent extraordinary circumstances. But not so for testifying experts. The attorney work-product exemption does not automatically cover the materials provided by you to the testifying expert. This includes e-mail transmissions. What if you put your theories of the case in an e-mail to the expert? Is this work-product? Or can opposing counsel force the expert to turn these over prior to a deposition? The answer is ambiguous.

The work-product protection of FRCP 26(b)(4) becomes even more tenuous when your impressions and thought processes are communicated to an expert, who in turn discusses them with your media consultant. In this circumstance, your thought processes have become several steps removed from your own brain, turned into visuals in the case. Given the potential power of this evidence, the opposing counsel will fight to keep it out, focusing on your role in creating it.

What if you put your theories of the case in an e-mail to the expert? Is this work-product?

THE WORK-PRODUCT RULE AND EXPERTS

FRCP 26(b)(4)(B) established that a party may not discover facts or opinions held by a consulting expert who is not expected to be called at trial. However, what if an attorney allows a testifying expert witness or a media consultant to review work-product materials? May the opposing counsel properly demand to see them? Federal Rule of Evidence (FRE) 612 states that if a witness uses a writing to refresh his memory while testifying, the opposing party is entitled to see the writing and to cross-examine the witness about it. Although FRE 612 is silent about depositions, some courts have held that it applies to depositions as well as to courtroom testimony.[7]

The cases are divided on whether the sharing of protected materials by an attorney with an expert witness waives the work-product rule.[8] In general, legal commentators have supported the application of work-product when the attorney shares this kind of information with others on her team during the course of trial preparation.[9]

Application of Attorney Work-Product to Visual Evidence Creation

Disputes involving attorney work-product protection in the circumstances surrounding the creation of visual evidence have been addressed by the courts on a case-by-case basis. In *Cisarik v. Palos Community Hospital,*[10] the trial judge held the plaintiffs' attorney in contempt for refusing to allow counsel for the hospital and others to be present during the filming of a "Day

---

7. See, e.g., *Sporck v. Popeil,* 759 F.2d 312 (3d Cir. 1985). (The plaintiff was not entitled to see all documents selected by the defense counsel for review by the defendant prior to a deposition.) *See also James Julian, Inc. v. Raytheon Co.,* 93 F.R.D. 138 (D.C. Bell. 1982). (An attorney provided a witness with a notebook to prepare for a deposition, which contained work-product. The court held that ER 612 trumped work-product, mandating disclosure.)
8. See Christa L. Klopfenstein, "Discoverability of Opinion Work Product Materials Provided to Testifying Experts," Ind. L. Rev. 481 (1999): 32.
9. Klopfenstein, "Discoverability."
10. 579 N.E. 2d 873, 875 (1991).

in the Life" video of the infant. The Illinois Supreme Court disagreed, finding that sufficient protection was insured by the foundational requirements of accuracy and fairness.[11]

However, in *Neuswanger v. Ikegai America Corp.,*[12] decided close in time to *Cisarik,* the Illinois Court of Appeals required an employer's insurer to disclose a videotape of an expert examining a machine involved in the death of a worker.[13] The court determined that work-product did not apply since the employer and the insurer had not been named as parties to the suit. In the alternative, if the rule did apply, the videotape was a "tangible thing." The trial court gave the added safeguard of permitting the deletion of the expert's audible thought process prior to the disclosure.[14]

In the body of the *Neuswanger* opinion, the court noted that:

> Illinois has taken a narrow approach to the discovery of attorney work-product. . . . Ordinary work-product, which is relevant material gathered in preparation for trial which does not disclose "conceptual data," is freely discoverable."[15]

The opinion in *Neuswanger* noted also that it was "not an attorney's work-product that is at issue, but [rather] . . . a consulting expert.[16]

The court added that when the material gathered or produced by an attorney or an expert is of a more concrete nature "and does not expose the attorneys or experts mental processes,"[17] it was not unfair to require that that information be shared prior to trial.

Any relaxation of work-product in this Illinois opinion can be argued to be of rather limited scope, given that the video showed

---

11. 579 N.E. 2d at 875.
12. 582 N.E. 2d 192 (3d 1991).
13. *Neuswanger v. Ikegai America Corp.,* 582 N.E. 2d 192 (3d 1991).
14. *Id.*
15. 582 N.E. 2d at 195, citing *Monier v. Chamberlain,* 221 N.E. 2d 410 (1966).
16. 582 N.E. 2d at 195.
17. 582 N.E. 2d at 195.

only the silent operation of the machine. The expert's commentary was deleted in the copy provided. It also had not been taken by a party to the lawsuit, but rather, by the decedent's employer.

HOW CONFIDENTIAL ARE AN ATTORNEY'S THOUGHTS IN THE CREATION OF VISUAL EVIDENCE?

In the absence of judicial interpretation to the contrary, the plain language of FRCP 26(b)(4) applies. Pretrial procedure expert Professor John Mitchell of Seattle University School of Law believes that this rule applies to the creation of visual evidence:

> This is an advocacy process. There is a difference between doctoring the substance of a visual because you don't like the outcome and changing it through a drafting process that attempts to base the visuals on the facts and the opinions of the expert. If a reason for the changes relates to the fairness and accuracy of the visuals, then this is a drafting process and the other side doesn't get it, it is work-product.[18]

For the most part, the courts have upheld the attorney work-product rule, preventing discovery by the opposing party in disputes over the foundation for visual evidence. But, as shown in *Neuswanger*, the practice is not uniform. So where does that leave a lawyer who has been an active participant in the creation of exhibits and doesn't want to reveal her strategies to the other side?

In the end, Professor Mitchell believes the courts will recognize that lawyers who go through drafts of visual evidence to get an accurate representation of their case theories are protected by the work-product rule. This kind of good-faith advocacy, distinguishable from a deliberate effort by a lawyer to twist the truth, is classic work-product, immune from discovery:

There is a difference between doctoring the substance of a visual because you don't like the outcome and changing it through a drafting process.

---

18. John Mitchell, interview with William S. Bailey, April 21, 2008.

The drafting process for visual evidence is classic work-product, based on the attorney's thought process. You aren't changing hidden things like data. The other side can figure out what you did by looking at it. Changes in color, position, and camera angle are obvious. These are not subtle or sneaky. It is also obvious that things like computer animations are done under a counsel's direction. You can't just go to the animator and say, "Make me a film." It starts with the lawyer, who has developed a theory of the case, based on the facts and the law.[19]

TAKEAWAYS—DEALING WITH EVIDENTIARY AND ETHICAL ISSUES

- *Lawyers often are uncomfortable about the foundations and ethical questions that surround the creation of visual evidence.*

- *The creation of visuals for a case is somewhat unpredictable.*

- *You may have to do multiple drafts of a visual evidence idea before it is in final form.*

- *Attorney work-product protection applies to many aspects of creating visuals.*

- *If you change your basic idea during the visual drafting process, you may have to turn over the prior versions to opposing counsel.*

- *If you are doing a video recording in your case, editing in the camera is wise, meaning don't start recording until you know what the end result will look like.*

- *If an attempt to create visual evidence involving an expert turns out badly, you always have the option of striking that expert and starting over with a different one.*

---

19. Mitchell, interview.

◆ *Admission battles over visual evidence focus on the lawyer's role in creating it.*

◆ *Ordinarily, FRCP 26 (b)(3)(A) protects the work-product of an attorney from discovery absent a showing of undue hardship.*

◆ *Be careful what you put in writing to your media consultant or expert in the process of creating visual evidence, as it likely will be discoverable.*

◆ *Try not to involve an expert directly in the creation of visual evidence until it is in a form that is close to final.*

◆ *Delete prior outmoded drafts of visual evidence from your computer, unless these were relied upon or created by an expert.*

24

ENHANCING REALITY

Reality is merely an illusion, albeit a very persistent one.

—Albert Einstein

When President Woodrow Wilson saw D. W. Griffith's *The Birth of a Nation* in 1916, he was so awestruck by the power of cinema that he described it as "writing history with lightning." While you may not have the resources or the need to film history on a Hollywood scale, video and computer animations have become important tools for lawyers in building their cases.

Like any powerful weapon of persuasion, video must be expertly and carefully handled. There always is some risk that it may be harmful in some unforeseen way, as in the example of *Scruggs,* discussed in the previous chapter. Self-inflicted wounds always hurt the worst.

This chapter will help you develop a general awareness of the foundation for video and computer-animation re-creations of events, as well as a protocol for evaluating the ways in which a judge and jury will receive them. Just like Hollywood studios

> Like any powerful weapon of persuasion, video must be expertly and carefully handled.

do "sneak previews" of new films, so must lawyers gauge the impact of a video or computer-animation re-creation in a case.

State v. Roth: Dueling Videos[1]

The 1992 Washington State murder trial *State v. Roth*[2] provides unique insight into the strategic use of video re-creations of the events at issue. The jury in this trial saw "dueling videos," one advancing the prosecution's theories and the other the defendant's.

Roth demonstrates the need to test the effects of any video prior to using it in court. If this is not done, showing the video in court may have unintended consequences, influencing the jury's decision in negative ways that you may not foresee. This is exactly what happened to the defendant in *Roth.* The jury's guilty verdict was due not only because the prosecution's video was effective, but because the defense's was not.

Randy Roth was a thirty-seven-year-old auto mechanic whose fourth wife, Cynthia, drowned in Lake Sammamish in Washington State on July 23, 1991. The Roths were in an inflatable rubber raft, which Roth claimed tipped over on top of his wife due to the wake created by a passing speedboat. Roth said she was trying to climb back into the raft at the time, having suffered a leg cramp while swimming nearby.

In Roth's story to the King County Sheriff's Department, he said he was able to flip the raft back over after about thirty seconds. He said he heard his wife cough, "as if she unexpectedly got water in her mouth." She was lying facedown in the water at that point. Roth said he "breathed into her a couple of times," but there was no response. In his version of the story, he climbed back into the raft and pulled his wife into it, rowing back to shore.

The trip back took about twenty minutes, and Roth did not attempt to call for aid from other boats in the water, nor did he yell for help to the shore as he approached. When Cynthia's

> The jury in this trial saw "dueling videos," one advancing the prosecution's theories and the other the defendant's.

---

1. The videos mentioned in this section are on the DVD included with this book.
2. *State v. Roth,* 75 Wn. App. 808, 881 P.2d 268 (1994).

sons came over to the raft after Roth landed, he told them to get a lifeguard, but not to draw attention to themselves.

A subsequent police investigation revealed that it was almost impossible to tip over the raft using the scenario described by Roth. Using Roth's raft, the police videotaped a woman hanging on to it as several speedboats passed close by. While Roth said in statements to the police that the speedboat was fifty to a hundred yards away, the raft did not even overturn when the police-driven speedboats raced by it at a distance of seven feet.

At the time of Cynthia's death, Roth had a life-insurance policy on her in the amount of $385,000. Roth's second wife, Janice, had died in 1981 when she fell from a cliff while hiking with Roth. He collected $100,000 as the beneficiary on Janice's life-insurance policy.

This was a tough circumstantial evidence case for veteran deputy prosecutor Marilyn B. Brenneman, known for her creative approaches to difficult problems. Although there were no marks on Cynthia Roth's body or any other overt evidence of foul play, too many things pointed toward murder. Her solution was to make the prosecution's evolving theory visual, showing that Roth killed his wife by pushing her under until

Marilyn B. Brenneman

she drowned. When the defense's version of events turned out to be highly improbable as well, Ms. Brenneman added this to the prosecution's video as a separate section. She disproved the defense theory as she proved her own. In bringing murder charges against Randy Roth, the police and the prosecution sought to use the videos of their speedboat demonstrations on Lake Sammamish. The prosecution team prepared another video in a swimming pool, using the same raft, demonstrating their theory of how Roth drowned his wife. A male swimmer, the same general size as Randy Roth, held a female swimmer the same size as Cynthia under the water.

The first camera position in the prosecution video showed the scene from the top of the water, with the male pushing down on the head of the female, who unsuccessfully struggled to surface. The camera quickly cuts from the view above the water to an even more powerful one beneath, where the female swimmer's desperate attempts to reach the surface and the downward shoves from the male above are more clearly seen.

The camera quickly cuts from the view above the water to an even more powerful one beneath.

Stills of Murder Method from Police Video

Underwater View

When confronted with these videos prior to trial, Roth's counsel had three potential responses.

1. Keep them out of evidence altogether.

2. Pick away at the flaws, pointing out discrepancies between Roth's description of what happened and what was shown on the videos.

3. Re-create Roth's version of the events that day in a defense video.

The court denied the defendant's motion to keep out the prosecution's videos. So, first in a swimming pool, and later out on the same lake where the event occurred, the defense reenacted Roth's description of the events in and around the raft.

The defense also reenacted an actual tip-over of the raft on Lake Sammamish, with the passing speedboat. Ultimately, it appeared to require some effort to make the raft tip as the defendant described, with the swimmer shown grabbing onto one of the gunnels and pulling back with counterclockwise force.

Defense Video at Scene: Raft Will Flip from Wake

At the trial, the jurors saw the videotapes of the two police reenactments, one in a swimming pool and the other on the lake where Cynthia Roth died.[3]

The jury had little difficulty convicting Roth of murder, which was affirmed on appeal.[4] While no written accounts exist of what the jurors thought of the videos specifically, obviously, by their guilty verdict, the jury viewed the prosecution version as far more believable.

In an attempt to gain greater insight into the fine points of general audience reactions to these videos, as well as the interplay between the videos, I showed them to groups of law-school students, having them fill out evaluation forms afterward. Upward of 80 percent of the students found the prosecution

At the trial, the jurors saw the videotapes of the two police reenactments, one in a swimming pool and the other on the lake where Cynthia Roth died.

3. "Drowning Reenacted by Defense," *Seattle Post-Intelligencer,* April 7, 1992.
4. *State v. Roth,* 75 Wn. App. 808, 881 P.2d 268 (1994).

video very persuasive, with corresponding criticisms of the defense video as weak and not credible.

Lingering Skepticism of the Prosecution

A number of the law students, after watching the dueling videos, voted that Roth was guilty. Nevertheless, they perceived certain flaws in the prosecution's version. The most prominent criticisms were the lack of physical evidence of a struggle prior to Cynthia Roth's death and the fact that the re-creation in the swimming pool did not account for other factors out on the lake that day, such as waves, wind, and weather.

However, these lingering doubts did not rise to a level sufficient to swing the pro-prosecution group to the defense side. On balance, even with the limitations, the majority felt that the prosecution videos were helpful and persuasive.

Can You Ever Make a Perfect Video?

In the end, two basic points of agreement emerged among the 80 percent majority who voted for a guilty verdict, based on the videos:

- The defendant's story was implausible. A raft could not tip over in the way that he claimed.

- The weakness of the defendant's video ended up helping the prosecution's effort to be more persuasive.

The fact that the prosecution video effectively shifted the burden of proof to the defendant was the best overall measure of its effectiveness.

The differing reactions to the *Roth* videos make it seem unlikely that any lawyer can ever produce the perfect video, one that all jurors will embrace. Some variation is likely with juror interpretation of videos and animations in legal cases.

But the solid 80 percent favorable rating of the *Roth* prosecution video, along with the strongly favorable comments it elicited, prove that a video does not have to be 100 percent

The most important lesson of *State v. Roth* is to always use a focus group in evaluating the effectiveness of this kind of evidence, no matter which side created it.

believed to be effective in tipping the balance. Clearly, this video was a strong factor for the prosecution team in *Roth*, shoring up their circumstantial case in a powerful way. This was combined with the evidence of motive, presented as the insurance proceeds Roth collected after Cynthia died, as well as the insurance payout when his second wife, Janice, had died.

The student questionnaire responses identified a number of initial hurdles the prosecution faced in this case. A significant minority believed that it was possible to tip over a raft in the manner claimed by Roth. Some held on to that belief, even after seeing the prosecution video. Still others wanted to see signs on Cynthia Roth's body that proved that the defendant repeatedly pushed her down in the manner shown on the prosecution video.

It is impossible for anyone to anticipate all the ways in which an audience will interpret a video or a computer animation. The most important lesson of *State v. Roth* is to always use a focus group in evaluating the effectiveness of this kind of evidence, no matter which side created it. This will tell you how close the re-creation is to hitting or missing the mark.

If the defense team in *Roth* had done a focus group, the ineffectiveness of its own video surely would have been revealed. A number of subjects laughed out loud when viewing the feeble efforts of the male swimmer to save the female in the first defense video. Obviously, the defense missed this potential effect entirely.

STATES V. MACHINE SHOP—USING A COMPUTER ANIMATION INSTEAD OF A VIDEO[5]

Considerations of cost and practicality often will preclude using the kind of live-action videos done by both sides in the murder prosecution of *State v. Roth*. Computer animations often are the best alternative, in that these do not involve any risk to human subjects and are easier and cheaper to produce than a live video.

---

5. Pseudonym. The animation for this case is included on the DVD with this book.

Even so, pay careful attention to the animation's foundation, making sure that it accurately reflects the scene and action of the event at issue. Use photographs showing people or objects in their correct locations, which an animator can then use to build the set and the characters who will appear in the animation.

I used a FRCP 34 scene inspection to create an animation rather than a video in the personal injury case of *States v. Machine Shop*. We modeled the behavior and conditions that led to the plaintiff's lathe accident. I used the photographs I took as the basis for the animation, taken with an eye toward proof of foundation accuracy for the judge in a later motion to admit.

The basic facts of the accident involved an eight-pound steel ring called a "boss spacer" that flew out of the lathe and hit the plaintiff in the mouth. Only minutes before, the foreman had come over and increased the speed of the machine, telling the plaintiff, "This is how we do it." When questioned later at his deposition, the foreman had no explanation for why the accident happened but did not blame the plaintiff or himself.

The lathe in question was examined by my engineering expert, who observed:

> Unacceptable levels of wear that would affect the ability of the chuck jaws to be properly tightened . . . [particularly] with a cutting speed that was two and a half times too fast.

The plaintiff suffered mandible and sinus fractures as well as the loss of multiple teeth. Extensive dental reconstruction was necessary after sufficient healing of his other facial injuries had occurred.

I felt that a computer animation could have a strong possibility of helping the plaintiff's case in a number of respects:

1. The drama of the injury, getting hit forcefully in the mouth with an eight-pound steel ring.

Pay careful attention to the animation's foundation, making sure that it accurately reflects the scene and action of the event at issue.

2. The shop foreman had increased the speed of the lathe only minutes before. Showing him doing this would increase the chance that he would be blamed.

3. The animation would tend to mitigate any defense arguments of plaintiff's comparative fault.

4. Since many of the jurors were unlikely to understand the operation of a lathe, the animation would help them visualize how a lathe operates.

I focused on the animation foundation during the FRCP 34 inspection of the shop. My client stood at the same lathe and demonstrated various motions and behaviors that he would do on the job, all of which was photographed, along with his holding an exemplar of the type of eight-pound steel spacer used on that day. I took multiple photos of the lathe. I then gave them to the animator, who now had a solid basis for re-creating what happened.

My client stood at the same lathe and demonstrated various motions and behaviors that he would do on the job.

The animator purchased a graphic of a similar lathe, then modified it to look like the one involved in this case, combining photographic detail into the composite image.

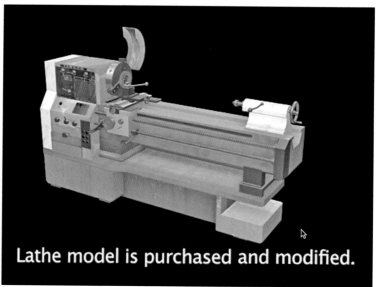

Lathe model is purchased and modified.

I provided the plaintiff's dental and medical records to the animator, along with imaging studies.

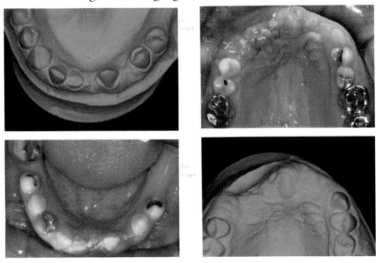

The animator then built a simple set of the shop, with the lathe and figures representing the plaintiff and his foreman added thereafter.

The animator then built a simple set of the shop.

Human models are added to the scene.

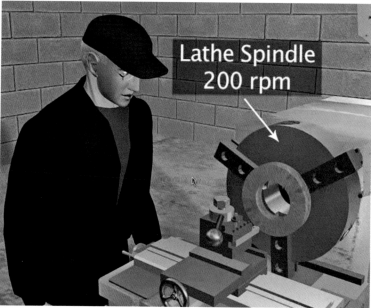

Lathe Spindle
200 rpm

I gave the animator a description from the various depositions of what happened.

As we learned in chapter 12, "Making Your Case Stick," one problem with animations is that they go by quickly. Since jurors do not like to see them multiple times, an alternative way to

One problem with animations is that they go by quickly.

stretch the effectiveness of an animation is to take still frames from it. This was what I had the animator do here, taking a freeze-frame just as the steel ring struck Mr. States in the mouth.

The final version of the animation was a simple and effective re-creation of what happened, similar in its overall ability to advance the theory of the case to the prosecution video in *State v. Roth*. I tested the animation on a focus group, who gasped audibly when the steel ring came flying out of the lathe and struck the plaintiff on the mouth. Subsequent follow-up revealed the following impressions by the focus group:

1. The correlation with foundation photographs taken at the scene and the simplicity of the animation made it credible, tracking with the real thing.

2. Though the foreman was equivocal in his deposition on whether or not he turned up the speed of the lathe, seeing him doing it in the animation convinced most viewers that he had, concluding that this was the cause of the accident.

I tested the animation on a focus group, who gasped audibly when the steel ring came flying out of the lathe and struck the plaintiff on the mouth.

3. The plaintiff was felt to be partially at fault for not having the guard down, but the fact that his supervisor had not said anything about it tended to mitigate the plaintiff's comparative fault.

TAKEAWAYS—ENHANCING REALITY

- *Jurors will look at animations critically, measuring how closely they match common experience.*

- *If each side uses a video or animation, there will be a "weak twin" effect. Not only will the stronger one win, but the weaker one will make the stronger one even more plausible than it would be standing alone.*

- *An effective video or animation can implant mental images that then become the jurors' reality.*

- *An effective video can shift the burden of proof because it is more real. An animation is less likely to do so, as it is less real.*

- *If there is no good video or animation concept that supports your theory of the case, it is better just to concentrate on poking holes in the other side's proof.*

- *It is better to do nothing at all than to use a video or animation that doesn't help your client.*

- *Wishing and hoping your video or animation will be effective doesn't make it so. It is critical to do a reality check with a focus group.*

- *Be vigilant for the unseen sucker-punch effect, where your own video or animation can prove the opposite of what you intend.*

25

EXPANDING TRADITIONAL
EVIDENCE RULES

Winning isn't everything, it's the only thing.

—Vince Lombardi

As the gatekeeper making evidentiary decisions, a judge expects each side to offer exhibits with a definite point of view. As Professor David Boerner of Seattle University School of Law has observed:

> Any lawyer is going to shape their evidence in a way that is most positive for them and most negative for the opponent.[1]

While evidence cuts in one direction or another, the trial judge has to ensure that it doesn't cross over the line of fairness. This chapter explores the background of this decision making.

---

1. David Boerner, interview with William S. Bailey, March 25, 2008.

Is It Real, Demonstrative, or Illustrative Evidence?

Evidence falls into one of three categories: real, demonstrative, or illustrative. Each of these has different foundation, timing, and use considerations. For example, real evidence is discoverable, while demonstrative evidence may not be, protected by the attorney work-product exception. Professor Robert Aronson of the University of Washington School of Law defines the subtle conceptual difference between the two:

> There's a difference between original evidence, like a photograph of the scene, and evidence a lawyer creates to advance a client's position. Evidence created by a lawyer didn't exist before.
>
> A photograph of the scene right afterward is real evidence. If there's no original scene left, then you have to turn this photo over under most circumstances. Real evidence is the murder weapon. Demonstrative evidence is a diagram of the murder weapon, used to show how the real one works.[2]

Changing from One Form to Another

While real evidence and demonstrative evidence are usually mutually exclusive, this is not always so, particularly when information becomes unavailable to other counsel. In these circumstances, demonstrative evidence may change into real evidence.

In *Neuswanger v. Ikegai America Corp.,*[3] an Illinois case where the plaintiff got hurt in a machine accident, the defense lawyer took a video of the machine shortly after the accident, with his expert on camera, making comments. Was this real evidence or demonstrative? The discoverability of this video hinged on this issue.

The defense lawyer refused to turn the video over to the opposing counsel. Given the close time proximity to the event, the court

Evidence falls into one of three categories: real, demonstrative, or illustrative.

2. Robert Aronson, interview with William S. Bailey, March 18, 2008.
3. 582 N.E. 2d 192 (1991).

determined it was more akin to real evidence. There was no other way for the plaintiff to verify the condition of the machine immediately following the event. Though the plaintiff was allowed to see the video, the defense could erase the expert's comments.

Illustrative Evidence

Evidence offered or admitted "for illustrative purposes only" is in a lower status category, often used as a fallback position when the court has foundation concerns about an exhibit. Common illustrative exhibits include expert diagrams drawn during testimony or charts of counsel summarizing evidence. Relevance and accuracy still matter, but less so, in that illustrative exhibits usually do not go back to the jury room.

While some lawyers may believe that illustrative evidence need not be disclosed before trial, judges often disagree. In Judge William Downing's courtroom, both demonstrative and illustrative evidence have the same disclosure rule:

> I've seen lawyers come to court with really important pieces of evidence and say, "Oh well, Your Honor, it's only for illustrative purposes and therefore I didn't need to produce it to counsel beforehand." My response is: "This illustrates your theory of the case. It can't be merely for illustrative purposes. You needed to disclose it prior to trial."[4]

The lesson from all this is that the label of real, demonstrative, or illustrative evidence may not mean much in terms of foundation, discoverability, or notice to counsel. Exceptions to the usual rules always exist. But it does help to have a working presumption of what category each piece of evidence in your case falls into.

Common illustrative exhibits include expert diagrams drawn during testimony or charts of counsel summarizing evidence.

---

4. William Downing, interview with William S. Bailey, November 14, 2008.

FOUNDATION BASICS

Foundation always takes time. You must master all the underlying details. If you wait until the last minute, you may miss something or lack the necessary time to make changes required by your judge. Early planning of visuals pays many dividends, the most important of which is understanding your case better. Illustrations also can be quite useful in depositions, scoring points with witnesses. If any of these are challenged, give the witness a pen and say, "Fix it." This approach locks testimony in with greater precision than words alone. It also anticipates foundation issues well in advance, giving you a chance to correct mistakes.

Strong foundation requires your hands-on participation throughout the creation of your visuals. Here are the essential steps:

> *If any of these are challenged, give the witness a pen and say, "Fix it."*

- Review documents and photos to understand what happened.

- Talk to fact witnesses.

- Visit locations and take your own photos or videos.

- Boil the case down to key points.

- Try to explain to your coworkers, family, or friends what happened. What confuses them? How can you clear this up visually?

- Talk to your experts. How can they help explain key points?

- Use an illustrator to turn key elements of the trial story into images.

- Constantly challenge yourself with the question, "Will the trial judge buy this?"

DO THE TRADITIONAL RULES REALLY WORK HERE?

High-tech evidence is different in many ways from traditional forms. Judge William Downing sees the tension this creates in deciding admissibility issues:

The people who wrote the rules of evidence in 1970 couldn't see these things coming. A witness in my courtroom recently was shown a Google Earth photograph of the neighborhood and was asked if it was fair and accurate. The witness hesitated for a second. I said to him, "Now the last time you were up in your satellite looking down at the neighborhood, is that the way it appeared?"

While this got a good laugh, the fact of the matter is nobody really has the personal experience to lay the proper foundation for a satellite photograph or aerial surveillance photograph. We take it for granted, but technically it would be very hard to lay the foundation.

But all these things, digital photography, Photoshop manipulation of photos, and computer-animation re-creations of an occurrence have so much potential for mischief. There really need to be some strong safeguards in place.

The source of these protections need to be in the professionalism of the attorneys, the discovery process, the sharing of any image generated for trial with opposing counsel, and then a close scrutiny by a court before it's allowed in front of the jury.[5]

A TWO-STEP PROCESS

High-tech evidence does need different foundation rules. It is best to envision this as a two-level process, first before the judge and then before the jury. This will involve repeating proof presented to the judge, so the jurors also can appreciate the foundation for what they are seeing. Judge William Downing explains why both steps are needed:

It's important to share the explanation of how the exhibit came to be. Were these photographs taken by a person who just happened to be standing there? Were

Judge William Downing

---

5. Downing, interview.

changes made in the lighting, visibility, or contrast? What about the way the photo was printed and processed? It's not just sharing the physical exhibit itself, but also the background. Who created it and what processes were followed?

The process itself must be explained and not simply the conclusory statement that it's a fair and accurate depiction. That's really the crucial thing.

For a jury to put high-tech visual evidence in the proper context, they need to hear how it was created. They need to have the benefit of cross-examination or *voir dire* examination, which may expose flawed assumptions or methodology before they see that exhibit.[6]

THE ROLE OF EXPERT OPINION

Unlike simple photographs, high-tech visuals do not have built-in foundation. Your experts often will be able to fill in this gap. In fact, early expert consultation will help you develop visualization ideas and strategy, backed up with scientific and technical resources.

Judge Downing believes that experts can save lawyers from making costly visual-evidence mistakes:

> Anticipate foundation, so that you don't find yourself at trial, out of pocket with substantial cost, for no benefit at all. There's really nobody else but an expert who a lawyer can consult with to get a good idea whether the planned exhibit will work. The key question is, "Will I be able to ask you on the stand that this is an accurate depiction?" It's a further incentive for expert consultation to withstand the scrutiny of cross-examination and objections by your opponent.
>
> This process is particularly true for computer evidence. You can spend a lot of time and money creating

> Unlike simple photographs, high-tech visuals do not have built-in foundation.

---

6. Downing, interview.

it, being very conscientious about getting it right and then ultimately still have a problem getting it in.[7]

PULLING IT ALL TOGETHER

Lacking the ease and simplicity of a photograph or simple diagram, computer-generated evidence usually is a multistep collaboration between lawyer, expert, and illustrator. Foundation is critical, and you take on multiple roles, including producer, director, and scriptwriter. The legal process places constraints on your choices that don't exist for computer graphics in other fields, such as marketing or entertainment. Even if this evidence comes in, it will be attacked by the opposing counsel and subject to juror skepticism.

Done correctly, a computer illustration or animation likely will be admitted, making jurors eyewitnesses to an event. Done incorrectly, if the evidence comes in at all, it will make you seem dishonest or even desperate. The possibilities here directly correlate to your attention to foundation, always thinking through to the end.

FOUNDATION BY NEGOTIATION

In recent years, a mutual amnesty between counsel on exhibit challenges has become more common. Kathy Cochran describes the trade-off:

> My hope always is to use my visuals in opening statement. Frequently, the other side does too. This leads to a negotiation between counsel out in the hallway. "I'll let you use yours if you let me use mine."
>
> More and more, the visuals of both sides mostly come in if they've been prepared properly.[8]

This leads to a negotiation between counsel out in the hallway. "I'll let you use yours if you let me use mine."

---

7. Downing, interview.
8. Kathy Cochran, interview with William S. Bailey, October 28, 2009.

TAKEAWAYS—EXPANDING TRADITIONAL EVIDENCE RULES

◆ *Into which category does each piece of visual evidence in your case fall?*

◆ *How will you get each piece admitted? Different standards apply to real, demonstrative, and illustrative exhibits.*

◆ *Traditional evidence admissibility rules did not anticipate foundation for high-tech evidence.*

◆ *Will your experts back up your visuals as accurate?*

◆ *Explaining the foundation of visual evidence is a two-step process, first for the judge and then, once admitted, repeating this for the jury's benefit.*

◆ *What is the potential for the visual to be used against you? Will you have to turn it over to the other side, even if you choose not to use it? If so, when?*

◆ *Should you agree to any kind of foundation amnesty with the other side, particularly when it comes to using visuals in opening statement?*

26

WINNING AN ADMISSIBILITY KNIFE FIGHT

Creative risk taking is essential to success in any goal where the stakes are high.

—Gary Ryan Blair

In November 2009, golf superstar Tiger Woods was involved in a messy, well-publicized marital dispute with his then wife. A Hong Kong–based tabloid newspaper company used informed guesses to make a minute-and-a-half-long digital animation of these events, "giving a vividness and a sense of concrete reality to what is basically conjecture."[1] Even though the production values were marginal and the soundtrack was in Chinese, this animation became an instant global sensation, with 1.7 million views on YouTube alone.

When interviewed about the background of this animation, a scriptwriter with the Chinese tabloid that produced it, Daisy Li, described her company's targeted appeal to the younger

---

1. Noam Cohen, "In Animated Videos, News and Guesswork Mix," *New York Times,* December 5, 2009.

demographic: "The print version of newspapers is shrinking. The young people don't like to read the newspaper."[2] The huge success of the Woods animation provided strong incentive for the tabloid to follow up with similar ones.

However, animations in public life are not confined to tabloids. The Italian murder trial resulting in the conviction of American college student Amanda Knox featured a prosecution animation of its theory on how the events occurred. Once again, the primitive technical quality did not seem to interfere with its persuasiveness.

Computer animations have the greatest potential power and risk of all the forms of visual evidence discussed in this book. Done properly, they give the judge and jury a vivid eyewitness view. Seattle University Professor John Mitchell sees them as just an extension of photographs:

John Mitchell

> There is an inherent suspicion of new things in the law. It's a throwback to when photos were first used in cases a century ago. In a real sense, computer animations are no different than a series of photos on poster boards.[3]

The viral circulation of the Tiger Woods animation shows the huge potential power in this approach to the reenactment of events. In a legal case, this leads to a metaphorical knife fight between the proponent and the opponent of the animation. Professor David Boerner sees it as inevitable that high-tech visuals will result in these kinds of pitched evidentiary battles:

> The animation process is longer and more drawn out than photographs, with multiple drafts and layers of involvement. The stakes go up significantly and the foundation becomes critical.[4]

The upside of a computer animation is counterbalanced by negatives that open a lawyer to potential credibility challenges.

2. Noam Cohen, "In Animated Videos."
3. John Mitchell, interview with William S. Bailey, April 21, 2008.
4. David Boerner, interview with William S. Bailey, March 25, 2008.

Jurors hold courtroom evidence to a different standard that what they see on television:

> A jury could take offense if a computer animation unfairly manipulates the outcome. You could be sowing the seeds of your own destruction, paradoxically providing ammunition to the other side.[5]

There is greater potential volatility with computer animations:

> Where do you start it and where do you stop it? Using these is a high-stakes bet. If all goes well, it might help you win. But if it goes wrong, it might be the single biggest factor in bringing you down, particularly in this time of high juror suspicion.[6]

David Boerner

CONSTANTINE V. PRINCE: THE ANIMATION COMES IN[7]

In *Constantine v. Prince,* representing the family of a twenty-two-year-old bicyclist who had been run down in a crosswalk, I weighed my options and decided in favor of Professor Boerner's high-stakes bet, going for an animation. Wrongful-death cases always are harder for the plaintiff's side, as the "dead men tell

5. Boerner, interview.
6. Boerner, interview.
7. Pseudonym.

no tales." Our pretrial focus groups showed potential issues not only around what the defendant driver could see of the crosswalk, but also whether the bicyclist safely entered it.

None of the eyewitnesses actually saw the impact, and one paramedic swore that our clients' son did not have a helmet on. The defense also made it clear that they would attack the bicyclist's character, dwelling on his supposedly alternative lifestyle, working as a bicycle messenger, with long hair and a Grateful Dead tattoo. The driver also claimed that his view of the crosswalk was blocked by cars in the right-turn lane.

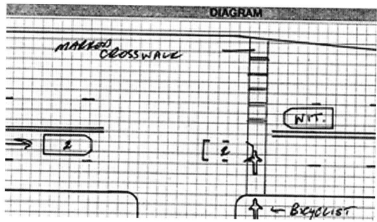

I didn't go with an animation until after unsuccessfully attempting to win summary judgment on liability, arguing that the bicyclist in the crosswalk was entitled to presume that the defendant would yield the right-of-way. After the trial judge denied my motion, ruling that the comparative fault of my clients' deceased son was a jury question, it was clear that I had to go with an animation. With both the defendant driver and the bicyclist in motion prior to the impact, changing position as they moved toward the point of impact, the bicyclist became ever more visible as the driver came closer to the crosswalk.

The goal of the computer animation in *Constantine* was to put the jurors in the driver's seat, allowing them to see exactly what the defendant saw as he approached the intersection. The defendant's excuse that cars in the right-turn lane blocked his view became untenable when presented in the animation. My

The goal was to put the jurors in the driver's seat, allowing them to see exactly what the defendant saw as he approached the intersection.

accident-reconstruction expert had plugged the data from the police investigation into his computer, which simulated the visual relationship of the SUV and the bicycle as they converged on each other.

The roadway was a straight four-lane arterial with marked crosswalks.

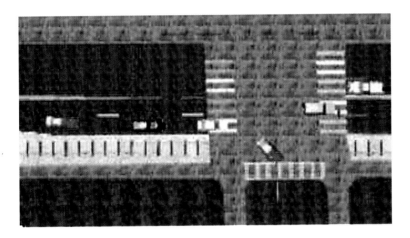

While the defendant had not told the officers at the scene on the day of the collision about cars in the turn lane blocking his view of the intersection, it became central to the defense's case.

*Photo showing the height of
the SUV and the bicycle*

Photo showing the crosswalk

The crosswalk as an animation

The bicyclist in the crosswalk

Time	X	Y	Z
0	-44	37	-2.65
0.25	-35.79	37.01	-2.57
0.5	-27.61	37.03	-2.59
0.75	-19.46	37.05	-2.59
1	-11.32	37.07	-2.59
1.25	-3.21	37.1	-2.59
1.5	4.73	37.12	-2.59
1.75	11.91	37.14	-2.57
2	18.31	37.16	-2.58
2.25	23.87	37.18	-2.58
2.5	28.66	37.19	-2.58
2.75	32.6	37.2	-2.58
3	35.76	37.21	-2.58
3.25	38.09	37.21	-2.58
3.5	39.78	37.21	-2.58
3.75	41.36	37.17	-2.59
4	42.93	37.11	-2.59
4.25	44.47	37.04	-2.59
4.5	46	36.96	-2.59
4.75	47.51	36.88	-2.59
5	49	36.8	-2.59
5.25	50.47	36.72	-2.6
5.5	51.92	36.64	-2.6
5.75	53.36	36.56	-2.6
6	54.77	36.48	-2.6
6.25	56.17	36.41	-2.6

Accident Reconstruction Calculations

The police photos showed that even if there had been cars in the right-turn lane, the bicyclist still would be visible.

Lighting was not an issue, and both sides agreed that the defendant was not speeding. A bicyclist with the same height and weight as the decedent was pictured on the corner from where the decedent entered the intersection; a patrol car was positioned in the right-turn lane. The police photos showed that even if there had been cars in the right-turn lane, the bicyclist still would be visible.

The most troublesome issue was the uncertainty over the bicyclist's helmet. There was no way to reconcile the conflicting evidence, so I told my animator to put a helmet on the bicyclist in the animation.

The Knife Fight Begins

The final version of our animation all but wiped out the defense liability arguments, visualizing the conclusions of the police detective assigned to the case. It is one thing for the jury to hear the detective give his perspective from the stand and quite another to see it on the screen. I had wanted to put the jury in the driver's seat, judging the defendant's behavior based upon their own experience as drivers.

If the animation was admitted into evidence, it seemed likely that the jury would believe that the defendant had plenty of time to stop and avoid the collision. After viewing the animation, the jury could only conclude that the driver wasn't paying attention. The animation also blew up his otherwise plausible-sounding claim that cars to his right blocked his view until it was too late.

The defense firm in the case hated the animation for all the reasons I loved it. They assigned their top appellate lawyer

It is one thing for the jury to hear the detective give his perspective from the stand and quite another to see it on the screen.

I stuck to the declarations of my experts and the animator.

to oppose its admission. Articulate and incisive in his briefing, well spoken in oral argument, he commanded a healthy respect. However, I could sense his underlying discomfort and urgency as we approached the bench to argue this motion. He did not like the animation one little bit and was determined to keep it out at all cost.

Facing a challenge based on a scattergun blast of details, I stuck to the declarations of my experts and the animator, making the points that the animation:

- Incorporated the police report and deposition testimony.

- Was based on my expert's time, distance, and speed calculations.

- Used an industry-accepted computer program to position the bicyclist and driver.

- Represented the animator's multiple scene visits and photos.

- Accurately reflected the defendant's available view.

- Would help the jury.

- Any deviations from reality would go to weight afforded the evidence, not its admissibility.

The Defense Fights Back

The defense attacked my accident-reconstruction expert's calculations and his decision not to show other cars or pedestrians in the animation. The defense's core arguments against the animation were as follows:

Inadequate foundation

- Time and position analysis misleading.

- No other cars or pedestrians seen.

- Ignores driver's need to scan ahead.

Based on speculation

- ◆ Body motions of bicyclist after impact.

Factual errors conflicting with testimony

- ◆ Bicyclist wearing helmet.

Confusing to the jury

- ◆ Exaggerated and unfair

The Judge Rules

The trial judge found that any testimony on the helmet would invite juror speculation and granted our motion *in limine* to exclude it. With that out of the way, the defense motion to exclude the animation was denied, though the judge did order a few modifications. The most significant one was that the bicyclist could not be shown wearing a helmet. The other was that the spiderweb impact pattern shown on the windshield was too confusing.

The defense motion to exclude the animation was denied, though the judge did order a few modifications.

The animation demonstrated that the defendant could have, and should have, seen the bicyclist.

One thing about the judge's ruling worried me—showing the bicyclist without a helmet. Given recent articles on bicycle safety that had appeared in the local press, I saw this as inviting a finding of comparative fault. Necessity's being the mother of invention, a way around this danger popped into my brain: revise the bicyclist from a human form to a stick figure with a circle for a head. This way, none of the jurors would be thinking, *Why doesn't he have a helmet on?* Two versions were prepared, one with no cars in the right-turn lane and the other showing a single car in that lane. Either way, the animation demonstrated that the defendant could have, and should have, seen the bicyclist. The jury returned a finding of 100 percent fault on the defendant and a $2.8 million verdict—on the defendant's birthday.

GEE V. HUBBARD: THE FOUNDATION OF THE DEFENSE ANIMATION GETS CUT AWAY[8]

In *Gee v. Hubbard,* a wrongful-death freeway collision case, it was the defense that decided to go with a computer animation,

---

8. Pseudonym.

in support of its theory that the decedent's disabled car appeared so suddenly that it was impossible for the defendant to avoid the collision. The emergency doctrine, giving wide latitude to a driver faced with a sudden emergency, was a real concern for plaintiff's counsel representing the decedent's estate, wife, and children.

The decedent sustained a high-speed blowout as he drove a sibling to the airport in the early morning, just before daybreak.

The tire deflated so quickly that it was not possible for the decedent to get from the fast lane over to the side of the road. He put on his flashers, kept his foot on the brake pedal, with the headlights on, and called for help on his cell phone.

Shortly thereafter, the defendant hit him from behind at high speed, with no preimpact braking. The impact occurred on a straight stretch of freeway, right next to a major downtown area. All the overhead roadway lights were working and there were no visual obstructions of the decedent's car as the defendant approached it. Just as in *Constantine,* the issue was, "What could the defendant see, and when could he see it?"

The issue was, "What could the defendant see, and when could he see it?"

The defense experts came up with the explanation that the defendant driver had just looked to his left for about three seconds when changing lanes.

Aerial view of accident scene

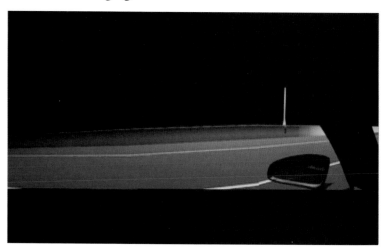

The defendant also alleged that a white Lincoln Town Car passing him to the left screened his vision of the decedent's car up ahead.

The Defense Animation—The Stalled Car Came out of Nowhere

The defendant in *Gee* assembled a formidable team of experts, working with the defendant to build an animation supporting the reasonableness of his failure to stop. In the dark and shadowy animation that resulted, indeed, the decedent's stopped car seems to "come out of nowhere," not allowing the defendant sufficient time to brake.

Animation: stopped car comes out of nowhere.

Plaintiff's Response

Randy Gordon, the plaintiff's counsel in *Gee,* was worried when he first looked at the defense animation. But after repeated viewing, he realized it didn't track with reality. He ended up going to the scene multiple times, sometimes with his experts and sometimes not. The animation had manipulated what was there to be seen, making the decedent's car seem to appear out of nowhere.

He ended up going to the scene multiple times, sometimes with his experts and sometimes not.

The Outcome—Defendant Gets Skewered by His Own Animation

Gee never got to trial. Professor Boerner's prophecy that an animation gone wrong might be "the single biggest factor in bringing you down" proved to be the defense's undoing in this case.

Randy Gordon

How the Plaintiff Kept Out the Defense Animation

1. EXPOSING THE MANIPULATION

   Mr. Gordon relied heavily on his instincts initially, comparing the computer animation to real life:

   > My initial reaction was, "I've driven down this road at night. This looks too dark Why is the decedent's car suddenly appearing out of nowhere? This doesn't happen in the real world."[9]

2. EXPOSING THE UNDERLYING CHOICES

   A key element in plaintiff's strategy to attack the computer animation was to expose the choices made by the defendant in its creation:

   > Any computer animation is a simplification of reality. Every time you make a change from real life, someone wins and someone loses. The defense experts manipulated a number of choices here, particularly the lighting.[10]

3. REVERSE ENGINEERING THE ANIMATION

   Mr. Gordon assembled a team of experts to assist him in reverse engineering the defense animation:

   > We had our own animator take apart what they had done, frame by frame, so we could see the choices that were made. Our experts carefully examined the photographic evidence of the scene.[11]

4. A KEY STRATEGIC CHOICE—SHOWING ACTUAL CONDITIONS

   Mr. Gordon was not satisfied merely to discredit the defense animation, deciding to photograph and film the actual lighting and visibility, using exemplar cars:

---

9. Randolph I. Gordon, interview with William S. Bailey, November 25, 2008.
10. Gordon, interview.
11. Gordon, interview.

We basically demonstrated in the ten seconds before the collision what you would have been able to see and when you would have been able to see it.

Their animation looked like a cartoon. Rather than doing an animation back, a war of cartoons, we went one step better—real life.[12]

Rather than doing an animation back, a war of cartoons, we went one step better—real life.

Plaintiff's re-creation: stopped car is visible.

5. Forcing the Defense Experts' Hands

Since the defense animation was based on expert testimony, Mr. Gordon went after them in depositions, with the goal of exposing all the manipulations.

The defense had their experts and their client endorse the animation and got caught. After the defendant's accident-reconstruction expert endorsed the animation as completely accurate, I said to him:

"You wouldn't endorse evidence that was inaccurate to a jury, would you?"

"Absolutely not."

"So you're saying this is absolutely accurate?"

"Yes."

---

12. Gordon, interview.

And then I tore it apart. All of a sudden, the defendant's whole case was in danger of being tainted by this animation. There were a lot of things they couldn't explain.[13]

6. Attacking the Animator on Details—Garbage In, Garbage Out

After the plaintiff's counsel identified and exposed all the "junk science" choices that the defense experts had made, he took the deposition of the animator, systematically exposing all the deviations from reality that resulted:

Q: What were your sources of information for this animation?

A: The defendant's experts, the defendant, and the defense counsel.

Q: Whenever there's a question of how something is going to be portrayed, that was determined for you by others?

A: Yes.

Q: You did no independent investigation of your own in this case?

A: Correct.

Q: Did you make an animation with a certain presumed speed?

A: Yes.

Q: In the final analysis you did whatever the defense accident-reconstruction expert told you to do?

A: Correct.

Q: What about the lighting in the animation. How did you determine that?

A: Our objective was not to do an accurate representation of the lighting, because we weren't out there the day the accident happened.

---

13. Gordon, interview.

Q: Are you suggesting that the lighting in the animation is accurate then?

A: No.

Q: Was there any occasion where the defendant said the animation was not right?

A: The main one was that he didn't have as much time to react as we were showing.

Q: You put a car between the defendant and my client in that animation?

A: Yes.

Q: Even though the defendant's own testimony was that he didn't remember seeing a car between him and my client's vehicle?

A: Yes, we did what we were asked to do.

Q: Do you know why the defense only asked you to use tail lights on the decedent's car, not flashers or brake lights?

A: I don't. It was the defense accident-reconstruction expert's decision.

Q: But the presence of brake lights would make a big difference in visibility?

A: It would make a difference.

Q: How did you pick the locations on the road for the streetlights?

A: We had to guess, looking at the photos taken that morning.

Animation: Tail lights hard to see

Real life: Bright tail lights clearly visible.

Q: I won't say garbage in, garbage out, but you did this based on what you were given?

A: That's exactly right.

7. NOWHERE LEFT TO GO

After a series of deft moves by the plaintiff's counsel in depositions, the defense suddenly found itself encircled:

> The more accurate we made it, the less they wanted to use it, as it became less and less favorable to their case. After they spent about $35,000, we put them in a position where they couldn't and didn't want to use the animation.[14]

8. VISUAL EVIDENCE CHOICES AND THE CREDIBILITY BANK

Throughout the case, Mr. Gordon kept in mind what evidence a jury would be likely to trust:

> My approach with everything in trial is to ask, "Is this putting money into the credibility bank or taking money out?"

By going consistently with photographic and film evidence, he got the upper hand. If the case had gone to trial, the jury would have believed his case, not the defense's.

TAKEAWAYS—WINNING AN ADMISSIBILITY KNIFE FIGHT

- *Computer animations are becoming more common in public affairs.*

- *While animations have inherent power that makes them worthy of consideration, they can also be risky.*

- *There is some inherent suspicion of new things in the law, which likely will make judges insist on a very solid foundation for computer animations.*

---

14. Gordon, interview.

- *The stakes go up significantly with the use of computer animations that attempt to re-create key events in the case.*

- *Because they magnify factual mistakes on the screen, computer animations open you to potentially damaging credibility attacks by the opposing counsel, making accuracy and foundation critical.*

- *The admissibility of computer animations revolves around the accuracy of the details. Smaller differences won't keep it out, but major ones likely will.*

- *Any computer animation is a simplification of reality. Are the choices consistent with real life?*

- *The opposing counsel will try to expose your choices in a computer animation as inaccurate, reverse engineering what you did, frame by frame.*

- *Doing a video of the actual conditions can be a successful strategy in opposing a computer animation.*

- *Animators are dependent on the information you give them. If the data and expert opinions they are relying on are proven to be wrong, it's garbage in, garbage out.*

- *Jurors trust some technologies more than others, with the ease of alteration or manipulation affecting their opinion.*

- *Ask yourself with each possible visual that you might use at trial, "Is this putting money into the jury credibility bank, or taking it out?" Don't risk the latter.*

27

TURNING THE WEAPON AROUND: DEFENSE INTO OFFENSE

Hitting is timing. Pitching is upsetting timing.

—Warren Spahn

The *Gee* case from the previous chapter points up the strategic reversals that can occur in the battle over the foundation and admissibility of visual evidence. The plaintiff's counsel had the opposition in retreat. The defense no longer wanted to use its own animation, since it was locked into an implausible version of reality. Rather than moving to exclude the defense animation, the plaintiff embraced it. Had the case proceeded to trial, the plaintiff's counsel would have impeached both the defendant and his experts with it.

The same strategy was used by my firm in *Constantine v. Prince,* after the defense felt obliged to come up with an animation of its own, demonstrating the opinions of their accident-reconstruction expert. This defense animation came in two parts. The first was an overhead view of the scene, showing the defendant making a right turn onto the adjoining cross street. The second part demonstrated how the body of the bicyclist might have hit the front of the defendant's SUV, been carried for a distance, and finally slid off onto the roadway.

After receiving the defense animation, we slowed it down to expose its basic elements, reviewing it frame by frame, revealing all the choices made by the defense in the animation. Two serious foundational defects emerged in the course of this analysis:

1. The right turn was being made illegally, in order to maximize the view obstruction to the defendant. The driver wasn't making the turn as close as possible to the right-hand curb, as required by statute.

2. The bicyclist smashed the window of the SUV in the real case. In the animation, the bicyclist's body never reached the windshield.

While my law partner Steve Fury could have made a motion to exclude or modify the defense animations for these reasons, the tactical decision was made to raise no objection, instead attacking the defense accident-reconstruction expert during cross-examination. In the end, this damaged the credibility of the defense expert, offering "cartoons" that didn't bear any relationship to the real facts of the case:

Q: How did you place the cars? How did you decide that's where you were going to place them?

A: Those were arbitrarily placed.

Q: You put this car here? This red car?

A: Yes.

Q: How did you decide to place it there? Again, just arbitrarily?

A: It is.

Q: What I'm concerned about is that it looks to me like you got this car over the center line. You know the rules of the road? You were a state patrolman for many years, right?

After receiving the defense animation, we slowed it down … reviewing it frame by frame, revealing all the choices made by the defense in the animation.

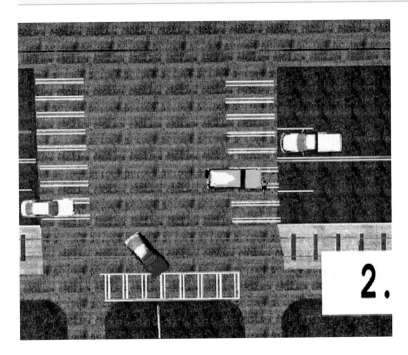

A: I do. I know the rules of the road.

Q: By statute, both the approach for a right turn and a right turn shall be made as close as practicable to the right-hand curb or edge of the roadway?

A: It's true. That's what the statute says.

Q: So we got this person here not going as close as practicable to the edge of the roadway, right?

A: That's correct.

Q: Did you have some reason why you picked having this car make an illegal right turn here?

A: I don't know that I would call it illegal.

Q: It's arbitrarily placed. So that it is, in fact, going into the far lane, an illegal right turn?

A: Technically, yes.

Q: Let's assume that he made a legal right turn, sir. Back there, there's no blocking of view, is there, if you move it back just a little bit?

A: Change the positions, you can change the view. There is absolutely no doubt about that. I'm not trying to insinuate anything otherwise.

Q: Let's talk about your other animation. For your computer reconstruction, you put in data for the defendant's speed as twenty-five miles an hour, correct?

A: That's correct.

Q: So we got here the point of impact, right?

A: That's correct.

Q: Body is on the hood?

A: That's correct.

Q: Riding on the car?

A: Yes.

Q: At one second, it starts to slide off?

A: Starting to, yes.

Q: I didn't see anywhere there, sir, that the entire body hit the windshield on this animation.

A: No, it doesn't. It comes up to the windshield.

The Trooper Was Speeding Faster Than 25 MPH

25 MPH Crash
Nothing Hits
Windshield

Trooper Windshield
Shattered in 2 Places

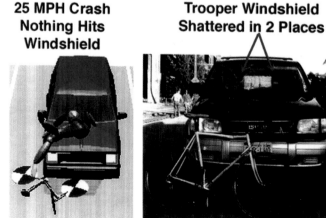

Q: But doesn't hit it?

A: That's correct. It's real close to the edge of the bottom of the windshield.

Q: But we don't have contact of the entire body with the windshield to cause this kind of damage.

A: No, not in an accident simulation you do not.

Q: The defendant has testified that the body was parallel with the bumper of the car.

A: Yes, that's true.

Q: According to your scenario here at the end of this at zero miles an hour we got the body perpendicular, don't we?

A: Well, yeah.

Q: So you've reconstructed a fifteen-mile-an-hour crash between a car with a bicyclist. It doesn't hit the windshield to cause the damage, correct?

A: No.

Q: And it doesn't end up with the body parallel to the front?

A: No, but it does end up with the body at the same distance.

Even if you can keep out an opponent's exhibit for lack of proper foundation or accuracy, you may not want to. Attacking the accuracy of an exhibit in front of the jury can be far more devastating than keeping it out of the trial. If an opponent's witness, expert or otherwise, vouches for the accuracy of exhibits initially, showing the errors in them on cross-examination can have a far-reaching and potentially devastating effect. This is precisely what happened to the defendant's accident-reconstruction expert in the *Constantine* case above.

Attacking the accuracy of an exhibit in front of the jury can be far more devastating than keeping it out of the trial.

TAKEAWAYS—TURNING THE WEAPON AROUND: DEFENSE INTO OFFENSE

◆ *Just because you can take out an opponent's visual exhibits through a pretrial motion doesn't mean that you should.*

◆ *Vouching for the accuracy of a visual that later is proven to be in error puts a witness, expert or otherwise, in jeopardy.*

◆ *Successfully examining an expert in front of the jury about errors he or she has made in the foundation for a visual exhibit can be very damaging to the expert's credibility.*

28

THE FUTURE IS NOW

I like the dreams of the future better than the history of the past.

—Thomas Jefferson

This is an exciting time to be a lawyer, with more real choices in how to present a client's case than ever before. Advances in technology have made visual advocacy available across a broad spectrum of subject matter and budget. While it once was true that only "big" cases had the resources for visuals, it is no longer so. Whether a routine traffic matter or an intellectual-property dispute involving hundreds of millions of dollars, visualization of information now is equally available and equally necessary.

THE TOP TEN TAKEAWAYS OF THIS BOOK

1. Find a theme.

2. Build a story around it.

3. Make it visual.

4. Go to the scene.

351

5. Set up the conflict.

6. Show the rule.

7. Reveal the choices.

8. Visualize the climactic moments.

9. Show and tell.

10. Foundation, foundation, foundation.

To be an effective lawyer today, you must be comfortable with a multimedia approach to the evidence, able to develop a theme that best explains the client's case, building it into a persuasive story with words and pictures. This starts with the best of traditional advocacy techniques, where solid preparation, strategic thinking, and skilled communication have been the keys to success, and then takes it to a higher level.

While possessed of a futuristic orientation, visual advocacy is based solidly on the well-established traditions of the past.

Every lawyer has the necessary creativity and skills to apply the techniques described in this book. It just requires a new way of thinking, with an awareness of how the visualization process intersects with the established rules of evidence. It also requires you to think critically about the wants and needs of your audience, which includes both judge and jury.

An important goal of this book is to educate you about the real opportunities that trial judges see for the adaptation of technology to the traditional methods of information presentation. Judges have a unique perspective, from their daily courtroom exposure to trials, knowing more about what jurors want. Their voices in this book point unmistakably to the need for cases to be made more interesting by lawyers who skillfully and appropriately visualize their messages.

Successful visual advocacy requires that you stay involved in the visualization process of your cases from start to finish. Leaving graphics artists to create exhibits without guidance is inefficient and potentially wasteful, cutting off the chance of fertile collaboration between you and creative consultants as the case moves forward. It also requires the vendor to give absentee lawyers a crash course in what has been done, often when trial is near and time is short.

While adept at rendering colorful images on a screen, most computer-graphics artists have little or no idea how to integrate the necessary legal foundation into the image-creation process. This is what you do best, with knowledge of the facts and the law, as well as the rules of evidence. Your steady and informed guiding hand better ensures that the images created by a computer-graphics artist will be appropriate, effective, and admissible.

In the twenty-first century, trial advocacy continues to be an art and a science. The active presence and informed judgment of lawyers, mixing it up and moving around in the courtroom, determines just the right blend and sequencing of a presentation. The visual lawyer of today must skillfully and imaginatively combine both low-tech and high-tech methods. Traditional demonstrative evidence, such as writing on butcher paper or using a scale model, is not obsolete. You must continue to think in terms of tangible, tactile, "high touch" exhibits, as well as "high tech" images on a screen.

The future is now. The research is irrefutable that multimedia learning works best. Our primary-school teachers were right: effective communication requires both show and tell. While jurors still decide cases on the substantive evidence, effective presentation maximizes your potential impact in our visual world.

The multimedia approach we have set forth not only works best, but also makes your work more fun and rewarding. We sincerely hope that this book makes a real difference in your lives, not only in your ability to get results for your clients, but also in your level of satisfaction in the practice of law.

Appendices

The Defense

Appendix A

DEFENDING WITH VISUALS

I have been up against tough competition all my life. I wouldn't know how to get along without it.

—Walt Disney

Competitive sports and politics share a common focus with trying cases—it's all about winning. All major collegiate and pro sports teams spend significant time watching their opponents' game films. Computer software assists in the process of breaking down plays and analyzing games. In politics, party strategists make detailed inquiry into everything that they can learn about the habits, techniques, and character of an election opponent.

The defense bar's visual trial techniques have reached a high level of sophistication, particularly in complex litigation. Just as in sports and politics, you ignore these at your peril. To be forewarned is to be forearmed. This appendix and the next will acquaint you with top defense lawyers' visual and storytelling techniques.

BASIC DIFFERENCES IN APPROACH

A basic difference of approach exists between plaintiffs' and defendants' lawyers. For one, the plaintiff has the burden of proof. Since the defendant doesn't need to prove anything to prevail, poking holes in the plaintiff's claims becomes a main focus. In turn, this influences the manner in which the defense shapes its trial story.

Though this analysis does not lend itself to absolutes, some common differences between plaintiffs' and defendants' counsel appear in the chart below:

PLAINTIFF	DEFENSE
Must prove defense's duty and breach.	Pokes holes in plaintiff's proof.
The defense's duty is broadly construed.	Defendant's duty is narrowly construed.
Goes back in time prior to the event at issue.	Focuses on the event at issue.
Seeks to simplify cause and effect. • Fewer defendants • Simple theories	Cause and effect complicated. • More parties • Other explanations
Paints damages with a broad brush	Dwells on the small details in medical records and complexity of proving causation.

Kathy A. Cochran

With some exceptions, such as medical-malpractice cases, defense attorneys have been slower initially to embrace visual advocacy. Insurance companies, which often pay the costs of a defense, were resistant to big artwork budgets. With the digital revolution, the cost of visuals became much less an issue, leading to greater acceptance and use on the defense side.

Kathy A. Cochran of Wilson, Smith, Dickerson and Cochran in Seattle, Washington, is regarded as one of the most visual and effective defense lawyers, serving as a visual consultant to other defense lawyers as her time permits.

She has seen a definite shift in the approach of the defense bar toward visual evidence:

> It used to be that most defense lawyers would choose the time-honored option of butcher paper over Power-Point, but no longer.
>
> Now I'm involved more in theme development and creative graphics.
>
> This adaption to presentation technology is driven by defense clients, as doctors, hospitals, and pharmaceutical companies use these types of media-driven communication techniques all the time. They expect the same from the lawyers who represent them in court. Defense counsel have adapted to this demand and even learned to like it.[1]

Michael Reiss, of the Seattle office of Davis, Wright, Tremaine, who has represented a number of Fortune 500 companies in employment cases, debunks the traditional notion that visualizing a defense case inevitably is seen by a jury as too slick:

> When we first started using PowerPoints, or visuals of any sort, there was fear by many lawyers defending big companies that jurors would hold a well-organized visual presentation against them as too slick. This is not true. All jurors and judges expect visuals now, with sophistication and good taste, using court time well.[2]

In modern trials, Kathy Cochran sees the use of visuals as more likely to depend on the lawyer's personal style than on the plaintiff or defendant designation:

> The difference in the frequency of use of demonstrative evidence really is more a reflection of the individual personality of the lawyer. Some are more comfortable with technology and more visual. Some lawyers

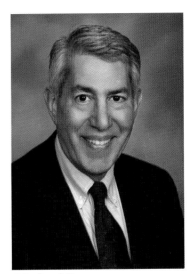

Michael Reiss

---

1. Kathy Cochran, interview with William S. Bailey, October 28, 2009.
2. Michael Reiss, interview with William S. Bailey, October 29, 2009.

are better educators than others, realizing the power of visual exhibits in the courtroom.[3]

The differing burden of proof results in a defense strategy that is more focused on the weaknesses of the plaintiff's case. The plaintiff's visuals take a big-picture approach, while the defense counterparts typically are far more specific. Ms. Cochran observes:

> Plaintiffs' lawyers tend to look at the issues in black and white: this is right, this was wrong. The defendants present in shades of gray, trying to show the complexities involved.[4]

Like plaintiffs' counsel, the defense avoids visuals that are too explicit, excluding gory elements that might be offensive to jurors. Ms. Cochran tries to assess the effect each visual will have, scrupulously adhering to good taste:

> Sometimes pictures can be a little too gruesome, leading to more cartoonish graphics. I start out with a real photo and then use some filters to make it seem a little less real. I've had jurors leave the box on occasion with even a cartoonish drawing, feeling like it was more information than they could handle.[5]

In addition to the differing degrees of specificity, the use of color in trial graphics also falls along party lines. Plaintiffs' counsel tend to use tones that arouse the emotions, while defense color choices reinforce cerebral detachment. Ms. Cochran's exhibits often incorporate shades of blue in her representation of hospitals, doctors, and drug companies:

> Each primary color tends to trigger distinct emotions.

In addition to the differing degrees of specificity, the use of color in trial graphics also falls along party lines.

---

3. Cochran, interview.
4. Cochran, interview.
5. Cochran, interview.

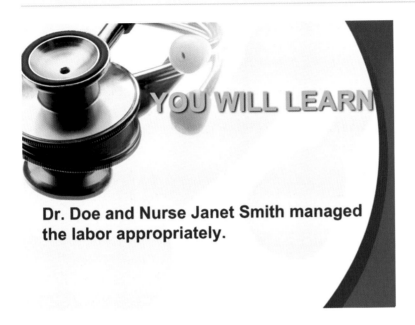

Dr. Doe and Nurse Janet Smith managed the labor appropriately.

Blue is classic, it's not angry, it's not a passion kind of a color. It tends to trigger a more intellectual response.[6]

THE DEFENSE STORY

In the competing versions of reality that make up a trial, it is equally important for the defense lawyer to come up with a good trial story. The basic storytelling rules are the same for plaintiff and defense counsel; each side just interprets the events in a different way. Veteran defense attorney Michael Bond of the Gardner Bond firm in Seattle, Washington, sees his task as no different than his opponent's:

> The issue always comes down to communication. Which side is telling a story that the jury is most likely to believe, one which tracks with their experience and perspective in everyday life.[7]

---

6. Cochran, interview.
7. Michael Bond, interview with William S. Bailey, September 30, 2009.

POSITIVE DEFENSE THEMES

The defendants need to tell a credible story that aligns with the evidence and common sense. Kathy Cochran adheres to this standard in defending her clients:

> It is very important for the story to be as close to reality as possible.[8]

When representing a corporate or institutional defendant, the defense story has to incorporate human interest for the jury. Michael Reiss looks for ways to put a human face on his organizational clients:

> I don't present actions in terms of "the company did this," but rather, the individuals working in the company. I present the decision makers as people, where they grew up, why they went to work for the company and why they like their jobs. These are the decisions they had to make and why.[9]

All accomplished defense lawyers agree that the tone of their story must not be negative, bullying, or otherwise lending itself to an interpretation that the defendant is mean or heartless. Mr. Reiss makes a point of being friendly and respectful toward the plaintiffs, leading the jury to his client's point of view through positive storytelling:

> Treating the plaintiffs with great respect is the key to how I try cases. In one well-publicized discrimination case, I described the named plaintiffs as good people with many strengths, using nice pictures of them to tell their stories.
>
> While the standard defense would be just to attack the plaintiff, effective defense storytelling in an employment case is positive: good employee, good company, things happening, no discrimination.

Treating the plaintiffs with great respect is the key to how I try cases.

---

8. Cochran, interview.
9. Reiss, interview.

My explanation for the outcome is merit based—
the plaintiff reached his limits, going as far as he could.
My story for the defense emphasizes the valid reasons
for this.[10]

Positive Visual Storytelling—The Plaintiff Is a Good Person

Even when she thinks a plaintiff's story doesn't make sense,
Kathy Cochran is at pains to avoid calling anyone a liar. Rather
than using such a hard-nosed attack, she gently will lead the
jury to this conclusion, presenting it as human nature to see
events in a self-serving manner:

> People tend to round off in their favor. They don't want
> to blame either themselves or fate for what happens.
> They look for some other target that they can feel bet-
> ter about.

> If any witness in a lawsuit is a liar, it should be obvious
> to the jury. They should reach that conclusion on their

---

10. Reiss, interview.

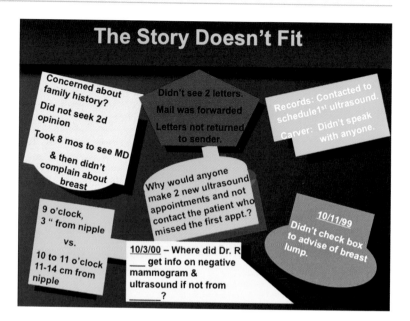

own. If I feed it to them and they don't buy it, I become the mean lawyer from the big bad drug company.[11]

THEMES

There is a natural tendency for defendants to hit back aggressively with a "we didn't do it" theme. Michael Reiss finds this approach limiting and counterproductive:

> Too many defendants are overly defensive. Simple denial of the plaintiff's claims is not enough. The defense needs to have its own themes, not defined by the plaintiff's story.

> In defending a case, the main thrust of my story is commitment to safety, fair procedure, building a product carefully, or being considerate of our workers.[12]

Just as a plaintiff's counsel uses the themes of making choices and personal responsibility in arguing for liability, so does the

Product assembly image reinforces defendant's responsible behavior

11. Cochran, interview.
12. Reiss, interview.

defense, only with a reverse spin. In the defense version, the plaintiff's bad choices are presented as the cause of the problem, with the bottom line being that the plaintiff is undeserving.

Brad Keller, of Byrnes and Keller of Seattle, Washington, sees the story-based struggle for the high ground as central to his success at trial. Who is the good guy, and who is the bad guy?

As a defense lawyer, one of Mr. Keller's main goals in his trial story is to show that the plaintiff either is undeserving or has sued the wrong entity:

> Does the plaintiff deserve the money? Is it fair to make the defendant pay? If so, how much? Every case really boils down to those simple things. If the jury gets past those two things, then I try to keep the damages as low as I can.[13]

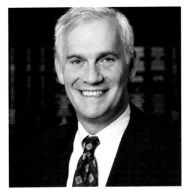

Brad Keller

THE PLAINTIFF'S CHOICES

Though he defends clients in a broad range of cases, including commercial business deals gone wrong, legal and medical malpractice, and products liability, Mr. Keller's themes at trial invariably center on choice, responsibility, and fairness:

> Every case involves people making choices, either that the plaintiff made or that the defendant was forced to make. By emphasizing these choices and responsibility, you're already two-thirds of the way there with the jury in establishing fairness. You just show how making choices inevitably leads to accepting responsibility, either for what people did or didn't do.[14]

DEFENSE THEMES IN EMPLOYMENT CASES

In employment cases, Michael Reiss identifies three elements of proof necessary for the plaintiff to prevail:

---

13. Brad Keller, interview with William S. Bailey, December 1, 2008.
14. Keller, interview.

My method is to
tell an evenhanded
fair-minded story
about the plaintiff,
simultaneously
educating the jurors
on the demands of
the job.

First, a pattern and practice of discrimination based on race. Second, statistics and expert testimony to back it up. Third, company policies, proven by documents.[15]

In counteracting the plaintiff's case, the defense focuses on the plaintiff's relative success in the very workplace they now are suing. Any plateau in their forward progress is explained on the basis of merit and job requirements:

> My method is to tell an evenhanded fair-minded story about the plaintiff, simultaneously educating the jurors on the demands of the job. What qualities are needed to perform well in this position? The jury becomes like a personnel manager, determining the overall fit of the plaintiff.[16]

In fact, it is not uncommon for Mr. Reiss to take the somewhat unusual tactic of actually praising the plaintiff or plaintiffs in the case:

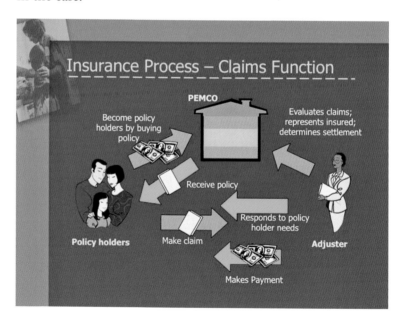

---

15. Reiss, interview.
16. Reiss, interview.

In a wage and hour class action involving insurance claims representatives, I used an organization chart to show why their work was so important. The description of the plaintiffs' duties and responsibilities matched my theme.[17]

DEFENSE THEMES IN MEDICAL CASES

The theme of 20/20 hindsight often works its way into medicine-based defenses, as explained by Kathy Cochran:

I will show what the doctor knew at the time of the incident versus what was discovered later, which might lead to a different judgment. I often come up with retrospective visuals to communicate what the doctor did and didn't know, or couldn't have known.[18]

---

17. Reiss, interview.
18. Cochran, interview.

She also commonly uses judgment as a theme in medical-malpractice cases:

> There are different reasonable judgments that can be made from the same set of facts. I often do highway or parallel road metaphors to serve that kind of a theme.[19]

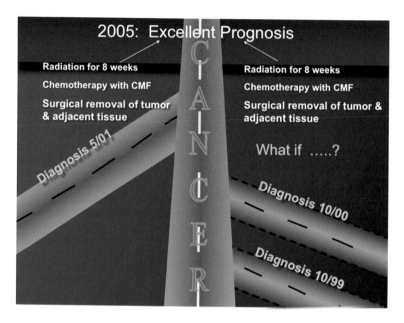

Ms. Cochran frequently uses themes reflecting the inherent complexity of medicine when defending medical-malpractice and drug product liability cases:

> The complexity of the anatomy and what the physician has to deal with tends to humanize the doctor to a jury. Then they actually understand how a mistake can be made without negligence.
>
> This puts my creativity to the test because I've got to take a complex thing and make it simple while still helping the jury to understand that it's complex. This challenge often leads me to metaphors.

This puts my creativity to the test because I've got to take a complex thing and make it simple.

---

19. Cochran, interview.

In a bowel surgery case, I used a graphic with a plate of spaghetti and a ketchup bottle. The physician has to get the bowel back into a small orifice. That graphic was one way of explaining how hard that is, used in tandem with what the intestines and peritoneal membrane look like in real life.[20]

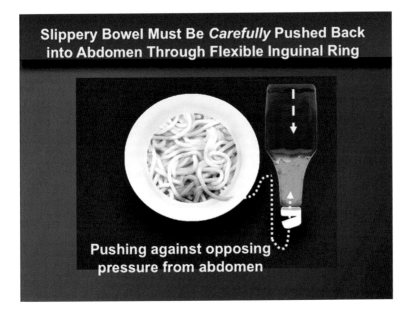

THE PROBLEM OF AN UNSYMPATHETIC DEFENDANT

In crafting the appeal of their trial stories, the defense counsel often faces a public-relations challenge of a client who is less likely to enjoy the natural sympathy of the jury. Kathy Cochran feels this rather acutely when she represents drug companies:

> It is hard to humanize pharmaceutical companies, as some people are angry at them. In that these companies are viewed as having a lot of money, there is a temptation for jurors to say, "Why not make them pay?"[21]

---

20. Cochran, interview.
21. Cochran, interview.

The challenge for the defense counsel is to find the human element and put it up front in the trial story.

Courtroom dramas in both films and on television portray David and Goliath struggles where the defendant is often powerful, bullying, and soulless. It is almost a contradiction in terms for a defendant ever to be the underdog. The challenge for the defense counsel is to find the human element and put it up front in the trial story. Brad Keller makes this a high priority in every case:

> Nobody has natural sympathy for a medical device manufacturer or a drug company. I get away from the image of my client as a profit-driven soulless beast and bring it down to a group of ordinary people who made decisions.
>
> In every business dispute, somebody made the decision. You've got to bring this person into the courtroom. People want to see the decision-maker, getting inside that person's head. This allows you to shift the David versus Goliath framework down to a much more human level.[22]

THE TRIAL STORY AND COMPANY CULTURE

The culture of a corporate defendant is a critical backdrop in the defense case. The work environment is presented as team focused. At the same time he builds up the defendant, Michael Reiss explains why the plaintiff didn't fit:

> In representing a well-known manufacturing company in a major class action employment case, my themes were built around this company's commitment to safety and quality. You have to show how it is a team. People understand sports teams and how they interact.
>
> The main thrust of our story was: "This is the culture of the company; we are proud of it and this is how it all works together." Our trial story and the themes were positive.[23]

22. Keller, interview.
23. Reiss, interview.

As a part of his trial story, Mr. Reiss also seeks to make the jurors more comfortable with the organizational structure of his corporate client. When the jury sees, through visual exhibits, where all the people fit together, the corporation does not seem as big or as impersonal:

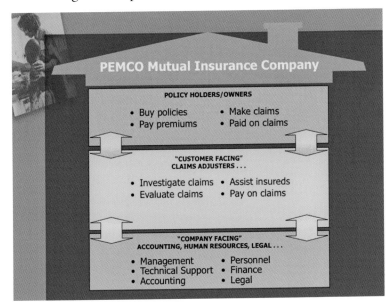

Organizational structures are effective visuals for the defense, giving the jury a feeling for how everything fits together.

With pay systems, I show the flaws in plaintiff's statistics and why our statistics are better. I use a funnel mechanism where we start with all these different ones and they funnel down into this other one.

Part of the message is to educate the jury about our company culture.[24]

Part of the message is to educate the jury about our company culture.

TAKING THE JURY ON A VIRTUAL SITE TOUR

After introducing the jury to the company culture, Michael Reiss builds on that foundation, making the jury experts on

---

24. Reiss, interview.

any relevant operation of the business. In a disability accommodation case brought against a truck manufacturer, Mr. Reiss realized that the jury would have to know how the trucks were built to intelligently decide the issues. For this reason, he created a virtual tour of the plant on video, demonstrating that no suitable job existed for the plaintiff.

He created a virtual tour of the plant on video, demonstrating that no suitable job existed for the plaintiff.

I needed to show the jurors on video how our trucks were built. Most people would assume that a big company ought to be able to accommodate a person with a disability someplace in the plant.

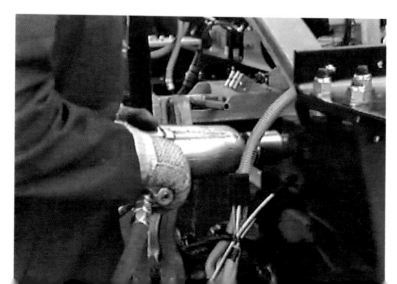

While different trucks require different kinds of assembly tasks, every single job involves the vibratory tools that the plaintiff was restricted from using.

Our video of the plant had to show the teamwork, the variety of jobs, and the constant use of vibratory tools.

In the end there was only one possible job that the plaintiff could do, welding. We tried him out in this, but he couldn't do it. While I could say all this in about thirty seconds, the jury wouldn't be able to see it for themselves. Since this was such a critical issue, I needed to visualize it, taking the jury to the plant. The video made the jury instant experts in how to build a truck.[25]

Every single job involves the vibratory tools that the plaintiff was restricted from using.

SHIFTING THE FOCUS

Defense lawyers tend to use different visual symbols in their cases. For example, in product-liability cases, the product itself often becomes the central prop in the defense presentation.

25. Reiss, interview.

Rather than act defensive, the strategy is one of robustly embracing the product. Brad Keller often has it prominently on display at the counsel's table throughout the trial:

> I like to portray the pride of the company in the product, rather than a defensive aura. I usually sit with the product right there on my table the whole time. It's a subliminal message that nobody on our side is embarrassed about it or trying to hide it. We're very proud of it, here it is. I've done it with external defibrillators, EKG monitors, and even a medical lab test. I want the jury to know that the product is a very real thing that real people use. It becomes a symbol, a point of focus in the courtroom.[26]

TAKEAWAYS—DEFENDING WITH VISUALS

- *Lawyers on both sides to a lawsuit now use visuals, themes, and storytelling techniques.*

- *Plaintiffs' counsel tend to focus on the big picture, while the defense emphasizes the fine details.*

- *Color choices in visuals differ between the plaintiff and the defense, with the defense trying to reinforce cerebral detachment.*

- *The defense tries not to be seen as mean spirited, while trying to discredit a plaintiff's case without attacking the plaintiff personally.*

- *A 20/20-hindsight theme attempts to keep the jury focused on what was reasonable at the time the decision in question was made.*

- *Defending cases that involve medical issues requires explaining complex scientific concepts, using visual analogies that draw upon common experience.*

26. Keller, interview.

◆ *Many jurors view corporations and institutional defendants as unsympathetic. The defense story, themes, and visuals try to personalize the defendant in more human terms.*

◆ *The elements of company culture presented to the jury will try to focus on quality, constant improvement, and fair procedures.*

◆ *The defense will try to put a human face on an institutional defendant through the use of an effective company spokesperson.*

THE DEFENSE PLAYBOOK

It's not what you look at that matters, it's what you see.

—Henry David Thoreau

This appendix examines the implementation of visual techniques in the defense case.

SETTING THE SCENE

Defense lawyers seek to emphasize elements of the physical scene that reinforce the theme or themes of their trial story. Strong defense visuals combine common sense, everyday experience, and the power of place.

A simple diagram of the scene helps the jury to understand the physical setup and the location of people in the story. Little real difference exists between scene diagrams used by either plaintiff or defense counsel, with the same goal of setting the stage for the trial story.

In a civil case brought against a police department by a wife involved in a domestic-violence incident, Aaron Weholt developed a scene diagram for the defense. The basic purpose of this was to give the jury a sense of where the responding officers were deployed.

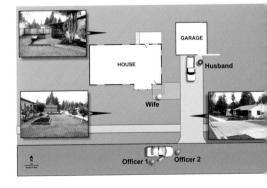

SCENE DIAGRAMS WITH THE DEFENSE THEME EMBEDDED

Defense themes often are embedded in diagrams. For example, the defense theme of poor choices by the plaintiff that result in an injury can be enhanced by adding information to photos of the scene. In the *Scruggs v. Snyder*[1] case, a small child was injured when crossing a busy highway adjacent to a state park. The child's adolescent sister was distracted from watching her brother by a softball game, which focused her attention in the opposite direction.

The defense for the driver built on a photo of the baseball diamond in question, which was next to a busy highway. The added graphics focused on the sister's being distracted and her choice to concentrate on the softball game rather than the safety of her brother.

In another case, Kathy Cochran realized that while most jurors are not medically sophisticated, they have been in a

---

1. Pseudonym.

hospital emergency room or visited a friend or relative who was an inpatient at some point. She used this near-universal experience as a backdrop to build a visual that reinforced her defense in a medical-malpractice case. The plaintiff claimed that the nursing staff had not regularly taken the patient's vital signs, leading to a medical catastrophe. The defense countered that the nurses were constantly aware of this patient's readings from the pulse oximeter in plain view.

Ms. Cochran explains the defense psychology behind this slide, which she created for the trial:

> The plaintiff's claim here was, "If vital signs were not written down on the chart, they were not taken."
>
> I have to bring the reality of everyday medical practice to the courtroom. Nurses don't always have to write something down. If that were the case, nobody would get any care. It's more like exception charting these days, when something is out of the norm.

I have to bring the reality of everyday medical practice to the courtroom.

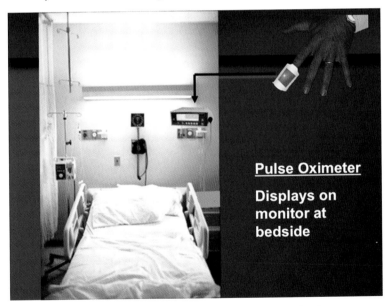

Pulse Oximeter

Displays on monitor at bedside

In this case, all the nurses had to do was look up to see this data every time they came into the room. This photograph reinforced the testimony of the nurses to this effect, going against the plaintiff's mantra, "If it wasn't written down, it didn't happen."[2]

Sometimes the defense seeks to capture activity in more than one room. This can require a more symbolic approach. In one medical-malpractice case in a hospital setting, Ms. Cochran used footprints to represent the routes taken by multiple staff members in covering an entire hospital floor, reinforcing the testimony on the care a patient received.

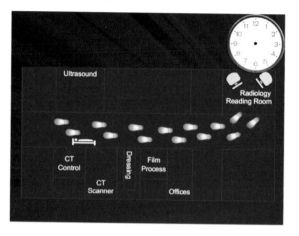

In another case, Aaron Weholt showed the helicopter flight of a patient from a local hospital to a specialized trauma center, reinforcing the defense theme that this was the patient's best chance.

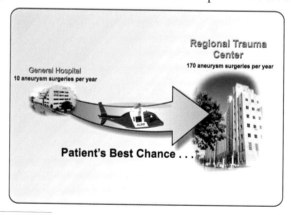

2. Kathy Cochran, interview with William S. Bailey, October 28, 2009.

IMPEACHING EXPERTS

In the battle of the experts, the defense can use visuals to attack the credibility of the plaintiff's experts. One approach to this is based on concepts of place, space, and distance. In the NITA case file of *Scruggs v. Snyder*, the defense tried to impeach the causation opinions of plaintiff's accident reconstructionist through visuals emphasizing the short reaction times and distances involved in the calculations of braking distance.

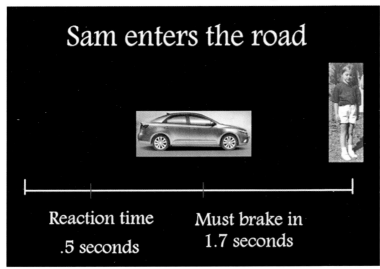

The defense often uses a timeline to compress a volume of information.

TIMELINES

The defense often uses a timeline to compress a volume of information.

> A timeline is a unifying device—it connects the dots and becomes symbolic. In many cases . . . the fight is about who knew what when.[3]

Using Timelines to Reinforce Trial Themes

Choice, personal responsibility, and lack of credibility or honesty are among the most frequently used themes in defending

---

3. Brad Keller, interview with William S. Bailey, December 1, 2008.

a case. Timelines string together events and facts that support those themes.

Medical Cases

Medical cases typically involve a series of events and providers caring for a patient. The defense uses the linear mode of a timeline to deflect the plaintiff's claims.

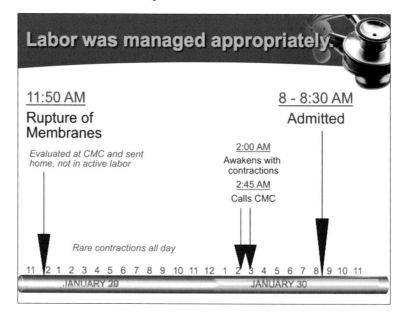

In pharmaceutical cases, a timeline also can show the state of knowledge of risks associated with a medication, as well as how much research was done on this and when.

Kathy Cochran favors timelines that are not just words, adding icons that capture the meaning and make the words more memorable. She used this approach in a case where the plaintiff had repeated emergency medical care, claiming that his active life was over. The plaintiff's multiple trips to the Middle East after the events at issue, visualized in a world map, became a feature in the cross-examination. Ms. Cochran decided just to show the route to the Middle East on the graphic, having the plaintiff testify from the witness stand as to all the travel times:

This showed that the plaintiff had a lot more energy than he was claiming.

Another timeline showed the plaintiff's various trips to the hospital, leading to the conclusion that he was a bit of a hypochondriac, with the icons of all of the ambulances stacked up.[4]

In another case, Ms. Cochran not only recorded the events of a patient's injury and emergency medical care over a several-hour period, but also visualized these events on the timeline, creating images of the medical attention given.

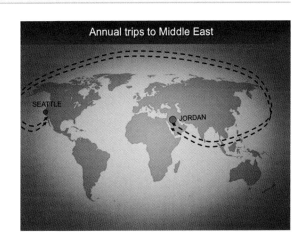

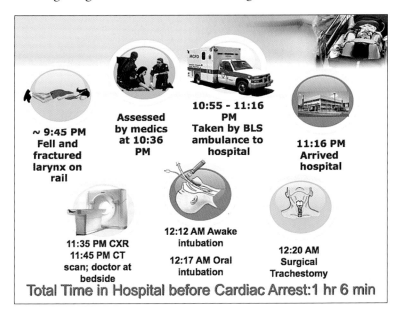

SHOWING NOTICE

Showing when the plaintiff knew or should have known elements of a claim is a common defense strategy. Visualizing the notice can have a powerful impact not only on the jury, but also on the witnesses in a case.

Showing when the plaintiff knew or should have known elements of a claim is a common defense strategy.

4. Cochran, interview.

For example, in a construction-defect case, the trial judge had ruled that the issue was whether "the plaintiff knew facts sufficient to put them on notice of the problem."

 had assembled a twelve-year history of water-leak complaints during discovery, but making this dramatic and visual at trial was a challenge.

In cross-examining the managing agent of the building, Mr. Bond went through a pile of maintenance records for the building. He divided these into four periods of two years each, putting an orange dot on a site plan of the building by each unit that had made a water-leak complaint during the period. He concluded his cross-examination on each grouping of complaints with the question, "Did this information give you any reason to believe that there was a problem with the construction?"

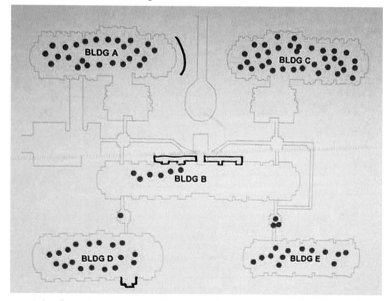

The first time around, the managing agent said, "No," emphatically. The second time, she said, "I don't think so." The third time, her response was an equivocal, "Maybe." By the fourth time, the buildings and grounds looked like they had the chickenpox. When asked the question again, the witness looked down and whispered, "Yes." A juror called out, "I can't hear you; would you speak up." The witness said, "Yes," loud enough for everyone to hear, making for a rather dramatic moment. This exhibit constituted a virtual notice scoreboard, providing a turning point in the case. Shortly thereafter, the plaintiffs took the defendant's last offer.

MAKING SCIENCE UNDERSTANDABLE TO THE JURY

A frequent challenge for the defense in medical cases requires that technical scientific studies be made intelligible and interesting. Kathy Cochran has developed visual techniques to make these articles more understandable:

> The scientific verbiage in an article often is not very helpful to a jury. I try to illustrate the scientific principles behind the verbiage, modifying illustrations in the article so they can be more easily understood.

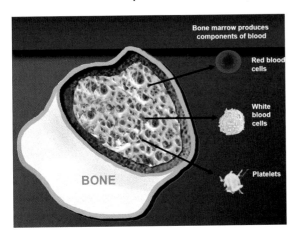

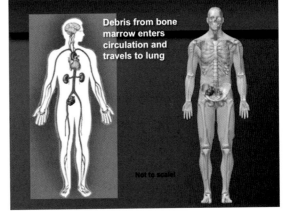

I always look for a sound bite in scientific articles, which is most often found in the abstract or the conclusion. But even a sound bite from an article needs to be presented by an expert who is a good teacher.

If I have a graphic with statistics from an article, I can turn those into an Excel chart with colors. Pie or bar charts usually

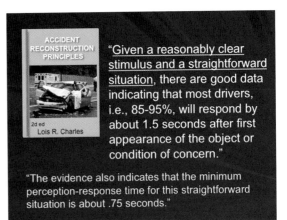

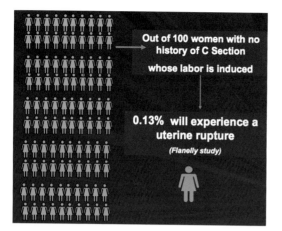

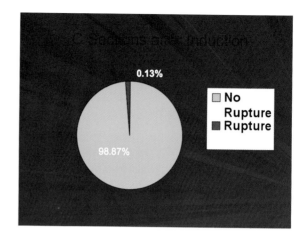

are the only real way you can communicate some of the complexity.[5]

VISUALIZING STATISTICS

Defense lawyers often are required to present statistical arguments in ways that will mean something to a lay jury. Defense visuals using statistics can focus directly on allegations made by the plaintiff, illustrating how the numbers don't add up. For example, in a case of claimed toxic exposure, Kathy Cochran compared the ozone level in the plaintiff's house to the levels in other locations:

> A cleaning company deodorized the fabrics in a house after a small kitchen fire, using ozone. The plaintiff came back more than 24 hours later and basically claimed that her life was never the same thereafter.

5. Cochran, interview.

This chart showed that the ozone levels in her house were well below other common environments.[6]

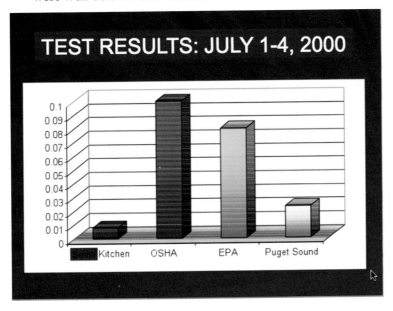

PLAINTIFF'S HISTORY AND CHARACTER

It is not uncommon for the defense to bring up background facts and character issues regarding the plaintiff in supporting its alternative theories of liability and damages. This can take many forms, including callouts from medical or employment records, as well as character traits revealed during the testimony:

> The accuracy of the history given by the plaintiff is critical to the defense case. Was there a prior medical condition? Other medication they may have been taking? Did the patient come back for follow-up testing as instructed? Did the patient promptly see another specialist when advised to do so?[7]

The accuracy of the history given by the plaintiff is critical to the defense case.

---

6. Cochran, interview.
7. Cochran, interview.

This technique can also explain the scientific implications of the plaintiff's medical history, as shown in the genetics case below, where a baby ended up with a very rare abnormality:

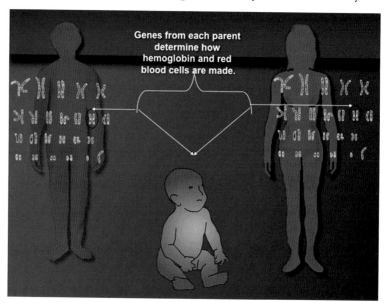

Our position that this baby was at risk for this condition independent of anything the doctor could have done really needed explanation.[8]

The use and abuse of medication comes up frequently in medical cases. Ms. Cochran will turn any pertinent portion of the plaintiff's medical history into a visual, emphasizing its importance to the jury:

> If use and abuse of medication is an issue in the case, I will show the jury how many pills we are talking about over what period of time.
>
> In a pharmaceutical case, a plaintiff may have taken multiple drugs, but blame his problems on one. A pill graphic like this can show the big picture.
>
> Medication graphics also can demonstrate a tendency to take the medications without learning anything

8. Cochran, interview.

about them. If so, then the story that "I wouldn't have taken this if I had been told" doesn't hang together. This same person is taking seven products. That's a context that a jury needs to know about.[9]

VISUAL ANALOGIES

At times, the defense will use visuals that draw analogies between everyday objects or processes and a technical or scientific principle. Kathy Cochran used this method in a medical-malpractice case involving the limitations of ultrasound:

Limitations of Ultrasound

> The plaintiff was claiming that a condition should have been picked up on the ultrasound.
>
> Ultrasound studies tend to be somewhat ambiguous. Nobody really can tell what they're looking at. Even though a lot of people have probably had one, they couldn't figure it out if they looked at the screen. I created this graphic to show that ultrasounds don't show everything.[10]

9. Cochran, interview.
10. Cochran, interview.

In another case, Ms. Cochran compared the force of a blow to the patient's throat to being hit by a baseball at high speed.

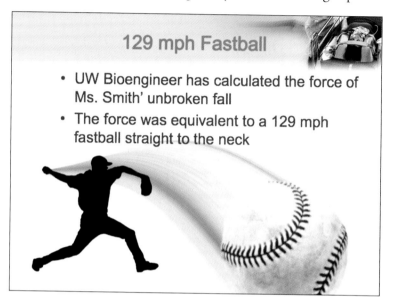

MEDICAL CHARTS

It often is difficult to read key information on medical charts. The defense uses callouts to make this readily understandable for the jurors.

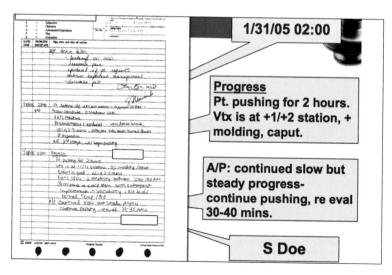

TAKEAWAYS—THE DEFENSE PLAYBOOK

The defense may use visual communication strategies against you. They may:

- ◆ *Create a context and a sense of place to reinforce case themes.*

- ◆ *Attack the credibility of opposing experts.*

- ◆ *Sort out information with timelines, which give form to the story and reinforce case themes.*

- ◆ *Show what the opposing party knew and when.*

- ◆ *Use visuals to make scientific concepts interesting and understandable for the jury.*

- ◆ *Use sound bites in scientific articles with visuals.*

- ◆ *Turn statistics into graphics.*

- ◆ *Make history and character issues visual.*

- ◆ *Create visual analogies between a scientific process and everyday experiences.*

- ◆ *Use visuals to interpret medical charts and imaging studies.*

ILLUSTRATION CREDITS

Introduction

P. 1: Duane Hoffmann, Hoffmann Legal Design

P. 2: (top) On Point Productions, (bottom) Duane Hoffmann, Hoffmann Legal Design

Part One

P. 3: Duane Hoffmann, Hoffmann Legal Design

Chapter 1

All illustrations by Duane Hoffmann, Hoffmann Legal Design

Chapter 2

P. 12: (top) used with permission of Walter Dauber, (bottom) Duane Hoffmann, Hoffmann Legal Design

P. 13: Duane Hoffmann, Hoffmann Legal Design

P. 14: (top) Duane Hoffmann, Hoffmann Legal Design, (bottom) Creators Syndicate by permission

P. 15–17: Duane Hoffmann, Hoffmann Legal Design

Part Two

P. 19: Duane Hoffmann, Hoffmann Legal Design

Chapter 3

P. 22: (top and bottom) Duane Hoffmann, Hoffmann Legal Design

P. 24, 25 (top and bottom): Robert Tourtelot

P. 26: Duane Hoffmann, Hoffmann Legal Design

P. 27: (top) Duane Hoffmann, Hoffmann Legal Design, (bottom) Robert Tourtelot

P. 28: (top) Robert Tourtelot, (bottom) Duane Hoffmann, Hoffmann Legal Design

P. 29, 30: Duane Hoffmann, Hoffmann Legal Design

Chapter 4

P. 33: (top) Robert W. Bailey, (bottom) Robert Tourtelot

P. 34: (top) Robert W. Bailey, 1 and 3 Robert W. Bailey, 2 Robert Tourtelot

P. 35: (top) Robert Tourtelot, 1 and 4 Robert Bailey, 2 and 3 Robert Tourtelot

P. 36: Tom Warner

P. 37: (top) Tom Warner, (bottom) Image © copyright Medical Legal Art (www.doereport.com). All Rights Reserved

P. 38: Tom Warner

P. 39: 1, 2, 4–6 Tom Warner, 3 Image © copyright Medical Legal Art (www.doereport.com). All Rights Reserved

P. 40: Duane Hoffmann, Hoffmann Legal Design

Chapter 5

P. 42: Robert W. Bailey

P. 43: Robert Tourtelot

P. 44: Tom Warner

P. 45: Duane Hoffmann, Hoffmann Legal Design

Chapter 6

P. 50, 51: Robert W. Bailey

P. 52: Duane Hoffmann, Hoffmann Legal Design

Chapter 7

P. 54: Robert W. Bailey

P. 55: (top) Robert Tourtelot, (bottom) Robert W. Bailey

P. 56: (top and bottom) Robert W. Bailey

P. 57: (top) Robert W. Bailey and Robert Tourtelot, (bottom) Robert Tourtelot

P. 58: 1, 3, 4 Robert W. Bailey, 2 Robert Tourtelot

P. 59: 5 and 6 Robert W. Bailey, 7 Robert Tourtelot (bottom) Tom Warner

P. 60: Robert W. Bailey and Tom Warner

P. 61: (top) Report W. Bailey and Tom Warner, (bottom) Tom Warner

P. 62: 1 and 4 Tom Warner, 2 and 3 Robert W. Bailey and Tom Warner

P. 63: Duane Hoffmann, Hoffmann Legal Design

Chapter 8

P. 67: (top and bottom) Robert W. Bailey

P. 68: Robert W. Bailey and Robert Tourtelot

P. 69: Robert Tourtelot

P. 70–72: Robert W. Bailey and Robert Tourtelot

P. 73: 1 and 2 Robert W. Bailey, 3, 5, 7–9 Robert W. Bailey and Robert Tourtelot, 4 and 6 Robert Tourtelot

P. 74–77: Images © copyright Medical Legal Art (www.doereport.com). All Rights Reserved

P. 78: (top) Image © copyright Medical Legal Art (www.doereport.com). All Rights Reserved, (middle and bottom) Tom Warner

P. 79: Tom Warner

P. 80: 1–8 Images © copyright Medical Legal Art (www.doereport.com). All Rights Reserved, 9–11 Tom Warner

P. 81: Duane Hoffmann, Hoffmann Legal Design

Chapter 9

P. 84: Robert W. Bailey

P. 85, 86: Robert Tourtelot

P. 87: (right) Robert W. Bailey, (middle) Robert W. Bailey and Robert Tourtelot, (bottom) Robert Tourtelot

P. 88: (top) Robert W. Bailey and Robert Tourtelot (bottom) Robert W. Bailey

P. 89: Robert Tourtelot

P. 90: (top) Robert Tourtelot (bottom) Robert W. Bailey

P. 91: Robert Tourtelot

P. 92: (top) Robert Tourtelot, (bottom) Robert W. Bailey and Robert Tourtelot

P. 93: (top) Robert W. Bailey and Robert Tourtelot (bottom) Robert Tourtelot

P. 94–98: Robert Tourtelot

P. 99: 1 and 2 Robert Tourtelot, 3 and 4 Robert W. Bailey and Robert Tourtelot

P. 100: (top) Tom Warner, (bottom) Image © copyright Medical Legal Art (www.doereport.com). All Rights Reserved

P. 101–103: Tom Warner

104 Duane Hoffmann, Hoffmann Legal Design

Chapter 10

P. 107–113: Robert Tourtelot

P. 114–116: Tom Warner

P. 117: (top) Evan Naylor (bottom) Tom Warner

P. 118: Tom Warner

P. 119: 1–5 and 7 Tom Warner, 6 Evan Naylor

P. 120: Duane Hoffmann, Hoffmann Legal Design

Chapter 11

P. 122: 1–3, 5 and 6 Robert W. Bailey, 4 Robert Tourtelot

P. 123: 7, 10, 11 Robert W. Bailey, 8, 12, 14, 16–18 Robert W. Bailey and Robert Tourtelot, 9, 13, 15 Robert Tourtelot

P. 124–125: Robert Tourtelot

P. 126: 1 and 2 Robert W. Bailey, 3 Tom Warner, 4 Robert W. Bailey and Tom Warner

P. 127: 5 Robert W. Bailey and Tom Warner, 6 Tom Warner, 7–12 Images © copyright Medical Legal Art (www.doereport.com). All Rights Reserved

P. 128: 13 Image © copyright Medical Legal Art (www.doereport.com). All Rights Reserved, 14–19 Tom Warner

P. 129: 20–24, and 26 Tom Warner, 25 Evan Naylor

P. 130: Duane Hoffmann, Hoffmann Legal Design

Part Three

P. 131: On Point Productions

Chapter 12

All illustrations by Duane Hoffmann, Hoffmann Legal Design

Chapter 13

All illustrations by Duane Hoffmann, Hoffmann Legal Design

Chapter 14

P. 156–158: Freemantle Media Limited, used with permission

P. 159: (top) Gallagher Law Library, University of Washington, (bottom) University of Washington Library

P. 160: (top left and right) Walker Smith, *The Everett Massacre*, 1917, (bottom) Everett Public Library

P. 161: Duane Hoffmann, Hoffmann Legal Design

P. 162: (top) Duane Hoffmann, Hoffmann Legal Design, (bottom) Everett Public Library

P. 163–164: Duane Hoffmann, Hoffmann Legal Design

P. 165–169: William S. Bailey

P. 170: On Point Productions

Chapter 24

P. 301: (top) King County Police Department, (bottom) John Lok, *The Seattle Times*

P. 302: King County Prosecutor's Office

P. 303: (top) King County Prosecutor's Office, (bottom) public domain

P. 304: public domain

P. 308, 309: William S. Bailey

P. 310: (top) William S. Bailey, (bottom) On Point Productions

P. 311: (top) Claude States, (bottom) On Point Productions

P. 312, 313: On Point Productions

P. 314: Duane Hoffmann, Hoffmann Legal Design

Chapter 25

P. 319: King County Superior Court

P. 322: Duane Hoffmann, Hoffmann Legal Design

Chapter 26

P. 324: Seattle University School of Law

P. 325: (top) Seattle University School of Law, (bottom) Seattle Police Department

P. 326: Seattle Police Department

P. 327: (top) On Point Productions, (bottom) public domain

P. 328: (top) Seattle Police Department, (bottom) On Point Productions

P. 329: (top and bottom) On Point Productions

P. 330: (top) On Point Productions (bottom) Seattle Police Department

P. 331: On Point Productions

P. 333P. 334 On Point Productions

P. 335: Washington State Patrol

P. 336: (top left) Google Earth (top right and bottom) On Point Productions

P. 337: On Point Productions

P. 338, 339: Randolph I. Gordon

P. 341: (right) On Point Productions (bottom) Randolph I. Gordon

P. 342: Duane Hoffmann, Hoffmann Legal Design

Chapter 27

P. 347: public domain

P. 348: William S. Bailey and C. Steven Fury

P. 350: Duane Hoffmann, Hoffmann Legal Design

Chapter 28

P. 351: Duane Hoffmann, Hoffmann Legal Design

Appendices

P. 355: Kathy A. Cochran, Cochran Productions

Appendix A

P. 358: Wilson, Smith, Cochran, and Dickerson

P. 359: Davis Wright Tremaine

P. 361: Kathy A. Cochran, Cochran Productions

P. 363: Michael Reiss

P. 364: (top) Kathy A. Cochran, Cochran Productions (bottom) Michael Reiss

P. 365: Byrnes and Keller

P. 366: Michael Reiss

P. 367–369: Kathy A. Cochran, Cochran Productions

P. 371–373: Michael Reiss

P. 374: Duane Hoffmann, Hoffmann Legal Design

Appendix B

P. 377: Aaron Weholt, Legal Media

P. 378: Dakota Solberg

P. 379: Kathy A. Cochran, Cochran Productions

P. 380: (top) Kathy A. Cochran, Cochran Productions (bottom) Aaron Weholt, Legal Media

P. 381: Paul Woods

P. 382, 383: Kathy A. Cochran, Cochran Productions

P. 384: Michael Bond

P. 385–390: Kathy A. Cochran, Cochran Productions

P. 391: Duane Hoffmann, Hoffmann Legal Design

About the Authors

P. 405: Ron Clark

P. 406: Robert W. Bailey

INDEX

About the Authors

William S. Bailey

My first real understanding of how visuals affect human thought came from my college roommate Gordon Ward. A talented artist, he taught me that art is much more than the ability to draw. Rather, it is a state of mind. Right after graduation from college, I had the chance to work with an award-winning "underground" filmmaker. While this was exciting for a time, my vision for the future soon morphed into something far more practical—law school.

My father was the first one to plant the idea. Raised in a strict "children should be seen and not heard" environment, he was exasperated by all my verbal challenges. One day, he slouched back in his chair and sighed. "Son, you like to argue so much, you might as well become a lawyer and get paid for it."

But it was more than just a weary paternal remark that led me to law school. Living in New Orleans as a child in the 1950s gave me an eye-opening view of Jim Crow racial discrimination. I became a political activist in college in the 1960s. A slogan from that time stuck with me, "If you aren't part of the solution, you are part of the problem." The urban setting of Northwestern University Law School in Chicago provided me opportunities to address issues of police brutality, prison reform, and the rights of mental patients.

I moved to Seattle after graduation, where working as a public defender put me in court nearly every day. Trying to help level the playing field of the justice system took everything I had to give and demanded more.

Teaching and writing about trial advocacy a bit later sharpened my skills further. If you try to explain things to others, you had better know what you are talking about yourself.

But serving as a juror in 1988 rocked my world. Thrilled at being chosen, my elation quickly dissipated. I struggled to stay awake. Why was this? I finally figured it out. As a juror, I had become a consumer of information. What had unfolded in front of me lacked entertainment value, all talking heads and no visuals. Nobody would ever watch a television show this boring, slow, and repetitive.

And then a terrible "aha" moment soon followed—"Oh no! I have been doing the very same thing!" Once the shock wore off, I vowed to change my ways, incorporating the power of images and storytelling in all future cases. No more talking heads.

I foraged for ideas over a far broader terrain, approaching cases more like a film director. I began to study marketing, behavioral psychology, design, script writing, advertising, symbolism, mythology, and religion. All of this has made me a better lawyer, with many more persuasion tools to apply on a client's behalf.

Once you become a visual advocate, there is no going back. It is our goal in this book to help you discover the power of stories, images, and words. It is a powerful force for justice that will benefit your clients.

—William S. Bailey
Seattle, Washington, June 2011

ROBERT W. BAILEY

My love of visual communication and a good story led me to the motion picture industry in Los Angeles. Like many creative types, I hoped to find work in the film business. After knocking on doors for a month, an opportunity to become a producer at a studio presented itself. Over the next few years, I became involved with the many facets of production, including writing scripts, storyboards, graphic design, art direction, directing, and editing. After several years of production work I left the studio and devoted the next year to writing a script for a motion picture. This experience sharpened my skills as a writer. I then relocated to San Francisco and did freelance work that included producing television commercials for attorneys.

One day my brother who worked as an attorney in Seattle called to suggest that I use my visual skills to help attorneys create exhibits. During this conversation, I had the creative idea to use storyboard illustrations to show the mechanics of an injury. This turned out to be a powerful tool for attorneys. My first client used the storyboards I created to successfully settle one of his cases. Soon thereafter, he retained me for another case, thus beginning my career as a trial consultant.

Four years later, I had helped win numerous cases using my visual communication skills. One of these included a high-profile case involving a nationally known rap singer. These successes led to an invitation to speak for the National College of Advocacy Case Workshops sponsored by the Association of Trial Lawyers of America (now the American Association for Justice). I have continuously been invited to speak and consult at these workshops for over fourteen years.

Over time, as I learned more about the psychology and strategy of courtroom communication, I began writing opening statements and developed a unique style of using visuals to show the whole story instead of one small portion of it. I also produced settlement videos, damages videos, and day-in-the-life videos.

Throughout this period, I continued to broaden my expertise as a writer and story consultant by participating in workshops and educational programs like Screenwriting (Los Angeles), Storymaking (Los Angeles), the Psychology of Creativity (San Francisco), and the Wisdom of Mythic Stories (San Francisco). As I synthesized this information for use in the world of law, I created new strategies for visual storytelling and spoke at over eighty CLE seminars and conventions throughout the United States. These presentations included the Art of Persuasion at Harvard Law School (sponsored by AAJ).

Over my twenty-year career as a trial consultant and visual communication expert, I have learned that showing the story has the power to deeply touch not only the minds and hearts of others, but my heart as well.

May these stories and images inspire you.

May your compassion for others deepen.

And may you become a visual storyteller.

—Robert Wilbank Bailey
Sonoma, California, June 2011